DATE DUE

| | | | |
|---|---|---|---|
| Nov 20 '81 | | | |
| Dec 11 '81 | | | |
| Jul 29 | | | |
| Oct 19 '82 | | | |
| Nov 17 '82 | | | |
| | | | |
| | | | |
| | | | |
| | | | |
| | | | |
| | | | |
| | | | |

# Vital Resources

Reports on Energy, Food,
& Raw Materials

# Vital Resources

## Critical Choices for Americans

Volume I



**Nelson A. Rockefeller**

**Lexington Books**
D.C. Heath and Company
Lexington, Massachusetts
Toronto

**Library of Congress Cataloging in Publication Data**

Commission on Critical Choices for Americans.
Vital resources.

(Critical choices for Americans; v. 1)
Reports of panels of the Commission on Critical Choices for Americans.
Includes index.
1. Natural resources–United States–Addresses, essays, lectures. 2. Energy policy–United States–Addresses, essays, lectures. 3. Food supply–United States–Addresses, essays, lectures. 4. United States–Economic policy–1971- –Addresses, essays, lectures. I. Rockefeller, Nelson Aldrich, 1908- II. Title. III. Series.
HC103.7.C55 1977 333.7 75-44718
ISBN 0-669-00413-8



Published simultaneously in Canada.

Printed in the United States of America.

International Standard Book Number 0-669-00413-8

Library of Congress Catalog Card Number: 75-44718

# Foreword

The Commission on Critical Choices for Americans, a nationally representative, bipartisan group of forty-two prominent Americans, was brought together on a voluntary basis by Nelson A. Rockefeller. After assuming the Vice Presidency of the United States, Mr. Rockefeller, the chairman of the Commission, became an ex officio member. The Commission's assignment was to develop information and insights which would bring about a better understanding of the problems confronting America. The Commission sought to identify the critical choices that must be made if these problems are to be met.

The Commission on Critical Choices grew out of a New York State study of the Role of a Modern State in a Changing World. This was initiated by Mr. Rockefeller, who was then Governor of New York, to review the major changes taking place in federal-state relationships. It became evident, however, that the problems confronting New York State went beyond state boundaries and had national and international implications.

In bringing the Commission on Critical Choices together, Mr. Rockefeller said:

As we approach the 200th Anniversary of the founding of our Nation, it has become clear that institutions and values which have accounted for our astounding progress during the past two centuries are straining to cope with the massive problems of the current era. The increase in the tempo of change and the vastness and complexity of the wholly new situations which are evolving with accelerated change, create a widespread sense that our political and social system has serious inadequacies.

We can no longer continue to operate on the basis of reacting to crises, counting on crash programs and the expenditure of huge sums of money to solve our problems. We have got to understand and project present trends, to take command of the forces that are emerging, to extend our freedom and wellbeing as citizens and the future of other nations and peoples in the world.

Because of the complexity and interdependence of issues facing America and the world today, the Commission has organized its work into six panels, which emphasize the interrelationships of critical choices rather than treating each one in isolation.

The six panels are:

*Panel I:* Energy and its Relationship to Ecology, Economics and World Stability;
*Panel II:* Food, Health, World Population and Quality of Life;
*Panel III:* Raw Materials, Industrial Development, Capital Formation, Employment and World Trade;
*Panel IV:* International Trade and Monetary Systems, Inflation and the Relationships Among Differing Economic Systems;
*Panel V:* Change, National Security and Peace;
*Panel VI:* Quality of Life of Individuals and Communities in the U.S.A.

The Commission assigned, in these areas, more than 100 authorities to prepare expert studies in their fields of special competence. The Commission's work has been financed by The Third Century Corporation, a New York not-for-profit organization. The corporation has received contributions from individuals and foundations to advance the Commission's activities.

The Commission is determined to make available to the public these background studies and the reports of those panels which have completed their deliberations. The background studies are the work of the authors and do not necessarily represent the views of the Commission or its members.

The Commission acknowledges the generous contributions of Nelson A. Rockefeller and Laurance S. Rockefeller and the gifts from other individuals and foundations, especially the Andreas Foundation, the Vincent Astor Foundation, the Brown Foundation, Mr. and Mrs. Frank Greenwall, the Reader's Digest Foundation, the Thomas J. Watson Foundation, and Mr. John Hay Whitney. The Commission also records its appreciation to the members of the Commission and its panels, consultants, and members of the staff who have participated in its work.

This volume is one of the series of volumes the Commission is publishing in the belief that it will contribute to the basic thought and foresight America will need in the future.

WILLIAM J. RONAN
*Acting Chairman*
Commission on Critical Choices
for Americans

# Members of the Commission

*Ex-Officio Members*

THE HONORABLE NELSON A. ROCKEFELLER
(Chairman of the Commission until
February 28, 1975)

THE HONORABLE HENRY A. KISSINGER

THE HONORABLE MIKE MANSFIELD
(Member of the Commission until
March 6, 1975)

THE HONORABLE HUGH SCOTT

THE HONORABLE THOMAS P. O'NEILL, JR.
Speaker
United States House of Representatives

LEO CHERNE
Executive Director, Research Institute of America, Inc.

JOHN S. FOSTER, JR.
Vice President for Energy Research and Development, TRW, Inc.

LUTHER H. FOSTER
President, Tuskegee Institute

NANCY HANKS
Chairman, National Endowment for the Arts

BELTON KLEBERG JOHNSON
Texas Rancher and Businessman

CLARENCE B. JONES
Former Editor and Publisher, The New York Amsterdam News

JOSEPH LANE KIRKLAND
Secretary–Treasurer, AFL-CIO

JOHN H. KNOWLES, M.D.
President, Rockefeller Foundation

DAVID S. LANDES
Leroy B. Williams Professor of History and Political Science, Harvard University

MARY WELLS LAWRENCE
Chairman and Chief Executive Officer, Wells, Rich, Greene, Inc.

SOL M. LINOWITZ
Senior Partner of Coudert Brothers

EDWARD J. LOGUE
Former President and Chief Executive Officer, New York State Urban Development Corporation

EDWARD TELLER
Senior Research Fellow, Hoover Institution on War, Revolution and Peace, Stanford University

ARTHUR K. WATSON*
Former Ambassador to France

MARINA VON NEUMANN WHITMAN
Distinguished Public Service Professor of Economics, University of Pittsburgh

CARROLL L. WILSON
Professor, Alfred P. Sloan School of Management, Massachusetts Institute of Technology

GEORGE D. WOODS
Former President, World Bank

Members of the Commission served on the panels. In addition, others assisted the panels.

BERNARD BERELSON
Senior Fellow
President Emeritus
The Population Council

C. FRED BERGSTEN
Senior Fellow
The Brookings Institution

ORVILLE G. BRIM, JR.
President
Foundation for Child Development

LESTER BROWN
President
Worldwatch Institute

LLOYD A. FREE
Former President
Institute for International Social Research

*Deceased

# Preface

In his Overview to this volume, the first in the fourteen-volume series of the Commission on Critical Choices for Americans, Nelson A. Rockefeller writes: "At no time has so much been happening so rapidly in so many facets of human life." This accelerated rate of change is dramatically evident in the brief period of four years since Mr. Nelson Rockefeller called together forty-two distinguished Americans to form the Commission on Critical Choices for Americans. During this period the Arab Boycott occurred, OPEC was created, a President of the United States resigned, the Vietnam War was ended, and the world faced new economic challenges and strategic considerations. The era of cheap energy was ended and the world faced the necessity of finding new and additional energy sources to meet not only its rising demands but its current needs. The problems of overpopulation reached critical proportions in parts of the globe and the whole world was awakened to the problems of providing food and shelter for the burgeoning population. The economic recession in the Western World brought new stresses and strains.

These and other events emphasized the need for reassessment and reevaluation of our public policies to meet new problems and opportunities. It was precisely to help a free people in a democratic society make sound judgments on how to handle such problems and to realize such opportunities that Mr. Nelson Rockefeller took the initiative in creating the Commission on Critical Choices. It had been the expectation that the Commission, working through a series of Panels, would have reviewed specific areas of public policy concern and reported publicly on the alternative choices before us.

In the Constitutional crisis initiated with the resignation of President Nixon, Mr. Nelson Rockefeller accepted the nomination by President Ford to be Vice

President of the United States and was therefore unable to continue his leadership of the Commission.

The procedure followed by the Commission was to develop background studies in various areas and to have the specialized Panels deal with the present and emergent situations and make their appropriate reports. Because of the changed circumstances incident principally to Mr. Nelson Rockefeller's assumption of the Vice Presidency, it was not possible to complete all of the Commission's projected works. However, three Panels continued their deliberations and were able to develop reports. These reports are presented in this volume along with Nelson Rockefeller's Overview. These Panels are Panel I: Energy and Its Relationship to Ecology, Economics and World Stability; Panel II: Food, Health, World Population and the Quality of Life; Panel III: Raw Materials, Industrial Development, Capital Formation, Employment and World Trade. Within the limited time frame, the other Panels were unable to complete their deliberations and to develop reports. However, the background studies prepared for all of the Panels are included in the fourteen volumes of this series.

As Acting Chairman of the Commission after Mr. Nelson Rockefeller became Vice President, I should like to make clear that the Panel reports in this volume do not necessarily represent or reflect the view of each or any individual Panel member. They do present significant insights on the conditions that confront us in the several fields of energy, food, and raw materials, and suggest alternative courses of action for dealing with them.

Nelson Rockefeller's Overview in this volume is itself a comprehensive and incisive analysis of major areas of concern to the American people and the critical choices they face for their future. He brings to this Overview, as he brought to the leadership of the Commission, a unique experience and expertise growing out of some thirty-five years of public service in federal, state and local government—with responsibilities both at home and abroad. Consequently, his comments on such subjects as energy and environmental protection, the challenge to growth, access to raw materials, food, science and technology, military security and foreign policy, are all cogent, critical and constructive.

Although he sees problems that confront Americans and all free societies as being serious and unprecedented, he finds grounds for optimism and an abiding faith in the future of American democracy. He writes here: "The spirit of America has been one of energy and creativity to meet the needs of individuals. It has emphasized individualism—individual economic freedom, individual political liberty, and individual responsibility. In our American law and in our society for these two hundred years, the focus has been on increasing opportunity for more and more individuals to attain that which their talents, capacities and aspirations could achieve." He sees an America that can continue on this progressive course of action with benefit for not only individual Americans themselves but for all mankind.

Nelson Rockefeller and his brother Laurance Rockefeller both contributed generously not only to the establishment and financing of the Commission on Critical Choices but also participated in its deliberations and other activities. In my judgment the contributions they and those associated with them in this enterprise have made have already helped awaken the American people to the realities of the world in which we live. They created awareness for the need to take constructive action to resolve the problems and to grasp the opportunities that are before us.

This volume and the thirteen other volumes totaling more than two million words provide an invaluable resource for all who seek to understand the critical choices that face Americans and the world in the years immediately ahead.

W.J.R.

# Contents

# List of Figures

# List of Tables

# Overview: Critical Choices and Emergent Opportunities

**Nelson A. Rockefeller**

Americans face unprecedented challenges in their third century as a nation. The world is being swept by vast winds of change transforming the old order and ushering in a new period of human history.

The swiftness and the extent of change is mind-boggling. At no time has so much been happening so rapidly in so many facets of human life.

Tomorrow's technologies are already outdating today's—while people have yet to accommodate to the transformations of yesterday.

The mechanisms exist to do more for more people now, and in the future, than ever before. At the same time, the finite limits of some vital resources and the impact of industrial development upon the environment pose new hurdles to the pursuit of sufficiency for all.

Ideas and values long held paramount are being assaulted by rival ideologies, shaken by discoveries, eroded by cynicism, and undermined by shifts in the economic and social pillars that supported them. The stabilities of the past are being replaced by the uncertainties of the future.

The Commission on Critical Choices for Americans was founded late in 1973 to look at these fundamental changes and assess their impact. Before describing the work of this Commission, however, I would first like to discuss the effect of some of the changes that have taken place and the resulting challenges we now face.

The United States of America emerged from World War II as the strongest country in the world, economically and militarily. Its influence extended into the cultural, social, and business life of much of the world. Its expertise—not only scientific and technological, but also managerial–was sought virtually throughout the globe. America's productive enterprise first sustained the war ravaged regions and then provided a base for their recovery and future development. So great was the outpouring of goods and services that assumptions of continuing abundance resulted. This, in turn, brought promises by government that were to prove impossible of performance–for example the "guns and butter" effort to carry on a major military effort in Vietnam with simultaneously expanded domestic federal programs.

But the heady days of the 1950s yielded to the disillusionments of the late 1960s and early 1970s. Amid the colder realities of the mid-1970s, as the time of the Bicentennial of the Declaration of Independence approached, American self-confidence received several severe jolts. The Watergate episode brought a major constitutional crisis and shook the faith of people in their government. The rout of the South Vietnamese army and the hurried American exodus from South Vietnam brought America's international influence to a new low in the post-World War II era. Inflation and a falloff in the rate of business activity brought economic hardship and increased unemployment.

In summary, the three decades from the end of World War II saw America through three periods: the first, one of unbounded optimism; the second, one of critical cynicism and nascent conflict; and the third, the dawning of an era of sobering realism.

In a sense, the assumptions of superabundance of the 1950s contributed to the emotionalism that characterized the conflicts of the late 1960s. These assumptions bore a responsibility also for the pervasive attitude that how one felt about things was more significant than the facts. This emotionalism, this "feeling" syndrome played its part in the over-commitment by government to programs, projects, and social promises incapable of fulfillment. The syndrome has by no means completely disappeared. Nor have the assumptions of continuing abundance lost their full impact. They are mitigated by the newly recognized realities, but they remain significant factors.

Another element contributing to the present state of affairs has been a shift from the traditional American ethic of each individual's responsibility for his own acts to blaming society for a vast spectrum of individual or group deficiencies. Not only has there been a diminution of individual or group responsibility for their actions, but there has also been placed upon government the charge to take remedial actions both to correct the deficiencies and to deter the antisocial actions. Accordingly, governmental programs have been instituted not only for traditional humanitarian or charitable reasons to help individuals or groups with public funds to better their lot, but also on the premise that such programs will protect society against antisocial behavior, delinquency, crime, and violence. A wide range of legislation to this end has been enacted as a result.

The pluses and the minuses of such legislation and governmental implementation of it are now coming under critical scrutiny. Again, more has been promised than has been accomplished. The negative results are beginning to claim public attention as well as the positive accomplishments. The reexamination of the public welfare system and the reappraisal of the youthful offenders laws and their practical results are instances of current importance. They are likely precursors of significant reevaluations of other programs as well. Indeed, there is a new questioning of the premises of such legislation. The renewed debate on the merits, the morality and the practical effectiveness of capital punishment is a case in point.

It might also be said that the far-reaching changes in the role of the federal government wrought in the days of the New Deal did not have their full impact until the 1960s and 1970s. World War II came so close on the heels of the New Deal social legislation of the 1930s that the nation's major attention and effort was devoted to the war effort and the immediate postwar recovery programs. Consequently, the sizable expansion of federal social programs culminating in the 1960s and the enormous growth of federal bureaucracy to administer them did not become the focus of widespread public attention until the late 1960s and early 1970s.

The urgent social reforms of the New Deal required federal action to meet human need. This brought the federal government into areas which heretofore had been the province of state or local government and the private or voluntary sector of American society. With the enormous financial capacity of the federal government—particularly its income tax resources and its borrowing ability—the successive Congresses and administrations, particularly in the 1960s, became the objects of all kinds of pressures for an ever-growing series of demands—for services, for regulations, for subsidies. As a result, the federal government has found itself involved in matters ranging from major health and welfare programs to the components of house paint and whether all-boy choirs are any longer legitimate.

In the effort to meet these demands, legislation has been enacted in which the legislative intent has been so broad and vague that it has resulted in a vast amount of court-made legislation. In the absence of clear and carefully thought out policy direction in the statutes, the courts have been faced with the need for practical interpretations that have a wide ranging impact on individuals and the society. Concern is again being voiced about the amount of "legislation" being made by the courts.

Equally significant, if not more so, is the vast amount of discretion left to the administrators—to the bureaucracy—to implement policy through rules, orders, and regulations rather than through duly-enacted laws. The volume and complexity of these administrative actions, the paperwork involved, the number of forms people have to fill out and the permissions they have to obtain, have already built up public resentment reflected in the "anti-Washington" and "anti-red tape" pledges of the recent presidential primaries and campaigns.

Even the elected representatives of the people find the large bureaucracy a formidable presence. Much legislation of a public policy character actually derives from the bureaucracy and the bureaucracy's experiences in administering existing law and coping with current problems and highly organized pressure groups. The bureaucratic supervision over observance of the law increases at least proportionately and, in all likelihood, more so if the funds are available for the purpose. It is small wonder that the number of lawyers in the federal government in 1975 had increased over 180 percent since 1970. In the same five-year period, the number of federal government accountants has gone from 45,000 to 75,000!

Put another way, we have moved a long way from the simple certainty of the law of yesterday to a point where, in more and more areas, one must go to the government bureaucracy to find out what the law and its maze of regulations are. The Internal Revenue Service, with its changing rules and regulations, can be a far more significant factor in personal and corporate life than individual or corporate behavior under many other civil and criminal statutes. Today, business often finds itself spending an inordinate amount of time on dealing with the complexities of tax policy and regulations instead of concentrating on productivity which historically gave the American economy its strength.

Ironically, the American Revolution was as much a struggle against bureaucracy as it was against George III. The frustrations and burdens vented upon the colonies by the British bureaucracy in London stymied colonial growth and individual initiative. Our forefathers revolted against a system that tried to regulate their trade and commerce to a design set by a distant bureaucracy.

Thus, the Declaration of Independence was not only a political declaration of liberty but a manifesto for economic freedom as well. The American Revolution challenged government domination of trade and set loose the forces that ended indentured labor services and ultimately ended human slavery in this country.

This economic revolution opened the vast heart of this nation to settlement and development by free men and women seeking to better their own lives. There was a belief, a fervent faith, that free individuals in a market economy could revolutionize the condition of ordinary men in this new world.

Two hundred years of human liberty and economic freedom produced an American enterprise and social system that gave ordinary people the widest possible opportunity. Under their drive and productivity, Americans achieved the highest standard of living in the history of man.

The United States developed a pragmatic balance between individual personal freedom and the common good. It achieved a productive balance between autonomy in enterprise, on the one hand, and governmental directions and restraints, on the other, in economic activity. These relations between government and the private sector have been dynamic—not static—a continually evolving political and economic relationship.

The American enterprise system has always included a significant role for government in economic life. The role involved not only the negatives of restraint but the positives of promotion as well. Indeed, this interplay between governmental action and private initiatives has been a key to our phenomenal national growth. A few examples will illustrate the significance:

a. The extraordinary agricultural production of America's farm families was made possible and stimulated by: (1) federal land grants for homesteads; (2) government construction of roads and canals; (3) the federal land-grant college system; (4) federal agricultural extension and other services; (5) federal farm credit and rural electrification programs; and (6) federal and state agricultural research programs.

b. The transcontinental railroad system which opened up this nation was made possible by federal grants of land and rights-of-way to the railroads.

c. The automobile industry—so important to our economy—owes its existence not only to American industrial ingenuity and private capital investment, but also to the billions of dollars invested by governments at all levels in our national highway system.

d. The worldwide preeminence of the United States aviation industry grew largely out of: (1) government research and development of military aircraft; and (2) federal government financial contributions to airports, airline operations, weather systems, and maintenance of the airways themselves.

These and other public spurs to economic activity were paralleled by government actions to protect the public interest: antitrust and business conduct laws; regulatory measures for safety, health, environment, and the like.

But the basic concept was to encourage the individual and private or voluntary enterprise—within a framework of law that sets the basic rules and seeks to protect the public interest.

Are the basic concepts set forth by the Declaration of Independence as sound today as they were 200 years ago?

Today there are growing claims that a dominant central government in Washington has placed impediments and nonproductive restraints upon individual activity, voluntary association, and economic enterprise. These claims merit our serious consideration despite the extraordinarily constructive and essential role played by the federal government throughout our history, despite the tremendous dedication of loyal civil servants who have made government work, and despite the continuing need for federal leadership and creative initiative.

There are those who see a danger that this central government and its bureaucracy, remote from the great productive regions of industry and commerce, remote from the farms, factories, mines and markets, remote from communities and their governments, is enacting laws and laying down edicts that unnecessarily stifle growth and productivity and bear little relevance to the actual scene.

There is increasing concern that in the pursuit of specific social objectives, the combined effects and broader consequences of legislation on individual liberties and freedoms are not adequately weighed.

There are those who warn that designs set in Washington are stifling individual and corporate initiative, thereby constraining growth, productivity, and the necessary increase in job opportunities.

And so we must ask ourselves: Is there a threat to human liberties today because economic freedoms are being restricted, initiative discouraged, and individual creativity thwarted?

Here in our land, do we run the risk of falling into the trap of thinking that human liberties and economic freedoms can exist, one without the other? They never have.

Throughout the world, the thrust for individual liberty has been challenged and blunted by doctrinaire assertions that economic security must be the prime object of society. It is held by some that only centrally-adopted and centrally-directed planning and programming, and implementation by an all-powerful government, can achieve economic security.

Suppression of human rights and civil liberties, to guarantee obedience to the dictates of an all-powerful state, is now the rule over much of the globe, and the rationale is economic necessity or security. Human liberties are not possible under the statism that now exists in most of today's world.

The risk here in America, however, may not be so much that we will take up the worship of the false gods of totalitarian ideologies; rather that we could drift into statism as a reaction to corruption, and by government's progressively legislating such overwhelming and detailed responsibilities for the ordering of the social and economic life of our society that liberty will be surrendered in the process.

The American federal system has been a bulwark against the over-centralization of government that has all too often impaired individual rights in other lands. Today, however, the power of the federal government with its impact on the daily lives of citizens has undermined the traditional role of state and local government. The enormous fiscal power of the federal government has become overwhelming and the federal grant-in-aid programs which were designed to help states and localities are now in fact inhibiting their ability to meet the most urgent needs of their citizens. The detailed regulations, the lack of flexibility, the mandating of priorities in the federal aid programs have resulted in a weakening of our federal system of government.

The genius of the American system lay not in a mass of detailed regulations but in the fact that government established a broad framework of policy and law to protect the interests of all and within which individuals, groups, and enterprises could operate with great flexibility.

The system also provided a reasonable continuity of policy that gave certainty as to the risks of investment, that sparked initiative and spurred competition, that provided reward for success and penalties for failure, that encouraged efficiency and economy, and gave assurance against confiscation of the product of one's labor.

How far has the nation retreated from this essential concept? With the present extent of governmental regulation and control, with the power of federal expenditures and range of federal taxes, can the historic individual, group, and corporate dynamism survive? Modest-sized and small businesses complain about the enormous amount of governmental licensing, inspection, regulation, taxation, and accounting required just to keep open. The costs can become prohibitive. Federal taxes, particularly the inheritance and estate taxes, have reached such a point as to make it increasingly difficult for family-owned farms and other family businesses to survive as such.

The line between governmental taxation, regulation, and operation of enterprise and that of the private sector is not set in concrete—nor can it nor should it be. However, if the dynamics of individual ambition and the energies that come from autonomy are to be harnessed for the productivity and social good of the nation, there is probably a point of no return in socialization and regulation of private effort. It is an interesting commentary that in the free world there appears to be a great rush toward such socialization and centralized planning and decision-making. Equally significant is the persistent complaint and difficulty in the planned and Socialist nations resulting from such over-centralization—and the almost frantic search for productivity and autonomy sufficient to provide it a chance of achievement.

In considering future directions in government-private sector relationships, the impact of any changes upon the productivity of enterprise requires more consideration than heretofore. The long-held view that America would automatically continue to outproduce the world, that American industry would continue to be the most productive, is no longer accurate. With the outstanding exception of agriculture, the rate of growth of American productivity has fallen behind all other leading industrial nations. This has, in turn, affected the American standard of living which today is no longer first in the rate of increase, but now ranks sixth in this regard.

The ability of America's economy to produce the needed goods and services and to supply the wherewithal for individual income, corporate income, and governmental income is crucial. The purchasing power of that income also rests importantly on the productivity of the economy both in terms of domestic needs and in the exchange of goods, services, and funds with other nations. All of this affects the ability of individuals to provide for themselves out of their income. All of this impacts on the fiscal ability of government to supply essential services and social benefits to the population. How to improve and increase the productivity of the nation is a basic question to be faced not in some distant future but here and now.

The elements involved are complex and interrelated but they are neither beyond our capacity to understand nor our ability to influence. They cannot, however, be isolated from the ideological, political, social, and moral context in which they have been placed. Accordingly, dealing with them can involve highly charged political, emotional, moral and social actions and reactions. A brief review of some of the major problem areas puts this in perspective.

### The Challenge to Growth

For the first time in our history, there is significant opposition to the concept of continued economic growth and the actual development of resources to that end. The debate here in the United States—and throughout the world—over growth versus no-growth is crucial for the future of the United States and the world.

In 1972 the Club of Rome set off the debate in its early reports which questioned both the world's capacity to sustain growth and the very desirability of growth. Its reports suggested that physical resources were inadequate and that disparities of distribution thereof, plus the inabilities of men and their institutions to cope with development, would foreclose continued growth and development. It found "limits to growth" to be essential to avoid future catastrophe and indicated human conflicts would make a shambles of the world, even before the alleged limits of physical resources were reached.

The Club of Rome studies found a wide audience. The authoritative ring of their postulates persuaded some, intimidated others, and challenged thinking people generally. Coming, as they did, at a time when environmental and ecological concerns were being voiced, and when the availability of cheap fossil fuels was being brought into far more realistic appraisal, the Club of Rome studies found a more hospitable reception than earlier doomsday prognostications. They also held an appeal for articulate personages who viewed with increasing dismay the spread of urbanism and the rapid growth and dispersion of population over the landscape.

The challenge of the original Club of Rome studies shook the complacency of the industrial world and the developing world. On analysis, however, the initial reports are better considered as provocation rather than revelation. Like all studies and all computer simulation projects, they are only as valuable as the assumptions upon which they are based and the nature and quality of the input they ingest. The Club of Rome recognized this, and considered the initial reports as but first steps in coming to grips with the future state of the world. Its more recent studies are far less doomsday in outlook on physical resources and human capacity to deal with the problems—albeit sober and deeply concerned for the future.

It appears clear that men can find the resources, provide the technology, and produce the material goods to meet human need. There is no real shortage of material resources. They can be developed. They can be managed. Indeed, the shortage of raw materials is not due to a basic scarcity but to the limited amounts currently available for cheap and easy exploitation.

With work, with ingenuity and increased expenditures of money and effort, most raw material shortages can be overcome and where the product is seriously limited, substitutes can be provided. But it takes not only intelligence and know-how to accomplish this result. It takes initiative, incentive, and huge capital investment.

There are nations of the world with limited material resources that have achieved phenomenal standards of living, which provide freedom of choice and high levels of culture for their inhabitants. There are nations of the world richly endowed with resources that have achieved even more spectacular results. But there are nations of the world amply supplied with resources that have yet to develop—or have actually retrogressed in—their contribution to human needs. And there are, of course, nations of the world lacking in resources, that neither have developed a dynamic for improvement nor scaled their claims and their ambitions accordingly.

The world's capacity to provide for humankind is not a matter of mere physical resources. It is a matter also of human will, human ingenuity, human determination, and human political and social organization.

On this score, there are serious difficulties, for the institutions created by men in different parts of the world vary widely in their commitment to improvement of every man's lot, or in their resignation as to every man's fate. Religious, cultural, ethnic, social, tribal, and political institutions and practices may either contribute to or retard the human being's effort to improve his understanding of the realities of his world and his drive to accomplish a better life for himself, his family, and the broader community. In America, all of these factors have contributed to our concepts of growth, progress, and productivity.

Historically, American institutions have been geared to growth—to settle a vast new frontier land; to provide a better living for an expanding population; to solve the problems of poverty; to ensure not only individual well-being but national security; and to provide expanded opportunity for future generations. This American ethic was a dynamic ethic. It assumed that work and development of resources would yield material, social, and psychological rewards. The American enterprise system was developed in the context of such a consensus. It assumed a dynamic, expanding, and changing demand—in both quality and quantity and variety of goods and services. It assumed a driving effort to meet such demand through invention, innovation, risk-taking, technological adaptation, and rationalization of production. It assumed the flow and ebb of demand and supply in a market economy wherein the role of government was to set the guidelines but not to dominate the process.

Committed to the idea of progress, America has looked to growth and productivity to enable the peoples of vastly different origins, of different economic, social, and cultural situations, to be able to achieve a plateau of living that would mitigate economic and social tension and help amalgamate the varied parts into a greater whole as a nation. Just this past year, we celebrated the success of this effort and the amazing realization of this idea in the Bicentennial observations.

America has been synonymous with growth. The concept of "The American Dream" may be nebulous in some respects but surely not in its emphasis on progress and the corresponding expansion of individual opportunity.

Those who espouse no-growth or restricted growth must face the problem as to how the poor and less advantaged are to advance their lot under such conditions. A static economy, or a significantly slowed economy, means unemployment and income limitation—and presents the problem of how to pay for social security, pensions, and other benefits whose liquidity depends upon sustained growth. The no-growth alternative appears to be to reduce the promised or committed benefits through inflation, with all the hazards such a policy entails.

One can indeed speculate how a democracy such as that in the United States could accommodate to a no-growth commitment. Such a policy would foreswear increased production, jobs, and income. It would look to a static or shrinking pie of goods and services somehow to be divided among the population. The social and political tensions thereby engendered would present monumental problems for our traditional institutions, oriented as they have been in the opposite direction. Clearly, the opportunity for individual self-development, for self-realization, would be restricted, as it is difficult to envision the implementation of a no-growth concept without the imposition of far more regulation and regimentation than has ever pertained here in peacetime.

The antigrowth alternative to our historic commitment to growth has not been, and in all likelihood will not be, put to the American people as a single proposition. No national referendum on the question "Do you favor a national policy of no-growth?" will be placed before the electorate. Rather, the no-growth concept will appear, as to an extent it already has, in pieces of legislation and administrative determinations. The no-growth implications of such piecemeal action may not be overtly evident, nor need the purpose of such actions be primarily designed as part of a no-growth scenario. Yet they may have far-reaching no-growth implications.

A major area, in point, is the environmental protection movement, which need not but frequently does have no-growth implications, if not results. It is significant that since the passage of the Environmental Protection Act and other parallel and complementary federal, state, and local legislation with this design, no new major airport has been built in the United States and the number of planned electric generating facilities has been reduced by significant numbers.

## Environmental Protection

Third-century America will wrestle continually with the act of balancing environmental considerations against other needs to serve the American people.

The whole development of America has involved an impact on the environment. From the first settlements in Virginia and the Pilgrim colony in Massachusetts, there has been a growing impact upon the North American continent's ecological balance. Indeed, civilization itself involves an effort to control environment for the survival, comfort, and convenience of man. The history of various civilizations is, among other things, a chronicle of what men did to the natural state of things to achieve their economic and social conditions and their cultural aspirations.

Moves to conserve the bounty of nature–conservation measures–have been known also throughout most of man's history. What has given impetus to the present day scale of action to protect the environment has been the vast extent of air pollution, water pollution, and soil pollution; the rapid gobbling up of arable land for urban sprawl; the enormous consumption of easily available natural resources; the magnitude of the task of waste disposal; and the extent of despoliation of natural beauty.

Clearly, for the health, safety, and comfort of both present and future generations, environmental protection measures are not only desirable but essential. Just what those measures should be will be a continuing question. There are areas of general agreement as to where action is needed. However, there is by no means agreement on a whole host of measures already put forward, and there is bound to be debate on such matters in the future. One man's environmental boon can be another's economic loss. For one, environmental exploitation may offer gainful opportunity. For another, the same may be environmental desecration.

The scale of values among the people in a democracy such as ours will vary widely. Since beauty may be principally in the eye of the beholder, preservation of scenic vistas can involve wide argument. The quaintness of an old neighborhood of ancient houses may be an historic monument to the observer but it may be a bit of an old slum to those who dwell in it perforce.

In American society the penchant for reform tends to push the pendulum of change to the more extreme position and a period of balance restoration has to ensue. Thus, in the zeal for conservation and environmental protection, measures have been taken that will require corrective adjustment to meet tests of practicality and to ensure compatibility with human needs for a growing population that expects a better life. At the same time, as more is learned about the impact of chemical and organic industrial processes on air, water, soil, and human beings themselves, new environmental protection measures will be enacted.

In a sense, each generation will have to come to grips with the problems of balancing environmental needs and desires against the pressing economic and social needs of the population. Different portions of the nation, different parts of the world, may face certain environmental problems in different dimensions and degrees of serious impact.

Some nations may place all-out industrial development ahead of any deleterious effect on the ecology. Others may be inclined to reverse the process. Even today the competitive position of some American industry in relation to foreign competition has been disadvantaged. The costs of meeting environmental standards and adjusting to changing regulations have increased the total price of a product to the point where it is not competitive. In other cases, environmental requirements have resulted in the closing of enterprises where the costs and other difficulties of compliance are prohibitive. Numbers of foundries in the United States went out of business because of the combined impact of environmental restrictions, smoke stack emission regulations, and new standards for working conditions set by the Occupational Health and Safety Act and the regulations issued under it. In other nations, foundries are being established that could not have met earlier American standards—much less the current ones.

Actually economic development and the protection of the environment are by no means incompatible. Balanced development is essential if a healthy environment is to be provided for the vast populations of the world. If these two objectives are pursued in common rather than as competing or opposing goals, enormous progress could be made.

On a broader scale, the interrelationships of the various parts of the world will determine the global environment. An atmospheric atomic explosion in China dropped some radioactive rain in New Jersey. A Liberian tanker, piloted by a Greek captain, ran aground in international waters and spilled oil that threatened American fishing grounds. Attempts by some nations to conserve the fisheries of the world and rare species of animals are frustrated by the trawlers of other countries and the unrestricted hunting and illegal poaching permitted by still others. How much, in the interests of its own people currently, can any one nation practice restraint and add to its costs in the interest of securing the world's environment when others despoil it for their own interests? The difficulties of arriving at a world consensus are formidable, as the recent Conference on the Law of the Sea demonstrated. But the problems remain and will be exacerbated if no concerted action is agreed upon and taken.

## Energy

It is not possible to speak of growth or of ecology without also speaking about the energy problem. The degree of development of a nation can be measured by its energy consumption. In the past, ready access to energy sources and the ability to tap them efficiently at low cost have been major factors in the industrial growth and strength of the United States. Abundant, locally available, cheap energy has been a major element contributing to America's high standard of living, and a major bulwark for national security.

However, the United States enters its third century in a new and precarious energy position. First, the era of cheap and abundant energy is gone. Second, domestic supplies of energy are not adequate to meet the United States' needs. Third, the dependence of the United States on foreign oil has reached the point where at times more than 50 percent of the total consumed has been imported. Fourth, environmental restrictions have hampered the development of nuclear- and coal-powered electric generating facilities and the exploration and development of new oil, gas, and coal deposits. Fifth, the rising costs due to inflation, plus the difficulties of raising capital, are deterrents to new energy source developments. Sixth, energy conservation remains more a verbal policy than a practical reality despite all the public attention devoted to it. Seventh, with over half of the supply of petroleum necessary for daily life in America dependent on foreign sources, OPEC nations could cut off supplies to the United States at any time and the supply could be interrupted by hostile military action. Eighth, new forms of energy—solar, geothermal, wind, urban waste, tidal, nuclear fission, organic from various crops, are still in the experimental stage and far from economic practical application on a large enough scale to substitute for present day coal, oil, gas, nuclear, and hydroelectric power.

Serious energy questions must be faced by American leadership, therefore, both to sustain the nation, its economy and its people's standard of living and to provide for any future growth and improvement in the American quality of life. The national security questions are urgent and are likely to become more so if actions are not taken to improve the domestic energy supply or to make access to foreign sources secure.

There has been a lot of wishful thinking on these issues. Conservation of energy—by which is meant reduction in its use—can cut demand. But extensive compulsory saving—or, for that matter, extensive voluntary saving—can have an adverse impact on sectors of the economy. Certainly conservation must be pursued and more fuel-efficient transportation, for example, must be developed and produced. However, the human needs, the necessity for jobs and income, for improved living for all Americans—particularly those at the lower rungs of the economic ladder—will require more rather than less total energy for the future, even assuming substantial conservation measures are also achieved.

Conservation, on any major scale, will require substantial capital investment now in thermal insulation, and more efficient machines, vehicles, and equipment. It will mean higher prices to encourage energy conservation and to encourage production from new energy sources at home. The Federal Energy Administration has indicated that this would entail deregulation of oil and natural gas—an end to governmentally fixed low prices.

One should not equate conservation of energy with automatic ecological improvement, as some people are wont to do. Actually, environmental improvement will require more energy rather than less. To purify water and air, to reduce the effluents from motor vehicles and airplanes, to reduce noise, involves more energy not less. There is, accordingly, a need to balance energy supply and energy potential with environmental objectives.

We must recognize, also, that the production of energy from any source has some ecological impact. The materials for solar energy collection and concentration must be produced. The heat collectors and other equipment will have their impact on aesthetics, space, and costs. Geothermal energy also will have its special risks, material costs, and effects. This is by way of saying that if one leaves the more traditional sources—oil, gas, coal, nuclear, and hydroelectric—one does not escape environmental considerations, although there is a tendency for certain anti-nuclear and anti-fossil fuel groups to do so.

The United States has the resources within its borders and the technology to achieve a substantial level of energy self-reliance, should it decide to do so. Offshore drilling for oil and gas, extensive development of coal mining, expansion of nuclear capacity, together, could achieve a large measure of energy self-reliance within a decade to a decade and one-half. Such an all-out effort would involve a very large capital outlay, streamlining of approval procedures, and a realistic pricing policy for energy—sufficient to justify the raising and investment of the large capital sums required.

From what is known of the world's resources, the world faces a depletion of both petroleum and natural gas resources at a rapid rate. There is therefore a need to turn to other more abundant energy sources—coal, nuclear energy, and, down the road, probably solar, geothermal, organic crop, and other energy possibilities. It is argued, in favor of a massive energy self-reliance drive now, that the lead time required for nuclear and coal plants is currently a decade and that an intensive research and development program should be undertaken for the more exotic sources, as yet economically unproven for large-scale use.

The financing of an all-out energy self-reliance program has been challenged because of its total cost and its alleged inflationary impact. Obviously, the nature of the financing itself would help to determine how inflationary such a massive program might be. If the program were financed by a combination of private and public effort—with the private energy companies permitted to charge adequate rates for their operating and capital costs, and government financing much of its share by a tax on energy use—the inflationary impact would be different than if prices of energy were kept artificially below market rates, as at present, by law, while the government sought to finance energy development by more federal debt without corresponding increases in taxes to amortize it.

The debate about the energy companies and whether oil companies should be allowed to go into the coal and other businesses—solar, geothermal, etc.—also bears on the question of financing. The large energy companies can provide both capital and expertise which could not be as well provided by smaller competitive companies restricted to a single energy source. The whole complex of discovery, production, marketing, and distribution would pose different problems if, as some urge, the large energy companies were to be split apart, whether horizontally, vertically, or both.

Again, the questions raised cannot satisfactorily be resolved on the domestic front alone. The international world has its enormous non-American energy organizations–Arab, Italian, French, German, Russian, and others. These, and others will be added, will be competitors for American-owned or -controlled enterprises–national or multinational. To date the large United States privately-owned energy companies, particularly petroleum companies, have provided the United States with an important vehicle for developing and assuring access to foreign energy sources.

It is suggested that major steps by the United States toward energy self-reliance would give the nation a freer hand in foreign relations, relieving the existing pressure from the OPEC nations, who would foresee the end of their influence due to their monopoly of foreign oil imports.

The early years of this third century will determine the direction the nation will take in energy. Failure to face the facts, to act positively to promote conservation, and to add new energy-producing facilities will be as determinative as positive action. The action or inaction on energy will affect both the domestic social and economic scene and the place of the nation in the world.

### Access to Raw Materials

From its beginning as a nation, the United States has stood for the "Freedom of the Seas," for access to the other nations of the world for trade and commerce. The United States has long been in the vanguard of the "free trade" countries, both for the export of American produce and the import of finished goods and raw materials.

For certain key raw materials, the United States relies on imports to sustain its industry–bauxite, chrome, and other materials in addition to petroleum. With a very few of these raw materials the United States has no adequate supply, but with others the imported materials are less expensive or more inexpensively fabricated than American materials or substitute materials. Accordingly, for reasons of competition with foreign nations, and for lower cost products for Americans, access to these materials is of major importance. A few of these imported materials are also of critical importance for national defense–chrome, for example, of which the United States does not have adequate supplies.

Stockpiling, the development of substitutes, or the discovery of new and cheaper ways of using ores are all methods open to consideration in order to free the nation from its danger of interruption of supplies from abroad.

Of increasing interest is the availability of strategic raw materials from the oceans, the Arctic, and from Antarctica. Here, again, vital decisions will be made either actively or passively regarding development of these potentialities for the benefit of the American people and people of other countries of the world–an important factor in the promotion of world peace.

How to finance these developments, the role of private industry, the role of government therein, are major questions to be faced. If international agreement on access to the oceans and Antarctica and the Arctic is not reached, should the United States go it alone?

## The United States Free Market in Relation to State-Planned Economies

As the second century of the United States came to an end, the relation of America's enterprise market economy to the planned economies of the Socialist states was brought into sharper focus than heretofore. The USSR purchases of large amounts of American grain in the free markets of the United States had a major impact on prices in the domestic market. They also set in motion probably the most serious discussion to date of the vulnerability of the free markets of the United States to bloc purchases by Socialist, planned economy countries. The potentiality for positive results as well as the possible disruption of markets was brought to public attention as never before.

What a free market country like the United States can or should do to protect itself against such disruption, accidental or intentional, raises major questions. A free market offers a foreign Communist, Socialist, or otherwise state-trading nation an opportunity to buy up American supplies, even if it should not need them, and, if they are in short supply, later sell them back to Americans for increased prices. What steps should the United States government take to protect our producers, our consumers, and our system itself against such foreign buying?

The whole area of how the state-planned national economies—with their central trading, buying, and selling—should relate to the American and other free market economies is one that requires far more attention than it has been given. Trade among these nations, and those that fall in between as partially planned economies, is surely desirable for the future and can be a major element in the preservation of peace. It may well mean, however, a major adjustment in America's traditional international trading approaches and, indeed, in some of its domestic policies—particularly in the antitrust field.

## Food and American Agriculture

One of the great strengths of America has been its agricultural production. In 1776, it took ten American farmers to feed one city person. By 1930 one farmer fed ten people. Today, one American farmer produces enough food and fiber for fifty-six persons—forty-four in the United States and twelve others overseas. The magnitude of this achievement of American enterprise is seen when it is realized that in the Soviet Union 30 percent of the population is in agricultural activity and the USSR still has to import foods for its people. After sixty years of Soviet promises and enormous costs in lives and suffering, the USSR finds itself required to import food from capitalist America. The Soviet state farms and collective farms fare poorly when compared with the initiative, inventiveness, and productivity of American farm families and the American industrial and governmental supports for their efforts. The agricultural exports of the United States are one of its principal earners of foreign exchange. Indeed, American food surpluses—together with those of Canada and Australia—are major bulwarks against famine in many other parts of the world.

The fact is that our foodstuffs and fibers are major and essential elements in our foreign trade and our balance of payments. It also should be pointed out that it is American agricultural science, technology, hard work, and productivity that make its surpluses. Other regions of the world could produce very substantial agricultural surpluses or contribute much more to feeding their own populations if they applied themselves to the task and overcame the ideological and institutional obstacles that stood in their way.

Major questions face the country as we look to the future. Should government policy encourage American farmers to produce more food through subsidies to export even more? Or would such production increases, added to other production, flood the markets and cut farm prices and income thereby? It must always be remembered that the effective market for agricultural products is the demand by those with purchasing power. Hence, the huge Soviet grain purchases were beneficial to the farmers who produce grain. The American consumer, however, paid higher prices for produce as a result.

As the American farmer depends for a significant share of his prosperity on the sale of produce abroad, he has a vital stake in American foreign policy—in America's ability to ensure the "Freedom of the Seas" to American commerce and hence national security. He also has a vital stake in the solution of the energy problem. Higher fuel costs or scarcities of fossil fuel can mean higher costs to the farmer or severe hardships as supplies become hard to come by. The price of fertilizer, the costs of plowing, planting, harvesting, and shipping are all geared to the costs of fuel and energy.

As America moves into its third century, one of its great strengths is the productivity of its agriculture, but the future outlook for continued productivity, although ever increasing, is bound up with the complex of other forces and the problems they engender.

## Science, Technology, and Increasing Productivity

As in agriculture, so in many other fields of endeavor, American technology through increasing productivity has given strength to the nation and benefit to the world. In its history, particularly this past century, American practical "know-how" has taken the findings of science, both here and abroad, and converted them into useful applications that have revolutionized the industrial and commercial world, have changed the face of military effort, and have brought new dimensions to human health and comfort. Because of its technological prowess the United States has gained the lion's share of the market for commercial aircraft, led the world in computers and electronic data processing, commercial communication satellites, vaccines for infantile paralysis, and hosts of other areas.

This particular interest and ability has been noteworthy, as well, in the fields of administration and management. American managerial knowledge and practices have influenced the whole world, particularly since the end of World War II.

The practical bent of Americans, their concern with "how to do," their concern for progress and medical benefit for the many from discoveries and inventions, have made the United States the world leader in technology. If there had been any doubt before, World War II, and its immediate aftermath, would have certainly dispelled it.

However, as America enters its third century the competition from other nations–Japan, Germany, other Western European countries, and the Soviet Union–presents a new and major challenge to America's technological supremacy. There are also challenges to the nation of domestic origins on a scale not heretofore encountered. The environmental movement has raised doubts and raised roadblocks to technological development. The stopping of the SST aircraft construction and the anti-nuclear development pressure groups are cases in point.

Although not necessarily so intended, governmental regulations respecting new products, new drugs, pollution control, and the like can act as a brake on technology–particularly upon experimental applications and testing. The American educational system has also undergone changes that have given less emphasis to technology than heretofore. American universities' significant ties with industry and government, so important in World War II and the postwar period, have been altered and in some cases even severed in the wake of the campus revolts of the 1960s.

These transformations raise questions about the future. America's lead in technology has been one of its hallmarks. It is a major means of creating a comfortable life-style for most Americans and a promise for all of them. It is one of the kingpins of America's world commerce and of its national security.

The unique relationship in the field of technology between government and the private sector–industries, universities, foundations–has been one of America's greatest strengths. The weakening of these productive associations raises questions regarding future American technological progress in both the civilian and military areas. The initiative, ingenuity, and pragmatic sense of Americans has stood them well for two centuries. It will take substantial effort and a positive commitment to ensure their continuation.

**Military Security and Foreign Policy**

The United States came out of World War II militarily stronger than ever before, but also more exposed than ever before. With the might of its conventional arms plus the atomic bomb the United States stood at the apex of military power. However, World War II and its aftermath saw the decline of British and French military power, the destruction and subsequent limitation by treaty of the Japanese military forces, and the decline of power in the other nations of what is loosely called "the free world." With the British navy no longer able to patrol the seven seas and no Western European land forces able to cope with the Soviet rising power there, the United States found itself the chief bulwark of power to balance the rising Soviet military presence.

The enormous buildup of military power by the USSR has already threatened the strategic balance between the Soviet Bloc and the Free World headed by the United States. By achieving at least parity in nuclear weapons, by an overwhelming land army and by a navy that has grown to such a point as to really challenge the sea lanes, the USSR has become a power of serious concern to the non-Communist world.

Soviet armed intervention in Czechoslovakia, Hungary, and East Germany quelled efforts in those countries to move toward a more liberal society. The Russian army units in the satellite countries remain both as a military force poised against NATO and as a domestic force to help keep the satellites in the Soviet orbit. The successes of Communist arms in Vietnam, the Angola incident in which Castro Cuban troops were utilized, Soviet support of so-called wars of liberation and covert operations, all indicate the determination to hold what is within the Soviet bloc and to expand its influence and control.

The Nixon Administration's opening of the door to China was a measure to help redress the balance of power. The Nixon effort at "détente" was designed to establish better relationships and communications with the Soviets to avoid surprise attack and looked to a relaxation of tensions and curtailment of the rate of Soviet nuclear, army, and naval buildup. The SALT agreement represents a major step in this direction.

The relationships with the USSR and with China remain two of the most vital problems confronting America. They have many facets and involve complex considerations. But, to date, the Soviet and Chinese expansionist aims have never been renounced; rather, they have been reiterated repeatedly. So long as this remains the case and the major military and naval buildup continues, America faces the necessity of its own preparedness and the necessity of a foreign policy that can provide a counterbalance to such a concentration of military power.

The disillusionment in the United States during and following the Vietnam War, the persistent challenge to military spending by certain articulate domestic groups, and the costs of escalating American military preparedness all pose serious obstacles to building a defense that can counteract the USSR's presence. This may be particularly acute with respect to American naval forces and necessary air cover. The "Freedom of the Seas" is not merely a doctrine but a vital necessity for the United States and the free world.

Surrounding this central problem are the relationships with America's allies and friends and the so-called Third World countries. In all of these activities, economics plays a major role and a strong American economy adds strength to the free world's position. There are major new forces rising in various regions of the world that demand recognition and that must be coped with. The tide of change runs so rapidly that America's responses will have to be not only wise and sound but timely in order to be effective. This means that America must anticipate emerging crises and be prepared to deal with them.

## The Morale of the People

The spirit of America has been one of energy and creativity to meet the needs of individuals. It has emphasized individualism–individual economic freedom, individual political liberty, and individual responsibility. In our American law and in our society for these two hundred years, the focus has been on increasing opportunity for more and more individuals to attain all that their talents, capacities, and aspirations could achieve. Through the drive, energy, creativity, and responsible behavior of free individuals, it was assumed that both a great nation would be built and a productive society established to improve the quality of life for everyone. The results of two centuries of such activity speak eloquently for the soundness of the concept and the vitality of the spirit.

The world today, of course, is far more complex and intertwined than that of 200, 100, 50, or even ten years ago. Industrialization, technology, mass communication, new health and life expectancy levels, changes in family and other traditional economic and social patterns have brought new stresses and strains on our political, economic, and social fabric. The individual is caught up in these massive developments and adjustment to secure the positive prospects they offer is complicated by the negative potentialities they could entail. In the search for betterment and in the effort to forestall regression, group activity is engendered to bring pressure or counterpressure on government or other institutions in the society. How the individual relates to such groups, how they may advantage or disadvantage him, become continuing concerns in a nation where individuality has been its hallmark and voluntary association and full freedom of expression have been canons of its faith.

How much Americans value individuality and individual political liberty and economic freedom–how hard and how much they are willing to work, sacrifice, and fight to sustain and advance these fundamental objectives–will determine the course of democracy not only here at home but in the rest of the world.

## The Work of the Commission on Critical Choices for Americans

To gain the future, we must analyze the past, appraise the present, and assess the future in the terms of the desirable and the attainable consonant with our living faith in the individual and our commitment to the cause of human dignity.

For free people to make the broad judgments and for their leadership to make the specific decisions involves no mean task. It involves the sorting out of the basic issues and concerns from the welter of data, opinion, contention and prediction that surrounds us. To assist in this process, to help identify the more fundamental issues, to examine the alternatives that may be offered in deciding, were prime purposes of the creation of the Commission on Critical Choices for Americans.

The need for a review of our approaches to problems and the need to develop new concepts to meet today's needs and tomorrow's requirements became increasingly clear in the late 1960s and early 1970s. While I was governor of New York State, it became evident to me that many governmental programs—federal, state, and local—and the institutional arrangements to implement them, had lost or were losing much of their relevance and capacities to meet the present and emergent situations. It was clear that we needed to review our approaches and develop new concepts which would permit us to reshape government programs to serve people better. A full-scale examination of the workings of our federal system in relation to the realities of today's world was needed.

It was for this reason that late in 1972, I organized a major New York State study regarding the Role of the Modern State in Our Changing Federal System.

Shortly after the work on this study began, it became evident that the problems confronting New York State could not be analyzed, much less solved, unless they were viewed in a national and even international context. It is no longer possible in this complex and interdependent society for a single state to meet the needs of its people and determine its own destiny from within its boundaries alone.

Late in 1973, therefore, I organized the Commission on Critical Choices to take over and greatly broaden the scope of the initial New York study. Forty-two prominent Americans from both political parties and from across the nation agreed to become members of this national commission. A list of the members appears at the beginning of this volume.

The secretary of state, the secretary of the treasury, and the majority and minority leaders of the Congress became ex-officio members. The first meeting of the commission was held in December 1973.

A study commission was not a new idea for me. I have always believed strongly that one of the best ways to deal with complex and difficult problems is to bring together a group of intelligent and concerned people and ask them to analyze the problems and develop new approaches to meeting them. In the late

1950s, for example, I served as chairman of the Special Studies Project of the Rockefeller Brothers Fund. The influential reports published as a result of this project were the result of more than 100 American citizens thinking and working together over a period of four years.

While I was governor of New York State, I frequently organized study groups and it was a result of these studies that many innovative programs were begun in New York.

When I organized the Commission on Critical Choices for Americans in late 1973, it had become clear that the institutions and values which had accounted for our astounding progress during the past two centuries was straining to cope with the massive problems of the current era. The increase in the tempo of change and the vastness and complexity of the wholly new situations which were evolving with accelerated change had created a widespread sense that our political and social system had serious inadequacies.

For too long, we had been operating on a basis of reacting to crises, counting on crash programs and the expenditures of large sums of money to solve problems.

The purpose of the commission was to help provide the factual basis and ideas so that we could look ahead and plan for the future. Its task was to analyze present trends, to determine whether they would be beneficial for the future, and, if not, to set forth the choices available to the American people to change these trends. The commission was not designed to do original research, but rather to bring together and synthesize and analyze the vast amount of research material that already existed.

As indicated by its name, the commission was not to make recommendations, but to place before the American people the critical choices they would have to make if they wanted a free, vibrant America in the future. It was a group of concerned men and women without axes to grind who voluntarily joined together to help determine the facts and formulate the choices before the American people.

The commission's work was financed by the Third Century Corporation, a New York not-for-profit organization. The Corporation received contributions from individuals and foundations to advance the commission's activities. No government funds were involved.

Because of the complexity and interdependence that exist in the world, the commission decided to organize its work on a basis that emphasized the interrelationships of the critical choices and that avoided the pitfall of looking at any one critical area in isolation. To accomplish this, we set up panels of members of the commission, with outside panelists, which grouped the interrelated areas together. Overlapping membership of the panels was worked out to ensure a coordinated consideration of the subjects under review. There were, in all, six panels:

*Panel I*: Energy and its Relationship to Ecology, Economics and World Stability;

*Panel II:* Food, Health, World Population and the Quality of Life.
*Panel III*: Raw Materials, Industrial Development, Capital Formation, Employment and World Trade;
*Panel IV*: International Trade and Monetary Systems, Inflation and the Relationship Among Differing Economic Systems;
*Panel V*: Change, National Security and Peace;
*Panel VI*: Quality of Life of Individuals and Communities in the U.S.A.

The members of each panel are listed at the end of this volume.

From its beginning, the commission was to have a two-year life and was to complete its work by the end of 1975. One of the major reasons I had resigned as governor of New York State in December 1973 was to be able to devote my time to being chairman of the commission. I had every intention of remaining as chairman until its work was completed. The year 1974, however, brought to this country a constitutional crisis and when President Ford asked me to be the vice president of the United States, I accepted. This meant that I had to resign as chairman of the commission. In February 1975, Dr. William J. Ronan took over as acting chairman of the commission.

Under Dr. Ronan's leadership, the reports of the first three panels were completed and these are included in this volume. I should point out that these panel reports do not necessarily represent a consensus of opinions of all the panel members, nor necessarily the view of each individual panel member. They do present the information deemed necessary for the leaders and people of this country to consider thoughtfully the critical choices we must make in the areas of energy; food, health, and population; and raw materials.

At the beginning of its work, the commission decided that the most urgent priority was to complete the reports of the first three panels. These reports would analyze the worldwide situation in key resources such as energy, food, and raw materials and would provide the background necessary before the commission could address the areas to be studied by panels IV, V, and VI such as U.S. security and the quality of the life within the United States.

Given the two-year time frame set for completion of the commission's work, there was not time to complete the reports of panels IV, V, and VI. A decision was made, therefore, to publish the studies and papers which were prepared for the commission's considerations by outstanding scholars in their fields. These background reports had been written by 128 of the best minds in the nation. The publication of these reports would give the public the benefit of their ideas and insights.

The various studies were organized into a series of fourteen books, each with clearly defined topics of interest. With the publication of these fourteen volumes, 128 outstanding authors are now reporting directly to the country on the critical choices we face both at home and abroad.

Although all the subjects dealt with in this series of books may not be of interest to everyone, this series in my opinion constitutes the best single source for learning about the factors and trends that will determine our future.

The following is a brief description of each of the volumes which have been published.

*Volume I: Vital Resources*. This book presents, in addition to this essay, the reports of panels I, II, and III. The reports set forth the key trends in these critical areas and discuss the choices before the American people. They show that critical choices in energy, food, population, and raw materials are interdependent. They also highlight the fact that choices in these areas cannot be made in isolation from each other nor in isolation from their impact on the economy, the environment, the quality of life, and our relations with other countries.

*Volume II: The Americans: 1976* is edited by Irving Kristol, the Henry R. Luce Professor of Urban Values at New York University and editor of *The Public Interest* magazine, and by Paul H. Weaver of *Fortune* Magazine. Sixteen distinguished contributors examine basic ideas about American institutions and how these ideas and institutions are changing. The areas discussed range from the federal system, education, diplomacy, security, and constitutional law, to the role of the family and the American dream.

*Volume III: How Others See Us.* Lloyd A. Free, of the Institute for International Social Research, here presents the results of a major poll of leaders and peoples of Western Europe, the Americas, and Japan, on how they view America and its relationship to them.

*Volume IV: Power & Security*. Edward Teller, nuclear physicist, Hans Mark, NASA Ames Research Center, and John S. Foster Jr., former Director of Defense Research and Engineering, Department of Defense, here outline the facts and clarify the interrelated issues of energy, technology and national defense.

*Volume V: Trade, Inflation, & Ethics.* Thirteen authors focus on urgent issues of domestic and international prosperity and stability, including export-import patterns, inflation, productivity, monetary reforms, petroleum, raw material exchanges, multinational corporations, and the ethical basis of international trade.

*Volume VI: Values of Growth.* This study of world population, food and the environment approaches immense problems in a historical and also ethical perspective, demanding the frequently lacking virtues of harmonization and common sense.

*Volume VII: Qualities of Life.* Twenty distinguished contributors look at the United States today and examine an array of subjective as well as objective factors associated not only with living standards and community planning, but also more amorphous though vitally important questions of attitude, value, meaning, and individual purpose.

*Volume VIII: Western Europe: The Trials of Partnership.* This is the first of a series of seven volumes of outstanding studies of regions of the world under the direction of Nancy Maginnes Kissinger. These volumes present the independent view of independent experts. This volume is edited by David S. Landes of Harvard University and includes essays by ten outstanding authorities. It shows that Europe's needs and priorities and its relations with the United States now evidence the cooler ties of a troubled partnership.

*Volume IX: The Soviet Empire: Expansion & Détente.* This volume, edited by William E. Griffith of the Massachusetts Institute of Technology, contains the thoughts of eleven authors and analyzes the present situation and projects future developments in the USSR and Eastern Europe, and their implications for United States policy.

*Volume X: The Middle East: Oil, Conflict, & Hope.* This volume, containing sixteen essays, is edited by A. L. Udovitch of Princeton University. It looks at the basic factors at work within the states of the Middle East and within the region as a whole, identifying the problems America should be concerned with, and outlining policy options available.

*Volume XI: Africa From Mystery to Maze.* Helen Kitchen, former editor of *Africa Report*, has assembled a group of eleven distinguished contributors who focus on the many different elements of a continent which will have an increasing impact on world affairs.

*Volume XII: China & Japan: A New Balance of Power.* China and Japan, as Donald C. Hellmann of the University of Washington and his six contributors point out, are global and regional powers that are changing the world in their own different ways.

*Volume XIII: Southern Asia: The Politics of Poverty & Peace.* Donald C. Hellmann's companion volume, covering the aftermath of the Vietnam War and the population-poverty equation in India, defines new concepts of interdependence in a region in which development is often considered beyond reach. This volume contains essays by five authorities.

*Volume XIV: Latin America: Struggle for Progress.* This study by James D. Theberge, Ambassador to Nicaragua, and Roger W. Fontaine of the Center for Strategic and International Studies, Georgetown University, measures the changes in the long-neglected continent and their potential impact on the United States.

These fourteen volumes represent an extraordinarily thorough development of the essential information we will need as we consider our choices, and make up our own minds, on the problems and opportunities of national and international life. I believe that the series will help provide the insights, the knowledge and the ideas we will find helpful in a rapidly changing world. Here indeed is a useful set of road maps and signs and directional markers as we move into our third century.

# I

# Report of Panel I: Energy and Its Relationship to Ecology, Economics, and World Stability

## I. Overview of Choices

Many critical choices confront our nation as it embarks on its third century. Perhaps none is more pressing than that concerned with how we can best obtain adequate and dependable supplies of energy, a matter about which Americans still have considerable uncertainty. We do not have a consensus of opinion on energy issues, and many Americans are not even sure what the key issues are.

Basic decisions on energy are urgently needed now; they are long overdue. But while indecision is surely harmful to the nation, the selection of the wrong course of action could be even worse. Policies affecting energy can influence our economic evolution and our social and political development for decades to come.

Our choices, moreover, cannot be made solely on the basis of what promises to give us the maximum amount of energy security, however defined. As a nation, we have other important objectives: a healthy economy, a strong private sector, a clean environment, a peaceful world. Thus, the energy choices we make must give adequate recognition to the close interrelations among energy, ecology, the domestic economy, national security, and the world community.

As far as can now be foreseen, the era of cheap and abundant energy for the United States has passed. Domestic production of oil and natural gas is inadequate to meet current needs, thus necessitating a heavy dependence on imports. These negative trends were evident even before the energy crisis of 1973 and, indeed, made that crisis possible. What is new is the realization that the United States can no longer rely on obtaining adequate supplies of foreign oil.

Yet, in the absence of domestic measures, U.S. dependence on foreign oil production continues to grow. At the same time, the prices of petroleum imports and of all other forms of energy have risen sharply, adding to consumer costs, reducing real income, and thus exerting a deflationary influence on the domestic economy. In addition, some producing nations have already taken action or are contemplating steps to reduce their exports of energy to the United States and its allies.

The high volume of imports exposes the United States to national defense and national security risks. Oil has already been used as a political weapon against the U.S. national interest, and as long as there is no viable alternative to foreign oil, this potential threat to the United States will continue.

The American economy and the American standard of living have been and still are dependent importantly on plentiful energy. To develop the necessary volume of domestic energy resources to support these activities will require large amounts of capital and will involve substantial lead times.

Given the character of American energy production, the capital required would have to come from both private and public sources. If domestic energy prices are permitted to reflect demand and if the profits therefrom are largely reserved for investment in energy development, the private corporations in the energy field and the existing public agencies, such as the Tennessee Valley Authority, could raise much of their own capital. Alternatively, the capital could come from direct government, taxpayer investment or from some private-public agency combination.

Conservation measures can reduce the demand for energy. Rising prices of energy can promote conservation, as can voluntary practices and governmental regulations. Some new forms of energy production, such as converting waste into energy, can make the objectives of conservation and energy policy wholly converge.

Both energy conservation measures and programs to increase energy production will have an impact on the environment. At the same time, environmental protection measures will have an impact on energy production and energy conservation. Although it is not popularly recognized, both energy conservation and environmental improvement programs, as well as energy production programs, will require substantial capital investment on energy inputs. Energy conservation and development programs also may involve a restructuring of the relationship between the private and public sectors and, in particular, a reassessment of those government policies—federal, state, and local—that impact on energy supply and demand.

Dependence on foreign oil in other industrial countries is much greater than in the United States. Arbitrary supply cutbacks and price hikes may well have a destabilizing effect on international relations. One must, therefore, consider these broader implications when discussing the problems of energy.

There are some who advocate that we should not adopt any new energy program or strategy. It has been claimed that the energy crisis was resolved when the oil embargo was lifted. In all OPEC countries (Organization of Petroleum Exporting Countries), actual production of oil at the end of 1975 was less, in some cases much less, than production capacity. This reduces the likelihood of another oil embargo or of another large price hike, and is the reason why some economists argue that OPEC is bound to collapse. To take any extraordinary steps would, in this view, close the barn door after the horse has escaped and, in fact, prevent the horse from getting back into the barn.

Moreover, there is concern that major efforts to achieve energy self-reliance may interfere with the attainment of economic and environmental objectives and may involve international complications. Accordingly, only a minimal type of self-reliance program, if any, would be considered desirable by those who hold this view.

We must recognize, however, that a decision not to adopt a major energy program of expanded production and increased conservation is also a choice. Its benefits must be weighed carefully against the economic and national security costs of our becoming even further dependent on foreign sources of oil. We must clearly face the issues raised by such a choice, particularly since the energy crisis that erupted at the end of 1973 was followed by a policy of, essentially, inaction and drift. There was considerable evidence by mid-1975 of what this policy involves:

1. The proportion of U.S. oil consumption accounted for by foreign oil has increased from some 29 percent in 1972 to about 35 percent by mid-1975.
2. U.S. expenditures for oil imports were running at an annual rate of some $25 billion in 1975, compared to $4.5 billion in 1972.
3. The international monetary reserves of the OPEC countries jumped from $5 billion at the end of 1970 to some $55 billion by mid-1975. For Saudi Arabia alone, reserves increased from $0.7 billion to $21 billion.
4. Electric utilities reduced expenditures for plant and equipment investments, and even cancelled previous orders on nuclear power plants.
5. The leasing of public lands containing fossil fuels for development and offshore oil drilling was not accelerated.
6. The reduction in the oil depletion allowance affected the rate of exploration and drilling for domestic oil.
7. The present system of controls threatened the adequate and equitable distribution of natural gas supplies.
8. Demand for energy was affected more by the economic recession than by ad hoc conservation measures, thus threatening an increase in OPEC's leverage over the world market once economic recovery gets underway.
9. Inaction encouraged the oil producing countries, including non-OPEC members, to raise prices further at the end of September 1975, with the prospect of even more price hikes during 1976.

These negative developments can be expected to continue if we choose to drift with no coherent strategies and programs regarding energy. The new federal energy legislation enacted in late 1975 contains a number of significant provisions. It does not, however, come to grips with the essential questions regarding the basic issue of whether or not this country should be self-reliant in energy.

If we choose an activist energy program, we must determine our objectives and how they can best be achieved. The argument in favor of energy self-reliance rests on the belief that increasing imports of foreign oil makes the United States and its allies vulnerable to economic, political, and national security pressures, including another oil embargo, disruptions of the sea lanes, and financial maneuverings. The OPEC price rise has already adversely affected the U.S. trade accounts and has contributed substantially to inflation and recession throughout Western Europe, Japan, and the United States. Reliance on imports also works to prevent development of ample domestic energy resources, which could otherwise stimulate the economy and increase employment—and give us a better bargaining position vis-à-vis the OPEC cartel, as well as greater national security. Moreover, even assuming a peaceful world and no OPEC price rigging, the long-range outlook for imports is not good because of the limited world supply of oil.

*The key choice, then, is whether we should adopt energy self-reliance as a national objective. If the decision is positive, we face a number of other significant choices:*

1. *If energy self-reliance is considered a desirable objective, should primary emphasis be placed on the expansion of domestic energy production, on energy conservation, or on oil storage?*

**Argument for Domestic Energy Production.** The United States is one of the few countries that has sufficient resources to be self-reliant in energy. We should develop these resources because they can potentially provide a long-term solution to dependence on foreign energy supplies. Utilizing appropriate technology, such development need not have an excessively adverse impact on the environment. Continued economic growth and an improved quality of life require more, not less, energy.

**Argument for Energy Conservation.** Saving energy through conservation can provide immediate results in achieving energy self-reliance, whereas the expansion of energy production generally involves long lead times. By conserving energy, there may be less need to develop those energy sources that could have especially adverse impacts on the environment. The implementation of energy conservation programs, up to a point, could be relatively easy and much less costly than those for energy development programs. However, energy conservation on a major scale and over an extended period of time could also require large capital expenditures and long lead times.

**Argument for Oil Storage.** Increased oil storage capacity would give us a relatively inexpensive form of insurance against a new oil embargo. Such a measure would be particularly effective if oil storage could be established on an early schedule, i.e., during the period when there is an imbalance between the production and consumption of energy in the United States and in the world. Oil storage also has the advantage that it can be used in a flexible manner and may create fewer disturbances of the environment and quality of life than some of the other strategies that are advocated.

2. *To encourage domestic energy production and conservation, how much reliance should be placed on the price system and how much on government programs?*

**Argument for Reliance on Prices.** Our market economy is based on the premise that prices are the most efficient allocator of resources. This applies to all sectors, including energy. Higher prices will stimulate private investment in the expansion of existing energy sources and in the development of new ones, and will also help encourage energy savings. Government allocation, however, promotes inefficiencies, requires the bureaucratic control of details, and is generally reflected in higher taxes and higher costs of services and products.

**Argument for Reliance on Government Programs.** The market economy leads to inequities. In times of crisis, such as military or economic warfare (which is applicable to the energy situation), government measures are needed to deal with the situation. This need not imply a permanent deviation from the market economy.

3. *In stimulating domestic energy production and conservation, how much reliance should be placed on private R&D and how much on public R&D?*

**Argument for Private Research and Development.** During the period from 1948-1955, the Atomic Energy Commission (AEC) spent many billions of dollars on the development of nuclear reactors. However, most of the economically viable proposals on reactor design emerged after the private sector entered the field. Most great industrial developments, including those in oil refining and production, have been pioneered and developed by private industry. If the appropriate economic conditions and favorable governmental policies prevail, the private sector could be a better job than governmental agencies.

**Argument for Public Research and Development.** The Atomic Energy Commission has spearheaded the development of nuclear reactors, which now appear on the world scene as a viable alternative energy source. Many have criticized the concentration on atomic energy, but most of the critics suggest that a similar public effort could solve the energy problem if the research objective were to be geothermal energy, solar energy, or one of several other suggestions. A broad and hopefully successful research program, including energy conservation, has been presented to the Congress by the Energy Research and Development Administration (ERDA), the successor organization of the AEC.

4. *To what extent should programs to stimulate energy production and conservation involve economic implications?*

**Argument for Economic Criteria.** Programs to develop our domestic energy resources and to conserve on energy use will require capital investments–the larger the program, the higher the cost. Up to a point, such investments could benefit the economy by accelerating economic recovery and reducing unemployment. Moreover, an all-out program to promote energy self-reliance could cost $1 trillion or more through 1985. This would invariably increase the proportion of total investment devoted to energy if only because such a large effort would reduce the availability of funds for other important sectors. This kind of program could thus promote continuing inflation by putting pressure on productive resources. It may be desirable to space the overall investment effort properly to bring it within acceptable economic limits, and to consider fully the economic costs in evaluating specific energy measures.

5. *How should the environmental implications of our energy programs be taken into account?*

**Argument for Enforcing Environmental Criteria.** Environmental considerations have been taken seriously only during the last several years. We have only begun to clean up the environment and to set limits to historic developments which, unless checks are enforced, could lead to irreversible and catastrophic consequences.

**Argument for Modifying Environmental Criteria.** Environmental legislation has caused the energy shortage to become more acute in several ways. One well-known example is the replacement of high-sulphur coal by oil and gas. This has been accomplished by imposing absolute standards, rather than by a detailed consideration of real health hazards. It is necessary to introduce modifications, at least during a transition period, so that environmental rules apply only in cases where a real health hazard exists.

6. *To what extent, if any, should energy programs be concerned with equity considerations?*

**Argument for Equity Considerations.** An equitable program is needed to encourage Americans to make temporary sacrifices in the national interest. The burden of any energy program must be shared, as much as possible, by different income groups and by different regions of the country. Ways should be found to compensate those people who suffer, without unduly impairing the production and conservation of energy.

7. *To what extent should energy programs be fashioned to take account of international implications?*

**Argument for Emphasis on U.S. Economy.** The United States should be concerned, first and foremost, with putting its own house in order. As it becomes more self-reliant through the development of its domestic energy resources and as it withdraws from the world oil market, more foreign oil will be made available to other consuming countries.

**Argument for Emphasis on Worldwide Aspects of the Energy Shortage.** The United States imports more than 20 percent of its energy requirements. Western Europe imports more than 50 percent and Japan more than 90 percent. The United States may turn out to be more vulnerable to pressures exerted on its allies than to pressures exerted directly on this nation. Therefore, it is important to develop a pattern of energy consumption and production which will permit the United States to influence favorably the world trade in energy, if feasible, through the export of energy. One important candidate for export would be coal.[a]

These overlapping and multilayered influences on energy complicate the making of choices–but by no means lessen the need to make choices. These general choices, in turn, provide the framework for decisions on which sources of domestic energy should be expanded and in what areas energy conservation measures should be directed. These specific decisions must be closely related to the basic choices. Fortunately, the United States is blessed with so many resources that it has numerous options as to what its energy policy can be. Most other countries have very limited options. At the same time, the United States must make realistic choices based on a full understanding of their implications.

A major danger in the pursuit of any energy strategy is the use of partial measures. There are complex interrelations within the energy sector and among energy and other areas, such as ecology and economics. These have to be fully considered in formulating any activist energy policy. Similarly, it is important to understand the energy situation in other countries and how U.S. policies may impact on them and on U.S. overall international economic and political

[a]A plan which would lead to U.S. exports of energy is detailed in a report to the Commission on Critical Choices for Americans by Edward Teller, entitled "Energy–A plan for Action." The report is included in Volume IV of this series, *Power & Security*.

relations. Especially vital is the need to relate all energy issues to world stability.

Further, the time dimension is an essential element to any energy program. Some programs require long lead times and will not have a significant impact by 1985 unless they are initiated very soon. Programs should be justified not only by their impact in the next few years or even through 1985, but by how well they meet U.S. long-term objectives. It is possible to visualize three time periods: between 1976 and 1985, when the United States and the other oil importing nations will have to rely heavily on OPEC oil; between 1985 and the year 2000, when the United States will have to rely heavily on newly generated energy resources, primarily, hydrocarbon, but also atomic energy; and the post-2000 period, when all nations will need new energy technology as the role of hydrocarbon declines.

We must be aware that certain choices are not irrevocable. Changes can be made if circumstances so warrant or if the effects turn out to be different than expected. Inflexible choices–such as excessive dependence on technological breakthroughs that do not occur–however, could be disastrous for the nation. Clearly, our ability to adjust and alter our choices, once made, will influence the relative desirability of alternative courses of action.

## II. The Critical Choices

### *Self-Reliance: A Sound Objective?*

A basic choice is whether the United States should continue to rely on foreign sources to meet an increasing portion of its energy requirements or whether the United States should adopt a policy of self-reliance in the energy field. "Self-reliance" is perhaps a more appropriate concept than "energy independence"; it connotes confidence in our abilities, while "independence" indicates freedom from external influence or control. "Self-reliance" is more positive, has fewer political or nationalistic connotations and reflects a process that encompasses varying degrees of achievement rather than the fixed objective that is implied by "independence." Any substantial self-reliance would enable the United States to be relatively invulnerable to foreign energy producers or to any modest import of energy.

Is energy self-reliance a desirable objective? Is self-reliance a desirable concept? Will it lead to more economic security and political freedom for the United States and its allies, or will it require a more controlled and centrally-directed society?

Those who urge that the nation achieve major self-reliance are especially concerned about the vulnerability of U.S. national security that is represented by oil imports and about the worldwide foreign trade imbalance. The Federal Energy Administration, in its *Project Independence Report*, estimates as a base case that by 1985, U.S. oil imports would total 3.3 million barrels per day (MBPD) at a world oil price of $11 a barrel (an annual outflow of $13.2 billion) and 12.4 MBPD at a $7 price (an annual outflow of $31.7 billion).[1] While these estimated figures may well change, they do not highlight the basic point that under present conditions, oil imports will continue to represent a heavy foreign exchange expenditure.

Imports bring the danger of politically-motivated supply disruptions due to embargo or war, which would threaten the national security interests of the United States. At the end of 1973, this danger was transformed from the theoretical to the practical, from possibility to reality. The Arab countries embargoed oil shipments to the United States and to other countries because of support for Israel. It could happen again. However, the oil fields in the OPEC countries are presently not working at full capacity (as they were in 1973). The increasing need for foreign exchange in countries like Iran, Venezuela, and Indonesia may decrease the effectiveness or even the probability of a new embargo by other OPEC countries in the near future.

An embargo is not the only danger. Buildup of Soviet sea power around the world, and especially in the Middle East, poses a real threat that, in case of world conflict, oil tankers might not be able to reach our shores. In these ways, a heavy reliance on foreign oil could jeopardize the national security of the United States, while subservience of the United States and its allies to a handful of oil producing countries could threaten the U.S. position as a world power.

The domestic economic stability of the United States could be affected by interruptions in supply and by large price increases. The OPEC efforts succeeded in aggravating unemployment and inflation and contributed to the subsequent recession. The quadrupling of world oil prices dramatically increased our oil import bill. The expenditures on oil by all consuming countries (including the developing countries) have increased drastically, even though the worldwide recession of 1974-75 has restrained the world demand for energy. The major industrial economies are poised for an economic expansion, which could substantially increase their oil import bills in 1976 and beyond. With world oil prices remaining high, and more likely to increase than decrease, certain oil producing countries are likely to continue to accumulate sizable foreign exchange holdings, which could well produce digestive problems for the international monetary system. This situation could expand the political leverage and influence of these countries in the United States and elsewhere.

Beyond threatening our national security and economic stability unrestrained oil imports work to delay domestic development of essential resources—oil exploration, coal, nuclear reactors, and advanced methods of oil and gas recovery—and to retard research in new energy sources—solar, geothermal, nuclear fusion, bioconversion—that may be needed if and when we run out of hydrocarbons.

On the more positive side, a domestic energy program geared to self-reliance would give the United States more diplomatic leverage in negotiating with the oil producing countries. This might help lay the basis for our achieving a stable, long-term arrangement with the OPEC that reduces the balance of payments burden of oil imports to both the developed and the less developed countries. The development of U.S. energy resources could stimulate the domestic economy and expand employment opportunities, especially for the scientific and engineering talent that has been developed by U.S. defense and space activities. Moreover, the use of tankers to bring in foreign oil poses possibly more of an environmental threat of spillage—accidental or otherwise—than does the development of some of our domestic energy resources, such as offshore oil/gas deposits.

There are thus good, sound reasons for a domestic energy program geared to making the nation more self-reliant in its energy supplies—and even contributing to the needs of our allies. However, this in itself does not justify going ahead and spending whatever is necessary to achieve self-reliance. The costs of energy self-reliance must be considered, including its impact on our ability to meet other desired objectives. We must recognize that there are various types or degrees of self-reliance, each with its own costs and benefits.

All beginning economic students are taught that there is no such thing as a free lunch. Someone pays. This basic economic proposition applies as much to energy and energy self-reliance as to other activities and objectives. There is a cost to our current essentially passive energy policy. There is a cost to an activist energy self-reliance program—not one cost, but a range of costs depending upon the scale and the composition of the program. If we consider the costs excessive, we may decide to reject the objective or scale down or change the composition of the program in order to bring costs to an acceptable level.

There is a concern that the concept of energy self-reliance runs counter to the kind of international economic system we have been working toward over the past quarter-century. That system, which we have by no means achieved and which has been subjected to setbacks, is designed to encourage the growing economic interdependence of nations. Toward this end, currencies have been made convertible, tariffs have been reduced—in many cases, eliminated—and capital controls have been curbed. National interests are not disregarded, but are seen as being best achieved through a healthy and efficient international economy, which takes advantage of specialization.

The OPEC policies clearly run counter to this goal. So also could energy self-reliance be regarded as retrogressive, wherein decisions are taken to promote the national interest with little or no regard for the international consequences. It might be considered a modern version of the old import-substitution approach to economic growth and security, which many less developed countries have found—the hard way—brought neither growth nor stability. Instead, it nurtured costly and inefficient industries which required continuing public subsidies to stay afloat. It may be ironic for the United States to adopt an import-substitution policy in energy at a time when many of the less developed countries are trying to extricate themselves from the adverse results of such policies.

Moreover, where do we draw the self-reliance line? If energy is considered a strategic industry worthy of our becoming self-reliant in it, what about steel? Or bauxite? Or sugar? Local and special interests, identifying with a concept of national self-reliance, will bring pressure that the principle be applied also to their industries. The protective tariff history provides ample illustrations.

Where do we draw the line internationally? At the present time, the United States is actively trying to negotiate changes in the European Community's Common Agricultural Policy (CAP) so that this region will buy more U.S. agricultural products. The CAP is based on the principle of agricultural self-reliance for its members. If we adopt an energy self-reliance position, how effectively can we negotiate a liberalization of the CAP? Or a liberalization of other trade barriers, current and future, against our goods by other countries? One negative impact of energy self-reliance, a policy designed to restrict our energy imports, may thus be the retardation of the growth of our own exports.

The argument against self-reliance is supported by those who regard the energy crisis as a temporary phenomenon, due mainly, if not entirely, to the machinations of the OPEC oil cartel, which they believe is bound to fail in the long run. Rather than pursue costly programs to accelerate the development of our domestic energy resources and undertake conservation programs which might impair our standard of living and way of life, they recommend that we either (a) wait for market forces to increase energy supplies and bring down world prices or (b) stimulate these market forces by a concerted policy to break up the OPEC cartel. Others regard the breakup of OPEC during this decade, either naturally or due to pressure by the oil consuming countries, as wishful thinking. Moreover, these people believe that the only way to reduce the long-run influence of OPEC is through a concerted program of domestic energy self-reliance.

It should be pointed out that the objective of self-reliance is vastly different from that of self-sufficiency. Self-reliance does not exclude all imports; it does not exclude the possibility of exports. It is a flexible objective whose pursuit could lead to the breakup of OPEC, a cartel which is not in harmony with the idea of free international trade. Self-sufficiency, on the other hand, connotes isolationism. It could lead to a host of trade restrictions—in which case the cure would be worse than the disease.

A strong argument in favor of self-reliance is that the world's petroleum and natural gas deposits are limited and around the year 2000 may be inadequate to meet the demand for energy. Thus, energy self-reliance for the United States through the development of nonhydrocarbon sources of energy could not only help secure this nation, but it could reduce the demand on the rest of the world's limited oil and gas resources. Indeed, the United States might even become a net energy export nation under certain "self-reliance plus" programs.

**Types of Self-Reliance.** Any decision regarding the desirability of energy self-reliance must recognize that there are different types or degrees of self-reliance. Maximum self-reliance may not be the most desirable; other types may give us more self-reliance than a do-nothing policy, but at less cost than the maximum type. The issues are: How much self-reliance? In what forms? How best to achieve them?

For convenience, two types of self-reliance are presented, involving four specific objectives. These are contrasted to an objective of no self-reliance. Although these categories are arbitrary, they do point out the nature of the decisions that have to be made.

| Type of Self-Reliance | Specific Objective |
|---|---|
| 1. Complete self-reliance | a. Net energy exports |
| | b. Balancing energy imports and exports |
| 2. Limited self-reliance | c. Limited energy imports |
| | d. Oil stockpile, standby facilities |
| No Self-Reliance | e. Uncontrolled dependence on imports |

It is clear why the first two objectives constitute complete self-reliance. The third and fourth constitute a kind of manageable dependence. While the third objective involves imports, they would be held to a manageable fraction, possibly 20-25 percent, of domestic energy consumption. In addition, the nation could protect itself against another oil embargo by preparing standby regulations to curb energy consumption, by storing more crude and refined oil, and by diversifying its foreign sources of supply. This objective is most compatible with our historical concept of national security. The fourth specific objective involves concentrating on energy storage and standby facilities to protect the United States from disruptions in foreign supplies of energy, but increasing our use of energy imports. The self-reliance so gained would be temporary—limited to the storage capacity developed. Critics point out that by itself storage only postpones the impact of the longer-term oil and gas shortages. The fifth, or "no self-reliance" policy, is criticized as exposing the nation to ever mounting imports and endangering national security.

Each type of self-reliance combines different ways of expanding domestic energy output, different ways of conserving energy, and different levels of stockpiling energy. Critical choices are required among these strategies, as well as within each of them. Trade-offs also will be required in selecting the degree of self-reliance best suited to our overall national security and economic and environmental objectives, as well as achieving the desired relationship in the public-private sectors. These factors are examined in Section III (critical trade-offs), Section IV (production strategies), Section V (conservation strategies), and Section VI (standby facilities).

**Quantitative Considerations.** Much of the public discussion on basic energy options has been devoid of quantitative assessments. At the same time, we have a plethora of numbers on the minutiae of energy production and how to conserve energy, and a lack of meaningful numbers for judging impacts of alternative policies, e.g., on capital requirements. Even though the published data are rough, they can provide orders of magnitude that may be meaningful in helping evaluate the alternative types or degrees of self-reliance objectives.

*Complete Self-Reliance: Balanced Energy Imports and Exports.* One type of self-reliance conforms to the original definition of our "energy independence" policy—zero energy imports. Domestic energy production would have to be sufficient to cover all of domestic energy requirements.

Published sources (detailed in Sections IV and V) provide the range of 1985 estimates for U.S. energy consumption, assuming maximum feasible savings, and for U.S. energy production, assuming the maximum feasible expansion of domestic energy output (see Table I-1).

These estimates indicate that while it may be possible to attain the self-reliance objective, it will not be easy. Looking at the averages, potential production just barely covers consumption, with almost no leeway for mistaken assumptions. A consumption of 96.8 quads in 1985 implies an annual growth of 2.5 percent from the 75 quads (35.4 MBPD) in 1973, a reduction from the annual growth of 3.4 percent during 1950-70. Production would have to increase from the 62 quads (29.3 MBPD) in 1973 to 99.0 quads in 1985, an annual growth of 4.0 percent, up from 3.0 percent previously.

The lack of a leeway is especially evident when we examine the range of estimates. If production approaches the lower end of the range, it will be unable to cover consumption, even if maximum energy savings can be achieved. Only if production exceeds 102 quads (a 4.2 percent growth rate over 1973-85) would there be some assurance that this self-reliance objective could be met. There are

**Table I-1**
**1985 Estimates for U.S. Energy Consumption**

| | | Range of Estimates | | Average of Estimates | |
|---|---|---|---|---|---|
| | | (quads) | (MBPD) | (quads) | (MBPD) |
| 1985 | Domestic Energy Consumption based on maximum potential savings | 91.8-101.8 | 43.3-48.0 | 96.8 | 45.7 |
| 1985 | Domestic Energy Production based on maximum potential expansion | 85.0-117.6 | 40.1-55.0 | 99.0 | 46.7 |

a number of estimates which indicate that production can indeed reach this level.

*Complete Self-Reliance: Net Energy Exports.* Another type of complete self-reliance calls for a level of energy production sufficient to cover all domestic consumption levels by 1985, and to contribute to exports. Accordingly, the 1985 production target might be set at 115 percent of the expected level of domestic consumption. What this implies is shown in Table I-2.

Table I-2 indicates the very little leeway that this type of self-reliance brings. If 1985 production is close to the lower end of the range of estimates, the production target will not be met. If 1985 production is at the upper end of the range and potential consumption savings are at the lower end, resulting in a consumption target of some 117 quads, the target can be met—but with no leeway. Only if both production and savings are close to the upper levels of the range or estimates is there any leeway to absorb mistaken assumption or to consider marginal changes in the mix of potential production and conservation programs.

*Limited Self-Reliance: Limited Energy Imports.* This type of self-reliance seeks to limit dependence on energy imports to a "manageable" fraction of domestic energy requirements, say 20 percent. This represents the amount of imports which would not disrupt the domestic economy if cut off. What this would imply is shown in Table I-3.

Even at the lower end of the production range, it would still be possible to meet the 1985 target, regardless of whether savings are near the lower or upper end of the range of estimates. If production reaches the level represented by the average of the estimate, 99.0 quads, there will be considerable scope to alter the mix of production and conservation programs.

This option provides more flexibility than the previous two in the combination of measures that may be needed. There is more scope for using economic, environmental, or other criteria for selecting various energy strategies. By requiring a less extensive energy development effort, this type of self-reliance

**Table I-2**
**1985 Production Estimates (Complete Self-Reliance)**

| | | Range of Estimates | | Average of Estimates | |
|---|---|---|---|---|---|
| | | (quads) | (MBPD) | (quads) | (MBPD) |
| 1985 | consumption—based on maximum potential savings | 91.8-101.8 | 43.3-48.0 | 96.8 | 45.7 |
| 1985 | production target—115% of consumption | 105.6-117.1 | 49.8-55.3 | | |
| 1985 | potential production | 85.0-117.6 | 40.1-55.0 | 99.0 | 46.7 |

**Table I-3**
**1985 Production Estimates (Limited Self-Reliance)**

| | | Range of Estimates | | Average of Estimates | |
|---|---|---|---|---|---|
| | | (quads) | (MBPD) | (quads) | (MBPD) |
| 1985 | consumption–based on potential savings | 91.8-101.8 | 43.3-48.0 | 96.8 | 45.7 |
| 1985 | production target–80% of consumption | 73.4- 81.4 | 34.6-38.4 | | |
| 1985 | production potential | 85.0-117.6 | 40.1-55.0 | 99.0 | 46.7 |

may involve fewer capital costs and fewer adverse environmental impacts than the complete types. However, it does involve import expenditures and hence risks dependence on foreign sources, however limited—a risk that may or may not be considered acceptable. This type of self-reliance may be pursued alone or in combination with a stockpile program.

*Limited Self-Reliance: Oil Stockpile and Standby Facilities.* This objective calls for no special measures to stimulate domestic energy production or to encourage energy savings. Rather, it concentrates on an oil stockpile and shut-in production facilities to protect the United States against supply disruptions.

In Section VI, we quantify various aspects of this option. One of its chief advantages over production and conservation strategies is its much lower cost—estimated to be billions of dollars compared to the hundreds of billions of dollars that the other options would entail. A disadvantage of stockpiling may be its limited period of effectiveness.

With no special efforts to curb imports, these can be expected to rise in line with growing domestic demand. The National Petroleum Council estimates that in 1985 petroleum imports could range from 5.4-12.5 million barrels per day, with a medium estimate of 8.4 MBPD.[2] This compares with actual imports of 3.5 MBPD in 1974.[3] At a price of $10 a barrel, the value of our oil imports could range from $20-$45 billion a year by 1985. As we have noted, imports are already above the lower end of this range.

*No Self-Reliance.* This option, calling for no special production, conservation, or storage measures, would involve uncontrolled dependence on imports. This entails a national security risk. Its economic implications are uncertain, but it obviously minimizes our bargaining leverage with OPEC and exposes the nation to energy price increases by OPEC countries, with adverse effects on efforts to control inflation and to stimulate business and employment.

The FEA estimated that the past embargo cost the nation some $10-$20 billion (annual rate) in lost gross national product during the first quarter of 1974. "The effect has been to put the economy on a growth that is $10-$20 billion lower than would have occurred without the embargo."[4] However, other factors of a cyclical nature, which were not directly related to the oil embargo, were also contributing to this decline. Thus, the embargo-induced loss may be much less than $10-$20 billion, especially since, over the long run, part of the loss can be made up. The FEA has also estimated that the embargo increased unemployment by 0.5 percent–a loss of 500,000 jobs–and was responsible for 30 percent of the subsequent increase in consumer prices.[5]

Paul MacAvoy, a member of the Council of Economic Advisors, has estimated the maximum cost of a selective oil embargo of one year by the Persian Gulf states against the United States at $7.7 billion by 1980, based on embargoed oil of 6.4 quads (3 million barrels per day).[6] The actual cost would probably be less as "lost" oil imports are replaced by domestic labor and capital imports. Indeed, MacAvoy maintains the impact on GNP might be less significant in 1980 with a one-year oil embargo than the four-month embargo in 1973-74 precisely because people and industry will have learned to adjust better to such disruptions.

Moreover, MacAvoy maintains that the problem with policies designed to curb imports solely through conservation is that "they are worse than the status quo, because they replace an (assumed) intermittent embargo by suppliers with a permanent embargo imposed on the demand side of the market–a permanent embargo prevents the unpleasant surprise of a temporary embargo, but by making permanent the cost increases during the temporary disruption."[7]

### *How Urgent Is the Need to Replace Our Petroleum-Based Energy Resources?*

A second, and closely related critical choice, concerns the desirability (or necessity) of replacing oil and natural gas as major energy sources. There is widespread concern about the medium-term adequacy of remaining petroleum resources, both in the United States and around the world. The fear persists that the United States will dangerously deplete its oil and gas supplies by the late 1980s or early 1990s. The National Academy of Sciences concludes: "World resources of petroleum and natural gas, discovered reserves and undiscovered recoverable resources, will be seriously depleted by the end of the century if present trends of world production and consumption continue."[8]

Moody and Geiger believe that U.S. crude oil production has already peaked, that Canadian production will peak by 1985, that Middle East production will peak in about 1995, and that crude oil production in the Soviet Union and China will peak before the year 2000.[9] To bolster this view one may cite the fact that the U.S. production of crude is now significantly below the levels at the time of the Arab embargo, despite the continued high demand for oil. (One should remember, however, that it takes at least three years to open new producing wells.) To be realistic, then, policies and programs designed to increase our energy self-reliance through at least the coming decade, must be fashioned to deal with this longer-term prospect.

Concern with the worldwide availability of hydrocarbons stems from projections of world demand overtaking supply. World demand for oil and gas has increased rapidly in the past due to growing populations, the spread of industrialization and urbanization, and higher living standards. The automobile—that symbol of affluence in most countries—is a key cause of the accelerating world demand for oil. Actually, after the recent and very large increase in world oil prices, demand has fallen noticeably due to the worldwide recession, which, at least in part, was due to the cost of oil. But, since oil and gas are considered to be indispensable in many of their uses, the price elasticity of demand—short-run and long-run—is considered by some to be low.

While demand continues to grow, the world supply of hydrocarbons is limited by what can be economically produced and, ultimately, by what is physically in the ground. Major new oil and gas discoveries, onshore or offshore, would serve to delay the time when we no longer have adequate hydrocarbons to depend upon. New discoveries will not add to the world's actual petroleum resources. Moreover, the easy locations where there are large hydrocarbon formations may have already been found. New finds of a substantial nature may prove to be difficult and costly to bring in. They may well occur in the Middle East, the Soviet Union, and China[10]—areas of the world to which the United States might not have access and on which it could not depend for uninterrupted supply.

The estimates on recoverable oil and gas reserves around the world are based on crude data and must be considered very rough approximations. The National Academy of Sciences estimates proven world reserves of crude oil at 600 billion barrels (350 quads) and proven reserves of natural gas at 2,100 TCF (210 quads).[11] Based on world production in 1973, oil reserves would last thirty years and natural gas reserves, forty-four years.

The Academy study presents three estimates of undiscovered recoverable crude oil, which range from 68-200 billion tons (400-1,300 billion barrels).[12] Its own estimate is 1,130 billion barrels, equivalent to an additional fifty-six years of production. Its estimates of undiscovered recoverable natural gas is 4,900 TCF, equivalent to 195 years.[13] Only a fraction of recoverable oil and gas is located in and around the United States, between 8-12 percent.[14]

Estimates of U.S. recoverable oil and gas resources are subject to continuing uncertainties. The latest estimates of the U.S. Geological Survey put identified crude oil reserves at 62 billion barrels and identified natural gas reserves at 438.7 TCF.[15] Undiscovered recoverable oil resources are estimated to range between 50-127 billion barrels, while undiscovered recoverable gas resources are estimated at 322-655 TCF. Estimates of the National Academy of Sciences fall within these ranges. At the 1974 rate of domestic production, according to the Academy report, our recoverable oil resources would last thirty-seven to sixty-two years and recoverable gas resources, thirty-six to fifty-one years. If we do not exploit all that is recoverable, our available resources would be depleted sooner.

In the long run, there is no doubt that oil will be exhausted. The question is whether this will happen in the twentieth or the twenty-first century. Many consider this difference of no great importance. Others believe that the rate at which new energy sources should be developed is itself a most important problem. Indeed, one may say that the more we develop our oil and natural gas resources in order to reduce our dependence on imports of foreign oil, the more we deplete our hydrocarbon supplies and hence become potentially more dependent on foreign oil supplies in the future. Moreover, a number of studies support the view that U.S. production of both oil and natural gas have reached their maximum rates—i.e., potential output has already peaked.[16] On the other hand, shortages of oil and gas are apt to lead to substitute production, such as in situ production of gas from coal and oil from shale. This might extend the availability of oil and gas.

There is some concern that we may be overestimating the size of our recoverable oil and gas resources. In 1972, the U.S. Geological Survey estimated our undiscovered oil and natural gas liquids at 450 billion barrels. In 1974, the estimate was lowered to a range of 200-400 billion barrels—in part due to using a lower water depth for estimating resources. The current "mean" estimate, using improved estimating techniques, is 98 billion barrels. This is still higher than some private estimates.[17]

The need for governmental action may be justified because of concern for depletion of our hydrocarbon resources, and because prices may not provide adequate signals for private action. For one thing, the time horizon, involving decades, is too great to warrant concern on the part of most private decision-makers. For another, prices are not now determined by demand and supply, as the actions of the OPEC cartel clearly demonstrated. Based on current world demand and potential world supply, oil prices might well be around $3 a barrel, instead of the OPEC price of over $10. Such a low price would discourage development of alternative energy sources and accelerate the depletion of hydrocarbons. Before we ran out, oil and gas prices would surely rise—but not necessarily in time for the decades of research, development, and commercialization that is needed before other new energy sources could adequately replace oil. The United States and other economies could be hit especially hard by the inability to adjust effectively to the large price swing that would result.

OPEC has thus served to accelerate the timetable—to underscore the need for a long-range response on our part to a situation that would have occurred even without OPEC. That response may require us to emphasize and accelerate those aspects of a self-reliance program, especially an R&D effort, that serve to diversify our energy supplies away from oil and gas.

A crucial determinant of policy action, therefore, is how fast the world is really running out of hydrocarbons. This is an issue of considerable uncertainty—

even among the experts. Published figures on recoverable reserves are imperfect indicators of our total oil and gas resources. They are simply the amount of oil and gas that has been developed for production. In the past, we have been able to accommodate large increases in demand, with reserve levels constant or even increasing. Identified reserves should be regarded as a flow of oil and gas, rather than an absolute stock—akin to business inventories. The more the demand and the higher the price, the greater is the incentive to explore and thus add to the total of identified reserves.

Both identified reserves and undiscovered recoverable resources are only a part of total resources—some 40-50 percent in the case of crude oil, but 80-85 percent in the case of natural gas. The higher the price for oil and gas and the better the technology of extracting the hydrocarbons from the ground, the more rapidly will uneconomical deposits become economical and thus be included in reserve totals. The high oil price is already encouraging a spate of extensive exploration and development activity, onshore and offshore, which should increase recoverable domestic oil and gas supplies. Engineering improvements, especially in tertiary recovery techniques and offshore drilling in deep water (beyond 200 meters), would also help.

If we believe that we are not likely to run out of hydrocarbons in any time frame that would cause us concern because economic forces operating alone and as a stimulus to technology will bring the necessary adjustments to supply and demand, then no special policies need to be introduced. However, the risks of being proved wrong could well be very severe dislocations to our economy and employment, impairment of our national security, and a serious jolt to our standard of living. Alternatively, if we believe we do face the real prospect of depleting our hydrocarbons and if we make an all out effort for self-sufficiency, the risk of being wrong could be very costly—a distorted use of resources that could also slow or check the pace of our economic advancement. Obviously, there are permutations and combinations in between these two extreme positions.

With respect to the development of alternative sources of energy other than oil and gas, we face other major choices:

1. Should the government assume primary responsibility for an accelerating R&D effort to develop alternative energy sources?

   *or*

   Should public action be restricted to efforts that ensure that price and profit expectations elicit an adequate private R&D response?

The high price of oil is already stimulating private investment in the development of alternative energy sources, such as solar and geothermal energy. However, the amount of investment so far is small. When these sources become more competitive with hydrocarbons, either through technological breakthroughs or further oil price increases, more private interest can be expected in their development. Will it be adequate? How can it be enhanced?

In this situation, we face another major choice:

> 2. Should we accelerate the extraction of our domestic oil and gas in order to reduce our dependence on oil and gas imports as rapidly as possible?
>
> *or*
>
> Should we slow down the development for domestic oil and gas deposits, so as to conserve them for future use?

With the former choice, we run the risk of using up our limited resources, leading to future shortfalls and ever greater dependence on foreign sources, unless we start to develop long-term substitutes. The latter choice involves an immediate increase in our already sizable dependence on foreign sources. The issue revolves around the present needs and value versus the future needs and value of our oil and gas deposits. How do we discount the future? In seeking the appropriate equation, one must consider that, apart from energy conservation, only more petroleum can help alleviate the energy shortage within the next few years.

## III. Critical Choices: Trade-Offs

In Section II, we presented two basic choices. If we choose *not* to be self-reliant and *not* to be too concerned about a possible depletion of our petroleum resources, then only a minimal kind of energy program may be needed—such as the one we now have, which is designed to make marginal improvements in efficiencies. On the other hand, if we believe that some type of self-reliance is desirable and/or that we need to prepare now for the replacement of oil and natural gas, then we face critical choices on the scale and composition of programs to accomplish these objectives. An extensive and concentrated energy program may well bring us complete self-reliance by 1985; however, this program may conflict with the achievement of other desired objectives. Either we accept this as a necessary cost, or we scale down our energy objectives and/or change the composition of the programs designed to achieve them.

Not everything need be, or can be, planned in detail. Trade-offs will develop as we go along. This is particularly characteristic of a market economy. It is even true of planned economies. A conscious awareness of the major trade-offs involved will help determine the relative desirability of specific energy proposals.

*Energy Objectives and the Desired Level of Government Influence*

The extent of government influence over our lives is already great. Federal, state, county, and local agencies have been set up to regulate a wide range of our economic and social activities. Government influence has been growing rapidly over the past decades. As new problems emerge, the government is often called upon to intervene.

A major program for energy self-reliance could expand government influence even further. The larger the program, the more the government influence—and interference. Programs that are beyond the capabilities of the private sector to undertake from a technological point of view, or to finance from a capital point of view, would involve some form of government assistance. The government would step in as a "lender of last resort," carving out more of an influence over the economy through direct and indirect controls and pressures, including the possibility of outright ownership and operation of enterprises. Conversely, if no energy program is undertaken and serious shortages of energy develop, the government may have to initiate new regulations, including rationing, in order to meet the economic, political, and social problems that will result.

The government is already heavily involved in the energy industry. Policies control how much oil and natural gas can be produced, the prices that can be charged for these fuels, and for electricity, the location of wells, the extent of competition in any one field, the fiscal incentives given producers, the fiscal charges that consumers must bear, the cost of transporting fuels from mines and wells to points of use, the safety and health standards in the production and transportation of fuels, the environmental standards in all aspects of energy production and use, also taxes on foreign fuels, speed limits, and many others.

Any new program to develop our domestic energy resources and to conserve on energy use may thus involve the following choice:

More government

*or*

Less government.

This is *not* a choice between only private involvement or only public involvement in energy programs. Much can be done, and already has been done, through private-public combinations. The need is to find workable partnerships and a desired balance between the two; to do so, we may choose to give greater priority to more government involvement or to more private involvement.

In order to expand domestic energy output close to maximum achievable levels, however calculated, a major R&D effort would be required through 1985 and beyond. The government could get involved by undertaking such R&D

directly, or by funding private R&D, or by constructing—or participating in the construction of—pilot plants and demonstration projects in areas of new technology, such as shale oil and coal liquefaction. Tax credits, subsidies, and price guarantees may be used to stimulate private investment in energy. Manpower retraining programs may support such efforts. An appropriate finance corporation may be used as an indirect government support and supplement to private energy investments. the price and supply of energy imports may be controlled, through quotas, tariffs, or taxes, in order to protect the desired domestic energy investments. Finally, the government may undertake direct operations in the extraction of fuels and the development of other energy sources—either by establishing new enterprises, alone or jointly with private enterprise, or by nationalizing existing private companies.

In the area of energy conservation, the government might impose minimum standards of energy efficiency on a host of products and processes, including automobiles, appliances, industrial processes, and the conversion by utilities of primary fuels to electricity. Labeling of energy efficiencies might also be required on energy-using appliances and equipment. Automobiles may be barred from certain lanes or specified downtown areas and may be taxed according to their weight or fuel economy. Tax credits or subsidies may be used to encourage more home insulation, more efficient electricity conversion, more investment in energy-efficient industrial equipment and processes. Some or all forms of energy consumption may be subject to direct taxation. The government may support R&D efforts in energy conservation and may undertake a broad program of public education on the need to conserve energy and how to do so.

This relationship between the scale of an energy program and the extent of government influence is especially valid when we consider broader economic impacts. In order that sufficient resources can be shifted to the favored energy sector, private consumption and nonenergy related investments may have to be restrained by measures that are more direct than general fiscal and monetary policies. These may include price controls, the rationing of raw materials and other supplies, import controls, tax incentives, loans, and capital allocations. These controls—and the inevitable efforts to close loopholes—could require an extensive bureaucracy and could expand considerably the influence of the public sector over our economy.

Policies that depend primarily on prices would generally involve less government interference. Complete dependence on the price mechanism may not achieve ambitious energy objectives, but policies designed to increase relative energy prices could work in this direction. These could include taxes, import tariffs, and domestic price floors. Also useful would be the easing or elimination altogether of both federal regulations that keep oil and natural gas prices below market levels and state regulations on increased oil production, such as "maximum efficient rate" limits and "proration" restrictions. A stimulus to private energy investment would be the accelerated leasing for private development of federal coal and shale bearing lands and offshore tracts and the streamlining of the licensing and approval procedures for new energy production, especially nuclear power plants.

High prices could encourage the energy producing companies to reinvest in the energy sector by raising profit expectations. A tax on excess profits that are not reinvested in energy activity might push along this encouragement. High prices also could curb the demand for certain types of energy and promote investment in energy conservation.

The problem is, how high is too high? At the extreme, we could ban all energy imports (thus getting instant self-reliance), and use prices to equate the domestic supply and demand for energy. Gasoline may go to the European level of $2 a gallon—or more. Lower income groups, certain industries (e.g., tourism) and certain regions (e.g., suburbs) would be especially hard hit. Such action would adversely impact on business and employment and would impair the quality of life of many Americans. It would be unpopular and politically most difficult.

An alternative choice is to reduce the scale of the energy program and to rely on the price mechanism as much as possible in order to achieve the desired relationship between the public and private sectors. The cost would be a somewhat lesser degree of self-reliance and a slower pace in replacing hydrocarbons.

The issue of more government versus less government can be presented in a specific form:

Removal of price controls

*or*

Oil rationing.

Those favoring less government believe that the private sector is capable of undertaking a major energy development program. This is seen as an area where private interests coincide with the national interest. However, businessmen are reluctant to make the long-term commitments that are needed as long as there is considerable uncertainty about the direction of U.S. energy policy and as long as their profit expectations are artificially held down by controls on oil and gas prices. Hence, the removal of such controls is regarded as a *sine qua non* for an acceleration in the private exploration and development of our oil and gas resources.

Those favoring more government involvement regard profits as already adequate to generate the desired private sector response. Accordingly, if the response is not forthcoming, more controls may be required over the activities of the oil and gas suppliers to encourage them to operate more in the public interest. In the meantime, the energy deficit could be covered by rationing existing supplies, especially oil, in order to reduce import dependence.

Either program could accomplish complete self-reliance. Neither is necessary if self-reliance is not considered an important objective.

*Energy Objectives and Economic Objectives*

We might have the best of both worlds if our economic growth could be sustained without the need for substantial additional supplies of energy. In the real world, however, this has not been the case. Past economic growth has gone hand-in-hand with rising energy consumption. The reasons are obvious. The agricultural revolution, the industrial revolution, the transportation and communications revolutions, the rise in living standards beyond subsistence levels—all these aspects of economic development in the Western world have involved large energy inputs. Man-power and animal-power do not suffice to fuel modern industrial economies. Mechanical power is the backbone of our economic system; it was fueled first by wood, then by coal, and now largely by oil and natural gas.

The generally held view is that this past relationship between economic growth and energy demand will continue. The Ford Foundation report, *A Time to Choose*, argues that it is possible to "uncouple" economic growth and energy demand, that is, the United States can achieve zero energy growth by the year 2000 and still sustain a positive economic growth. A 40-50 percent reduction in the level of energy consumption, relative to the historical trend, the report argues, would still not prevent a more than doubling of GNP from 1975-2000.[18]

Most other observers, however, are skeptical. Although there is some evidence of a decline in the energy-intensity of production (energy input per unit of output), they believe that zero energy growth would precipitate major economic disruptions and a lower standard of living for the American people. Moreover, some do not regard a doubling of GNP over a quarter-century period as sufficient to meet employment and other national and international objectives.

If we believe that future U.S. economic growth *does* require increasing supplies of energy—or that the risks to the country of following policies based on the zero energy growth are too great—then we face another critical choice:

More economic growth

*or*

Less economic growth.

Policies designed to promote more economic growth immediately, in order to raise domestic income and employment levels, might conflict directly with our longer-term energy objectives. By generating a large demand for energy, such policies might bring pressure (a) to increase our demand for foreign fuels (and thus hinder the attainment of self-reliance objectives), and/or (b) to accelerate the use of our domestic energy resources (thus hastening the depletion of our hydrocarbons).

Alternatively, policies involving less economic growth might help us meet our energy objectives by lessening the growth rate of energy demand and reducing the potential drain on our energy resources. However, the social consequences of a low economic growth rate include high unemployment among the youth and less-advantaged groups, as well as reduced revenues to federal, state, and local governments. These are some of the trade-offs involved.

Moreover, a major program looking toward energy self-sufficiency might stimulate economic growth because of the construction, equipment fabrication, transportation, and distribution activities involved. Accordingly, we may decide to seek *both* the energy *and* the economic objectives. In such a course of action, we may well face another key choice:

Restrict Consumption and
Nonenergy Investments

*or*

Tolerate More Inflation (Forced Saving).

A major energy program to achieve complete self-reliance and to replace hydrocarbons will be costly. Unfortunately, there are no acceptable estimates of just how costly. There have been very few attempts to estimate the capital and operating costs of efforts to expand domestic energy production and to conserve on energy use. This is a critical deficiency that deserves prompt rectification.

Part of the problem stems from widely differing assumptions about how much can be achieved through energy development and how much through conservation measures, and also from widely differing recommendations as to the role and extent of public policies, the technology to be used, the R&D effort required and the composition of the energy program (both between production and conservation, and within each category). Our traditionally short-run analytical techniques might not prove useful for the long-time horizon, to the point that margins of error are likely to be very large.

It seems not unreasonable to assume that the capital costs of an energy program designed to achieve complete self-reliance by 1985 and to prepare for the replacement of hydrocarbons could reach around $1 trillion (1973 dollars) in the period 1975-85. The National Academy of Engineering made what it calls a "guesstimate" of $490-610 billion.[19] Dr. Edward Teller estimated the capital costs of producing 116 quads (54.8 MBPD) of energy by 1985 at $590 billion.[20] Total costs could run over $1 trillion, however, if we include all the investments that are needed to support an extensive energy program–in infrastructure (transportation, distribution), in the supplier industries (rigs, pipelines, railway cars), in energy conservation programs, in environmental safeguards, and in those investments including R&D that will not contribute to output until after 1985. As past experiences amply demonstrate, cost overruns are much more likely than cost shortfalls. Actual future costs, even allowing for inflation, are more likely to exceed than fall below current estimates.

In addition to capital requirements, operational expenses must also be taken into account in assessing the relative costs of the various ways to expand our energy supplies. Some sources, such as hydropower, have minimal operating and maintenance costs. In others–underground coal mining–such expenses can be very significant. As yet, there are insufficient data to permit a reasonable quantitative comparison of these costs for the various energy sources. Still, they must not be ignored.

Despite the considerable difficulties in getting meaningful cost estimates, we can posit certain relationships. First, the greater the scale of the energy program, the higher the costs. While technological breakthroughs may actually lower costs for certain energy sources, this is too speculative a basis for estimating future costs. Second, costs will tend to rise at an increasing rate, increasing marginal costs. With fossil fuels, for instance, marginal costs will rise because it becomes more difficult to extract additional BTUs of energy, due to less accessible locations, the need for deeper wells or mines, and the need to utilize more expensive recovery technology. Third, the more the scale of a national energy program increases and the greater the costs, the more likely it is that other economic objectives will be pushed to lower priority. There is also the question of the impact of a major national energy program on inflation generally.

At present, domestic labor resources are considerably underutilized. A large energy program could help employ these resources, particularly in construction activities. This could help generate economic activity within the United States, narrowing the gap between potential and actual GNP, while not necessarily contributing to inflation.

Once resources are more fully utilized, however, we may still be committed to large energy investments which, in combination with other desired programs–defense, housing, transportation–may put pressure on total resource availabilities. Over the coming decade, investment in a number of key sectors may not be as expansive as in the past–highways, educational facilities, capital improvements by municipalities, and possibly even automobiles. Many believe that these sectoral weaknesses could cause further structural unemployment. The need, then, is to devise a national energy program that makes effective use of our currently underutilized resources and compensates for these slack sectors, without reviving long-run inflationary pressures and other economic distortions.

The relationship between the energy sector and the domestic economy is complex. Because the industry is capital-intensive, energy investments may not generate as much long-run employment as investments in other sectors. However, such investments could provide an important short-run boost to the economy and to employment. Moreover, the secondary effects of having an adequate and stable energy supply will have a very positive influence on the economy and employment. The alternative—an energy shortage—would mean less business activity and less employment.

What are the economic consequences of a large energy program? In 1973, some 25 percent of the nation's investments were allocated to energy and energy-related activities. An energy program of some $1 trillion over the coming decade could raise this to some 30-35 percent. To accommodate such a program without inflation, we must either (a) reduce the level of investments in other sectors of the economy and channel the released resources to the favored energy sector and/or (b) reduce the total domestic consumption of goods and services and again divert resources to energy investment. Either course would probably involve more government influence over the economy.

We thus, could face the following prospects:

Reduced growth in nonenergy investments

*or*

Reduced growth in private consumption

*or*

Increased efficiency in utilizing our human and material resources.

The third prospect is obviously preferable because it will minimize the distortions of an energy program on other areas of the economy. But if we cannot be more efficient, we face the first two prospects.

Alternatively, we may decide to accept the inflationary consequences as resources are bid away from other activities. Indeed, with large energy programs, this may be the only realistic course of action. As already indicated, however, there is no such thing as a free lunch. Inflation will not solve our problems. It only masks the fact, and only for a time, that real living standards are declining. Moreover, inflation brings a host of other distortions, which became painfully evident during the early 1970s.

As a result of a major program to expand domestic energy supplies, U.S. industry may be forced to use high-cost energy while other countries utilize lower-cost fuels. This risk would be heightened if the world price of oil were to decline some time during the coming decade, possibly in response to a world energy surplus. We have stated that the era of cheap energy has come to an end, but the long-run impacts of the increased oil price on world demand and supply of energy have yet to appear. They could be substantial.

A policy of non-self-reliance means continuing dependence on energy imports, to the extent that these are the cheapest source of energy. This may involve fewer economic distortions, such as inflation, than a large-scale domestic energy development program, as long as we have access to imports and the world price rise is moderated. There is no special reason, however, to assume that the OPEC price of oil will remain where it is or will rise only moderately. The 400 percent arbitrary increase of oil prices by the OPEC countries has certainly been one of the major factors contributing to the 1973-74 inflation plus recession. It may well be, therefore, that further inflation could result from arbitrary increases in oil import prices. With a major domestic energy self-sufficiency program, whether or not it contributes to inflation during its development, there at least would be an expansion in U.S. domestic energy capacity. The policy of non-self-reliance might produce inflation by leaving the nation without an enlarged domestic energy capacity and thus more at the mercy of inflated foreign oil prices.

A policy of non-self-reliance runs the real risk of short-run supply disruptions; however, this risk could be eased, to some extent, by efforts to encourage the surplus oil producing countries to invest in the United States, thereby giving them a stake in the well-being of the U.S. economy.

It should be noted that any sharp shift in the present patterns of energy production and consumption, caused either by higher oil prices or by government regulations, can precipitate serious short-term problems of adjustment. Some industries will suffer capital losses—the airline companies, for example, have been suffering heavily from higher fuel costs. New regulations for automobiles may significantly affect not only this industry and its suppliers, but could spread to the travel and recreational industries. Sharp shifts may also worsen the trade-off between inflation and unemployment—the so-called Phillips curve. We may have to suffer both higher rates of inflation and higher rates of unemployment.

Indirect policies might ease these problems by providing more time for adjustment; however, they may not always be adequate to meet the stated objectives. Also, sharp shifts in prices and policies are sometimes more effective in altering demand and supply than a series of more gradual shifts. Where this is so, this is the trade-off we may prefer.

No policy can give complete assurance against big price increases or big price decreases. It is the essence of a critical choice that it must be based on predictions of an uncertain future.

### *Energy Objectives and Environmental/Quality of Life Objectives*

We must recognize that there may be a trade-off between energy objectives and environmental objectives. Efforts to accelerate domestic energy production run the risk of environmental degradation. The greater the scale of a national energy program and the greater the need to develop domestic energy resources, the greater is the potential conflict with environmental considerations. This, of course, is part of the general trade-off between the environment and overall economic activity.

All aspects of the energy industry—in fact, all human activities—have potential environmental impacts: exploration, extraction, production, refining, transportation, generation, transmission, and ultimate usage. These impacts have many causes:

1. Air pollution:
   a. burning of coal by electric utilities
   b. burning of gasoline by automobiles
   c. emissions by oil refineries.
2. Water pollution:
   a. offshore oil spills
   b. excess water usage by coal gasification and liquefaction plants
   c. heating of water by power plants.
3. Land Degradation:
   a. surface mining
   b. subsidence of underground coal mines
   c. tailings of oil shale
   d. pipeline ruptures.
4. Safety:
   a. collapse of hydroelectric dams
   b. sabotage of nuclear facilities
   c. cave-ins of underground coal mines
   d. burning of oil and LNG (liquefied natural gas)

There is clearly a need to find ways of making a better environment compatible with ample energy. The trade-off can be eased somewhat by emphasizing conservation programs as one means of achieving our energy objectives. When it involves the more efficient use of energy, conservation is generally—although not always—thought of as being more compatible with the environment than the alternative of expanding domestic energy output. It must be remembered, however, that some forms of energy conservation require additional use of energy. The critical choice here is whether a conservation program by itself would be adequate to give us complete self-reliance. If it cannot, then we still face the basic choice of cutting back or delaying the setting of our environmental standards for the sake of energy and economic objectives or cutting back on our energy objectives by reducing the scale of our energy program, or finding new approaches that satisfy both requirements to some extent.

It is important to note that a policy of import dependence, whether limited or not, may also have adverse environmental implications. For example, the tankers carrying foreign oil have, up to now, been the principal source of oil spillage in the oceans, partly because of accidents, but largely due to the way the tanks are cleaned out. The breakup of a supertanker close to shore could have disastrous consequences to beaches and marine and bird life. By comparison, the damages resulting from leakages from offshore drilling have been minimal. In addition, the transport of foreign LNG poses safety hazards of unknown magnitude for U.S. ports and facilities.

### *Energy Objectives and Equity Objectives*

As with other large national programs, we must be aware of the crucial trade-off between efficiency and equity. Efficiency does not necessarily go with equity—in energy or in other areas. The need for a trade-off applies as much to price-oriented programs (taxes, price floors, import tariffs) as it does to nonprice measures (automobile tax based on weight or mileage efficiency). In any program, people and companies will be required to make sacrifices in the national interest. Should they be compensated? If so, in what manner—and how can this be done without excessive government interference? What will be the impact of the various energy programs on income distribution?

Equity considerations are important in their own right. In addition, with the end of the era of cheap energy, it may be necessary to shift public opinion in favor of a national energy program in order to meet major energy objectives. This necessitates an equitable approach. Public support requires that the energy program is not, and is not seen to be, a vehicle for enriching a handful of people or companies. The program may have to be carefully devised to spread the burden, as much as possible, among different income groups and different regions. Even without a special energy program, high energy prices themselves will cause income shifts that policymakers must fully recognize.

The key issue is the appropriate balance between efficiency and equity. Some individuals and groups are burdened more than others by measures to conserve on energy use or to expand domestic energy production. Even the nationwide reduction in the speed limit, which has saved lives in addition to saving energy, was vigorously opposed by truckers because it limited the number of trips they could make and hence reduced their potential incomes. Higher automobile taxes, fees, and tolls, which could bring substantial fuel savings, place an extra burden on those people who have no alternative but to use their cars to get to work. Higher prices for producers of domestic oil and natural gas may benefit these producers at the expense of consumers, especially the lower income groups that can least afford to pay higher energy prices. However, higher prices may also accelerate the production of domestic oil and natural gas and thus help us meet our national energy and economic objectives.

**National and Regional Considerations.** We face an especially critical choice in the need to reconcile legitimate regional interests with the achievement of national energy objectives. Indications are that this is a very serious issue which, if unresolved, could jeopardize the chances of success of any serious energy development program. Where the interests are irreconcilable, should we tone down our national objectives in order to accommodate regional interests, or should we work to make the national interest prevail, possibly by compensating municipalities and states for sacrifices that are in the national interest?

Certain regions may be adversely affected by energy expansion programs. The processing of shale oil on the surface would leave the problem of disposition of the vast tailings in Colorado, just as coal tailings in the past were problems in West Virginia. Despite years of safe and successful operation, the siting of nuclear plants is still a controversial issue. Some 90 percent of New England's electric power is generated by oil imports from the Middle East and Venezuela; this region has an obvious interest in lowering world oil prices. On the other hand, Texas, Oklahoma, Louisiana, and other oil producing states have an economic interest in raising price controls on oil and natural gas.

How do we reconcile regional or local interests with one another and with the national interest? If we cannot, do we jeopardize the chances of success of any serious energy development program? To what extent do we wish to promote regional energy security, in addition to national energy security—and how do we do it? These are some of the critical issues we face.

## *National and International Considerations*

A fifth critical issue is whether we, in the United States, should be concerned about helping our allies obtain adequate supplies of energy. And if so, how? Should energy security be sought in strictly nationalist terms, without regard to the interests of our friends? Should the search for long-run substitutes for hydrocarbons be pursued unilaterally or multilaterally? How much financing assistance should be given to the less developed, oil importing countries, which are experiencing very large balance-of-payments deficits because of higher oil prices and an inability to offset this—as the developed countries have—through expanded exports to the OPEC countries? How much of this balance-of-payments support should be conducted on a bilateral basis, and how much through multilateral arrangements?

One of the potentially grave consequences of the higher oil prices has been the tendency of a number of developed countries to try to protect their own balance-of-payments by exporting armaments and nuclear reactors, despite limited safeguards on their use. The misuse of such exports could trigger worldwide instabilities.

A self-reliance energy program that includes the domestic conservation and development of energy would help the demand/supply balance in other countries. As we reduce our energy imports—or at least limit their increase—more oil is made available for other countries. A self-reliance program that also enables the United States to export substantial amounts of oil and coal would reduce the dependence of its allies on Middle Eastern oil suppliers. We would then be in a better position to assist them in case of real or threatened supply disruptions.

A policy that reduced U.S. net energy imports to zero would prevent large foreign exchange expenditures on petroleum imports, which otherwise might weaken the dollar exchange rate. And by curbing the foreign exchange earnings of the oil exporting countries, this would reduce the need to recycle their surplus funds. At the same time, the pressure on domestic resource availabilities that might accompany programs for complete energy self-sufficiency could bring considerable inflationary pressures, with adverse impacts on the international economy.

It is also conceivable that a policy of complete self-reliance might lead the United States into a situation in which, once its needs are met, it does not really care how other countries cope—how they pay for their oil imports or how they obtain recycled petrodollars. We may be less inclined to renew agreements on energy sharing in times of crises, or to get involved in new discussions on price and access.

At the other extreme, a policy of no self-reliance would lead to a growing volume of U.S. oil import, which would enable the oil producing countries to put increasing pressure on the other energy consuming nations.

With policies of limited and unlimited dependence, we still have a direct interest in price, access, and recycling. To protect ourselves, we might utilize capital and technological transfers to encourage the widespread development of energy resources in the non-OPEC countries. This would enable us to diversify our sources of energy supply, while, at the same time, we increase the world energy supply and promote the economic growth and purchasing power of these non-OPEC countries.

Limited imports might enable us to curb the most expensive energy investments, in either conservation or production, by taking advantage of world supplies to a limited and predetermined extent. This reduces the chance—but by no means eliminates it entirely—that our economy will be saddled with much higher energy costs than other countries.

Storage is another economic insurance policy. All oil consuming countries have a strong interest in maintaining access to foreign sources of oil and to an equitable allocation of supplies whenever access is disrupted. The maintenance of a global stockpile, as opposed to national arrangements, would involve a considerable degree of cooperation among the energy importing countries.

The long-run development of substitutes for oil and natural gas will involve an extensive and expensive R&D effort in such areas as solar, fusion, geothermal, and bioconversion energy. We can choose either to go it alone or to work with and coordinate our R&D activities with other countries. Going it alone would involve international duplication and wasteful efforts. To be sure, the United States is one of the few countries that has the resources (people, material, capital) to go it alone and thus gain certain technological advantages over other countries. The issue is whether this is the best use of these resources.

One must keep in mind that an international effort could get bogged down by national jealousies, disagreements, footdragging, and indecision. On the other hand, an extensive domestic energy development program, while designed in part to curb imports, could have an adverse effect on U.S. exports if the pace is so fast that it is accompanied by resource pressures and inflation.

Finally, a U.S. commitment to work with other nations in R&D could promote greater international exchange of information, talent, and materials. It could conceivably bind the cooperating countries closer together economically and politically. Such a course will not be easy to pursue, but it has great potential benefits if successful.

## IV. Strategies: Critical Production Choices

### *Energy Production, Conservation, and Storage*

Conservation, increased energy production, and storage are the general strategies for achieving any desired level of self-reliance. In this and the next two sections, we examine the critical choices that have to be made within each strategy, and the factual details and projections upon which such choices must be based. As we examine the critical choices, we should be aware that for any objective, all these strategies may be appropriate. The issue is the optimum combination among the strategies and the decisions needed within each of them.

One basic choice concerns the priorities between saving energy and producing more energy. The issue of priorities revolves around the comparison of the social costs and the benefits of conservation with the social costs and benefits of production—matters which cannot easily be quantified. Even though it may cost more, in dollar terms, to save a unit of energy than to produce an additional unit, the effort to save might be preferred if a high value is placed on the social benefits of savings—or if the social costs of producing that added energy (e.g., pollution) are considered excessive.

Conservationists complain that these social considerations are not always taken into account. Indeed, they believe the nation's public and private institutions are heavily biased toward production. They emphasize that actions must be avoided which threaten adverse social impacts decades from now. In particular, they want social and environmental costs to be internalized as much as possible, so that producers and users of energy have an economic incentive to reduce these costs.

Those urging energy production, on the other hand, believe that the social costs incident to enforced conservation are ignored, that costs related to developing domestic energy sources are often exaggerated, and, as a result, our domestic production capabilities have been unduly retarded. They contend that we still have nuclear capabilities and substantial fossil fuel deposits; energy reserves are more limited by technology and price than by geology. They argue that technological advances can provide a *long-term* solution to dependence on foreign energy sources, without excessive impact on the environment. Moreover, they believe that overemphasis on conservation may have a negative impact on the economy and on the quality of life of Americans by making permanent the temporary costs that would accrue from another oil embargo.

These are obviously questions which cannot be settled in principle, but only in specific instances. Measures to expand domestic energy output are useful both to increase self-reliance by 1985 and to replace petroleum in the decades thereafter. Some conservation measures could have a fairly immediate impact on energy consumption, but appear to be limited in their longer-run impact. They would, however, gain us valuable time. A stockpile program may also give temporary self-reliance, but may do little to protect us against a depleting supply of hydrocarbons or increases in the price of oil.

### *How Much Can Production Expand?*

In this section, we examine some of the critical issues involved in the scale and composition of programs to expand domestic energy production. We look at production increases from the point of view of the potential amount of energy output in 1985, according to various published sources. None of the data in Tables I-4 and I-5 are original. The projections generally assume no additional economic, environmental, or other regulatory restraints. The factors limiting production are mainly technology, the availability of people and material, and, in the case of coal, basic demand. However, other assumptions vary widely, as indicated by the wide range of the estimates.

The projections are limited to 1985. It is essential, however, that we broaden our horizons beyond 1985. We cannot justify a program just because it balances demand and supply in 1985; it also must be consistent with our objectives for 1985-2000. However, those who would extend the view into the twenty-first century may wish to reflect whether they could have predicted the present situation in 1950.

As can be seen in Table I-4, estimates of potential domestic energy production in 1985 range from 85.0-117.6 quads of BTUs. Compared to the 62 quads actually produced in 1973, this represents an annual increase of from 3-5.75 percent.

Table I-5 presents estimates of potential production according to the major

**Table I-4**
**Potential Domestic Energy Production–1985**

| | quads of BTUs | MBPD of oil equivalent |
|---|---|---|
| a. Federal Energy Administration (11/74)–Accelerated supply: $11 oil | 104.2 | 49.2 |
| b. National Petroleum Council (8/74)–medium case | 88.4 | 41.7 |
| c. National Academy of Engineering (5/74) | 100.7 | 47.9 |
| d. Ford Foundation (9/74) | | |
| –Historical Growth | 105.0 | 49.6 |
| –Technical Fix | 85.0 | 40.1 |
| e. Joint Committee on Atomic Energy (5/74) | 87.1 | 40.1 |
| f. Institute of Gas Technology (12/73) | 117.6 | 55.5 |
| g. Commerce Technical Advisory Board (3/75) | 94.0 | 44.4 |

sources of energy. The estimates are taken from the reports specified in Table I-4, together with projections of ERDA. Not all reports estimated the specified energy sources. This table shows that the average of estimates of potential energy production is 99.0 quads, (46.7 million barrels per day of oil equivalent), somewhat below the midpoint of the range of aggregate estimates.

The wide range of estimates indicates the impact of differing assumptions, especially when long-run projections are made. We must thus treat any one projection with considerable skepticism; even the ranges themselves must be considered only approximations. Nevertheless, certain conclusions are evident:

1. Oil and natural gas are likely to remain our principal energy sources through 1985.
2. Coal and nuclear power are capable of major increases and could make important contributions to our total energy supplies by 1985.
3. The "new" energy sources will make only minor contributions by 1985–although their development during this period is probably essential for a significant expansion in later decades.

Should we set a target for 1985 energy production? If so, at what level? From a technical point of view, we might achieve a production level of from 85-118 quads (40-56 MBPD). Output could be even more if we can increase our coal exports, which in 1973 totaled 53 million tons and accounted for 9 percent of total coal production. If this percentage can be raised to 20 percent, the equivalent of 180 million tons, we could add some 4 quads of BTUs to the 1985 totals.

The desired level of domestic energy production is dependent on a number of factors, in particular on the level of domestic energy consumption, the type of

**Table I-5**
**Potential Domestic Energy Production, by Source**

| Energy Source | (Energy Produced) 1973 quads of BTUs | Range of Estimates on Potential Energy Production–1985 quads of BTUs | Average of Estimates of Potential Production–1985 quads of BTUs | MBPD of Oil Equivalent |
|---|---|---|---|---|
| 1. Oil | 22 | 23.3- 35.8 | 29.3 | 13.8 |
| 2. Natural Gas | 23 | 15.1- 30.1 | 25.0 | 11.8 |
| 3. Coal[a] | 13 | 16.0- 25.0 | 21.4 | 10.1 |
| 4. Nuclear | 1 | 6+ - 21.8 | 13.5 | 6.4 |
| 5. Coal Gasification | 0 | 0 - 3.6 | 1.7 | 0.8 |
| 6. Coal Liquefaction | 0 | 0 - 2.8 | 0.8 | 0.4 |
| 7. Shale Oil | 0 | 0.2- 2.5 | 1.4 | 0.7 |
| 8. Solar | 0[b] | 0.1- 0.6 | 0.4 | 0.2 |
| 9. Geothermal | 0[b] | 0.2- 1.0 | 0.5 | 0.2 |
| 10. Bioconversion | 0[b] | 0.8- 2.5 | 1.6 | 0.8 |
| 11. Hydro | 3 | 3.0- 4.1 | 3.4 | 1.6 |
| TOTAL | 62 | 85. -117.6 | 99.0 | 46.7 |

Source: Sources specified in table I-4, plus ERDA.

[a]Excludes coal used for gasification and liquefaction.

[b]Insignificant amounts.

self-reliance that is chosen, and the degree of concern about our depletion of petroleum resources. The less we conserve, the more energy has to be produced to meet any given level of self-reliance. Indeed, if energy consumption continues to grow at its past rate of 3.4 percent, it will reach 116 quads (54.8 MBPD of oil equivalent) of energy by 1985. This is very close to the top of the range of estimates of potential energy production.

Energy conservation measures can provide some leeway. (See Section V for a discussion of potential savings through conservation.) The more effective they are, the more adequately can domestic energy production cover domestic energy consumption and the better the possibility for some exports. Similarly, a lowering of our energy objectives—such as adopting a limited rather than complete type of self-reliance—could also give us more leeway, to the extent we are willing to continue to rely on and pay the costs of imports.

Let us now examine the key issues surrounding the production potential of each of the major energy sources—the resource, economic, technological, and other considerations that are behind the range of estimates presented in Table I-5.

**Oil.** Domestic oil production provided some 22 of the 76 quads of energy (10.4 of the 35.9 MBPD) consumed in the United States in 1973—a share of nearly 30 percent. Oil imports reached 13 quads (6.1 MBPD) that year, bringing the overall consumption of petroleum to 46 percent of the nation's total energy usage. Domestic oil output appeared to reach a peak around 1970 and has been declining since then. The depletion or reduced yields from existing wells has not been offset—as it had in the past—by the discovery of new oil deposits and the bringing into production new and high-yielding wells. The fact is that up through 1972, real oil prices had been declining. In constant 1948 dollars, the price of a barrel of oil declined from $2.60 in 1948 to $1.85 in 1972.[21] This discouraged investment in domestic exploration and drilling, especially since profitable opportunities were opening up abroad. The growth in refining capacity also slowed between 1970-73, partly due to a variety of governmental policies. As a result, imports cover an increasing portion of our needs for refined products.

We have earlier presented the issue of whether the United States (and the world) can count on sufficient oil resources to meet its long-term needs.[22] We have seen that while it is unlikely to be a problem through 1985, it could emerge as a critical problem sometime thereafter, especially if we are unable to develop fully our recoverable resources.

Where are these resources to be found? Which areas deserve the highest priority in terms of exploration and development activity—onshore, offshore, or Alaska? Should priority be given to the discovery of recoverable oil resources, or to the economic utilization of known but hitherto unrecoverable resources? Should we even set priorities—should we proceed on all possible fronts simultaneously in the hope that the economic and technological bottlenecks will somehow be removed? One should realize, of course, that many of these choices will actually be made by industry. But incentives, disincentives, and general public policy will make their contributions.

There are no easy answers to any of these questions, especially since there is considerable uncertainty about how much oil can be potentially extracted using any one particular strategy. The U.S. Geological Survey believes that the greatest potential still lies onshore, in the lower forty-eight states.

The lower forty-eight states are estimated to contain nearly two-thirds of the total remaining oil reserves and nearly half of the nation's undiscovered recoverable oil resources. The importance of Alaska is seen by the fact that it contains one-quarter of the nation's oil reserves and as much undiscovered recoverable resources onshore as lie offshore the lower forty-eight states.

Project Independence calls for onshore oil producing areas to account for one-half of total oil output by 1985. Nearly one-half of this is to come from new secondary and tertiary recovery techniques. Alaska is expected to account for over one-quarter of total U.S. oil output, with about one-half of this coming from the North Slope. The outer-continental shelf (OCS) around the lower forty-eight states is projected to contribute one-fifth of total oil production by 1985, mainly from the Gulf of Mexico.[23]

A major resource is the oil in known oil fields which cannot yet be

**Table I-6**
**Location of Oil Reserves and Undiscovered Recoverable Resources**
(units–billion of barrels)

| | Reserves[a] | Undiscovered Recoverable[b] Resources |
|---|---|---|
| Total onshore and offshore | 62.0 | 50-127 |
| Total onshore | 55.8 | 37- 81 |
| Lower 48 | 39.7 | 20-64 |
| Alaska | 16.1 | 6-19 |
| Total off shore | 6.2 | 10-49 |
| Lower 48 | 6.0 | 5-13 |
| Alaska | 0.2 | 3-31 |

Source: USGS, Circular 725, pp. 4-5.

[a]Includes demonstrated and inferred reserves.

[b]Totals are not obtained by arithmetic summation, but by statistical methods.

economically recovered. The average recovery rate, estimated at 30 percent,[24] delineates the potential for improvement. Secondary methods of oil recovery involve flooding the wells with water or using gas pressurization to get at the oil. Tertiary recovery methods comprise the injection of chemicals or the use of underground combustion (in the first instance, oil is mobilized by lubrication; in the second, by a decrease in viscosity). Improvements in such recovery techniques could help transform part of the unrecoverable resources into recoverable reserves. Other potential oil supplies could come from mining of the shallow reservoir beds of oil fields[25] and from the outer-continental rise. New technologies will have to be developed if the latter resources are to be developed. (The use of shale oil and liquefaction of coal are discussed separately below.)

Achievable oil production will be as much influenced by economic forces as by the size and availability of oil reserves and resources–if not more so. As long as private companies are involved in the exploration, extraction, and production of oil, the expectation of profits will influence the scale of their activities. Prices not only have to exceed costs, but also by a margin that adequately compensates for the risks involved. And the drilling and extraction of oil in the hostile environments of offshore areas and Alaska involve more risk, more lead time, and more costs than do onshore activities.

The jump in world oil prices has already stimulated new exploration and drilling activity and the reworking of wells not yet abandoned. However, because of the long lead times involved–the development of a new onshore field may take three to five years and an offshore field ten years–the resulting production increases will reach significant levels only by the early 1980s. This is why overall oil production is expected to continue its decline during the next few years despite the new investments.[26]

**Natural Gas.** The demand for natural gas has increased sharply over the past two decades, at an average annual rate of some 5.7 percent.[27] Because gas is a clean burning fuel, it is preferred for many uses. It is also a feedstock for the petrochemical industry. About half of the gas consumed in the United States provides heat for industry; over 20 percent is used to generate electricity. In the past, demand has been stimulated by the abundance of gas supplies, in part obtained as a by-product of drilling for oil, and by its relative cheapness under governmental price regulations.

Proven reserves rose from 144 quads of BTUs (144 trillion cubic feet) in 1945 to a peak of 293 quads (293 trillion cubic feet) in 1967.[28] Since then, additions to reserves have failed to keep pace with production. This is generally attributable to the absence of discovery of further huge onshore gas deposits and to price controls on gas transported interstate. The producing companies complain that, with drilling and exploration costs rising faster than the controlled gas price, they cannot get a reasonable return on further investments in this industry.

We have earlier examined the current estimates of gas reserves and undiscovered recoverable resources. At the 1974 rate of production, these recoverable resources would last from thirty-six to fifty-one years. This consists of measured reserves (eleven years), inferred reserves (nine and one-half years) and undiscovered recoverable resources (fifteen to thirty-one years).[29] Some two-thirds of these reserves and resources are estimated to be located onshore in the lower forty-eight states.[30] A good portion is to be found in association with the extraction of oil deposits.

Technological efforts to retrieve the natural gas that is trapped in tight geological formation, using either high nuclear explosives or hydraulic methods, may succeed in expanding gas supplies, especially after 1985. Substantial amounts of gas are believed to be in place in tight sand reservoirs in the Green River Basin of Wyoming, the Piceance Basin of Colorado, and the Unita Basin of Utah.[31]

Almost all long-term projections of future gas supplies assume that future gas prices will more closely reflect true market conditions; that is, controls over the wellhead price of interstate natural gas will be eliminated or substantially eased. Even so, no substantial output gains are expected because of the need to offset the rapidly declining output from existing gas fields. For the first time since 1971, annual production fell below 22 quads in 1974.

Until new investments come on line, the prospect is for very tight supplies of natural gas, necessitating interruptions of service at times. One study group on natural gas concluded that "... a serious scarcity of natural gas supply is inevitable in the 1975-78 period, with no means of supplementing the availability of natural gas. Thus, there is no way to avoid regional curtailment of existing gas customers."[32]

Assuming a high price for gas and an accelerated supply program, the FEA projects output will rise only to 25.5 quads by 1985—an annual growth from 1973 of only 0.8 percent. Other sources (see Table I-5) put output in 1985 as high as 30 quads. (If prices continue to remain low, natural gas output in 1985 could actually be considerably below current levels.) But even with higher prices, the output of gas from wells not associated with oil production is expected to continue to decline through 1980 in the lower forty-eight states because of the lead times involved in developing new gas wells. Such nonassociated gas accounts for two-thirds of the total gas produced in the United States.

By 1985, the FEA projects that 57 percent of our gas supplies will come from the lower forty-eight states, 30 percent from the outer continental shelf bordering these states, and 12 percent from the North Slope of Alaska.[33]

Both liquefied natural gas (LNG) and synthetic natural gas (SNG) could help supplement domestic natural gas supplies. The problem is that the costs of both are significantly greater than for conventional gas.[34] Moreover, LNG from foreign sources has the added problem of security of supply and the safety of LNG tankers from accidents, including collisions. (The contribution from coal gasification is discussed separately.)

**Coal.** Coal's contribution to total U.S. energy consumption has fallen from 90 percent at the turn of the century to around 17 percent at present. The decline reflects competitive inroads from oil and gas. These are cleaner and more convenient sources of energy. Oil, in particular, is more versatile and is the only energy source that is used to fuel the burgeoning number of cars on the road. The inability to develop a reliable and economical desulfurization process in the face of environmental regulations has been a major factor in the 1960s in prompting the electric utilities to convert from coal to oil in an effort to comply with air quality standards.

Over the past five years, the output of underground coal mines has been affected by reduced labor productivity, stemming in part from the implementing of the Mine Health and Safety Act of 1969 and partly from generally poor labor-management relations.

The development of the nation's vast coal deposits—in terms of BTUs, the United States has several times more coal than the Middle East has oil—is being held back by a web of uncertainties. Although Project Independence calls for a much heavier reliance on coal to fuel the economy in the coming years, the industry is skeptical about the national commitment to coal. It is concerned about strip-mining legislation, the leasing policy on federal coal lands in the West, and the implementation of the Clean Air Act, which restricts the burning of high-sulfur coals by the electric utilities. The industry is also uncertain about the direction of the national policy toward nuclear fuel, an energy source which has already received substantial federal assistance and which competes directly with coal in the generation of electricity. Changes in future availabilities and price of oil and gas also worry the industry. The net result of these uncertainties has been to hold back the major investments needed to expand coal production.

Total coal resources have been estimated at up to 72,000 quads (3.2 trillion tons), of which one-half has already been identified. Those reserves that are recoverable using current mining technology, and at current prices have been calculated at 9,800 quads (434 billion tons). In 1973, domestic production came to some 13.5 quads (600 million tons). At that rate of output, recoverable reserves would last over 700 years.[35]

Existing technology for getting the coal out of the ground and for processing it is considered adequate for both underground mining and surface mining. Much of the western mineable coal—which accounts for about one-half of the nation's coal reserves—is located in federal lands and can thus be mined without interfering with private property rights. The only technical (as opposed to economic or environmental) limitation to a major expansion of coal output is a shortage of men and materials and transport difficulties. The underground mines are faced with a shortage of skilled miners at a time when management-labor relations are unstable. The surface mines in the West are capital intensive and show high labor productivity. But they also face a shortage of power shovels, draglines, and continuous drilling equipment.

The western mines face a major transportation problem in getting coal to their eastern users. Locomotives, gondola cars, and hopper cars are all in short supply. Railroad tracks throughout the nation need to be improved. Only one coal slurry pipeline exists; many more may have to be constructed. Many of these labor and material bottlenecks, including the need to modify boilers to accept western coals, while serious, are capable of being resolved as production expands.

Some two-thirds of our coal output is used to generate electricity by the utilities. (Most of the rest goes for export, coke, and industrial uses, such as metallurgy.) Electrical generation is expected to remain the principal use of coal; however, a fraction may be used for processing into gas and oil. A major technological breakthrough in the desulfurization of coal could make an important contribution to the attainment of our national self-reliance objectives, as well as help conserve our domestic petroleum resources for uses where there are no adequate substitute fuels.

Projections (see Table I-5) indicate a potential expansion of U.S. solid coal output from 13 quads (577 million tons) in 1973, to 16-25 quads (710-1,110 million tons) by 1985. These projections generally exclude the amount of coal required to produce synthetic gas and liquids. From a technical point of view, we may actually be capable of tripling our coal output; however, demand for this high-sulfur fuel, which has limited versatility, appears to be more of a restraint than supply bottlenecks. Homes, factories, railroads, and electric utilities have all been converting away from coal. Indeed, the shift to oil by the electric utilities, especially those on the Atlantic coast, has been an important reason why the nation's oil imports increased so rapidly in the 1960s.[36] Between 1969-72, nearly 400 coal-fired boilers, accounting for about 7 percent of the nation's total generating capacity, converted from coal to oil.[37]

Coal could play an important role in any strategy in which the export of fuels is seriously considered. Our western, low-sulfur coal fields and the similar field in the Cook Inlet could become highly competitive in world trade. Do we want to become net exporters of energy or do we want to use coal to offset our oil imports?

Most of the output expansion is expected to come from western surface mines, where the sulfur content and the cost of extraction is lower than in the East. Moreover, nearly all of the coal can be recovered from a surface mine, compared to only about 50 percent from an underground mine. However, production cannot be accelerated rapidly. The output from existing mines can often be stepped up, but it takes an average of five to six years to develop a new underground mine and some three to five years to develop a surface mine. The Beluga coal fields in the Cook Inlet might go into operation in as little as three years. Nevertheless, the main problem is developing the demand for the coal in the United States and abroad.

**Nuclear Fission.** Some forty-seven nuclear power plants were in commercial operation in the United States by the end of July 1975. They accounted for some 8 percent of the nation's electricity generation.[38]

Estimates of installed nuclear capacity by 1985 have been dropping as delays in approvals and construction mount. Most recent estimates (see Table I-5) range from 6-22 quads (141,000-517,000 Mwe). The National Academy of Engineering believes that, with an accelerated construction and development program, it might be possible to reach 19 quads (447,000 Mwe) by the end of 1985. The Project Independence Task Force on Nuclear Energy believes that an accelerated program could produce 17 quads (400,000 Mwe) of energy in 1985, and account, by then, for some 45 percent of the nation's total electric energy production.

The possibility of developing a breeder reactor must also be considered. Up to now, efforts to produce a demonstration plant have been fraught with difficulty and the target date for completion of the Oak Ridge, Tennessee, plant has been put back to 1982. The breeder reactor, if it proves commercially feasible, would increase available uranium supplies manyfold. With present nuclear technology, the existing uranium source of power is in short supply and could be a limiting factor in nuclear plant expansions. Other improvements in nuclear technology, which require less time and less research expenditures, may ensure the future availability of fuel for reactors. One possibility is the introduction of fuel-cycles utilizing thorium, an abundant element.

**Coal Gasification and Liquefaction.** It is possible to obtain a synthetic gas from coal. A number of alternative conversion processes are actively under development. Industry sources believe commercial production can come as early as

1978, using the surface-mined coals of the West. Other sources do not expect significant commercial production before 1985.

The derivation of low-BTU gas from coal is now at a commercial stage, using existing technology. With second generation technology, it could be commercial as early as 1980-81. Pipeline gas from commercial plants may be delivered by 1984. Commercial liquids may be obtained from coal by about 1983.[39] Unfortunately, the projected cost of pipeline-quality gas is high—around $2.50 per million BTUs, the equivalent of $15 per barrel of oil and five times the price ceiling now in effect. This cost may be reduced, however, by the underground conversion of the coal into gas.

Conversion projections of synthetic gas supplies in 1985 range up to 3.6 quads (3.6 TCF) under the uncertain assumption that it will become economical to produce such gas by then.

The several coal liquefaction processes now under consideration may produce a variety of emissions. Process air emissions will contain $NO_X$ and CO, as well as particulate matter and sulfur dioxide. There will be, at least, one solid waste stream, consisting of the ash removed from the solvent refined coal product. Unless recovered, sulfur would also constitute a solid waste.

A significant expansion in high-BTU gas and liquid products is technically possible during 1985-2000, possibly using *in situ* or underground processes. Although the gasification and liquefaction of coal itself requires considerable energy and hence is not that efficient on a "net energy" basis, the synthetic gas and liquids could be an important supplement to declining oil and natural gas reserves and can be used for purposes where coal is not appropriate. Research efforts to raise conversion efficiencies are currently underway.

The gasification of high-sulfur coal to produce a low-sulfur gas is one of the ways to reduce the $SO_2$ emissions associated with the burning of such coal. However, strip mining will probably be required to a large extent to obtain the coals for conversion to gas, bringing on problems of land degradation. A gasification plant also will consume large amounts of water, which could be an environmental threat to areas where water resources are limited. Moreover, there is danger of water and thermal pollution, as well as a problem in disposing of the coal ash from the processed coal.

The net environmental impact of coal gasification may be a reduction in the extent of air pollution by sulfur oxides and particulate matter. However, coal consumption would rise, with the attendant problems of mining impacts and solid waste disposal. Most projections indicate no significant output by 1985. Production of methanol from coal, to be used as boiler fuel, may reach some 0.6 quads (0.6 TCF).[40]

**Shale Oil.** The United States has extensive deposits of oil shale-bearing rocks, especially in the Green River Formation of Colorado, Utah, and Wyoming. When heated, the rocks yield shale oil, which can be refined into the normal range of petroleum products. Total resources in the Green River Formation are estimated at over 10,000 quads (1,800 billion barrels). Only some 6 percent of the deposits, mostly located in Colorado, are considered accessible and economical to mine under today's technology and prices.[41] Even so, shale oil reserves of 600 quads (100 billion barrels) represent a huge supply.

The federal government owns four-fifths of the nation's oil shale-bearing land in these western states. However, the leasing of the land has been delayed as has the development of lands already leased. This partly reflects the fact the economic feasibility of shale oil development has not yet been proven. Retorting is a major problem. So too is a lack of water for the shale–three barrels of water are needed for every barrel of shale oil recovered. Water in this region is already committed to other uses and extensive amounts might have to be imported. An enormous volume of solid waste–some 40-50 acre feet per day from a 100,000 barrel-per-day plant–is produced that must somehow be disposed of.[42]

To overcome these and other problems, it has been proposed that *in situ* retorting of the shale oil be undertaken. An underground explosion would shatter the formation enough to enable a combustion process to release the oil and drive it to the surface. This technology continues to be in an experimental state–there is a very small-scale "pilot" plant near Rifle, Colorado–and large-scale commercial application of *in situ* processing is unlikely by 1985.

Projections of the volume of shale oil that can be obtained in 1985 by above-ground processing range from 0.2-2.5 quads (0.1-1.2 MBPD). At a volume of 1 quad, it is estimated that five major mines would have to come into production every year for ten years.[43] Using *in situ* processing, total production could reach 2.5 quads (1.2 MBPD) by 1985 and 4.5 quads (2.1 MBPD) by 2000[44]–assuming all the technological and environmental problems can be resolved.

**Solar.** The sun is an inexhaustible source of energy. It is already being utilized on a small scale as a source of commercial energy in a number of countries, including the United States. The early applications of solar energy are expected to be in the heating and cooling of buildings, where the technology is fairly well developed.[45] Substantial technological advances will be needed to produce steam for industrial processes. The National Science Foundation estimates that a successful solar development program could cause a significant number of buildings to be solar heated by 1980 and solar cooled by 1985. Solar energy can also be utilized to generate electric power, either through the conversion of sunlight to heat and steam or through use of solar cells. Further technological advances are required, however, because conversion efficiencies are very low and the cost of solar electricity is many times more expensive than that generated by conventional sources.

Projections indicate that, with an accelerated development program, solar sources could provide up to 0.6 quads (0.3 MBPD of oil equivalent) of energy for space heating/cooling by 1985.[46] FEA estimates of the potential conversion of solar radiation to thermal energy and electric power average from near 0 by 1985 to 8.3 quads by 2000 (3.9 MBPD of oil equivalent).[47] Whatever solar electricity is generated will mainly be in the southwestern United States, where it will be more competitive with fossil fuel sources.

**Geothermal.** Geothermal energy is obtained by utilizing the heat inside the earth. This stored thermal energy can be used for heating, cooling, or generating electricity. It has been tapped successfully for many years in a number of diverse locations, such as The Geysers (near San Francisco); Larderello, Italy; and the Wairakei field in New Zealand. Nearly a dozen U.S. states, mostly in the West, are actively investigating their geothermal potentials. Just as with oil and gas, there is no consensus at the moment as to the size of U.S. geothermal resources or how soon they can be exploited. However, it is estimated that some 60 percent of the geothermally prospective areas are on federal lands that have not yet been released for exploration.

Dry steam can be utilized by existing methods, but further technological advances are needed for the wet steam/hot water fields.[48] There is a special need to prevent corrosion and deterioration of equipment and to minimize adverse environmental impacts. And, in contrast to fossil fuels, it is not possible to transport geothermal "fuel." The energy must be exploited at its source.

Because of geological, technological, and economic uncertainties, there is a wide range of opinion as to how much geothermal energy can be obtained by 1985. (There is also considerable uncertainty as to how long a particular well will continue to supply geothermal energy.) Estimates for 1985 vary from 1,900 Mw of electric power to 30,000 Mw. The Project Independence Task Force in Geothermal Energy presented a range of 20-30,000 Mw (0.6-0.9 quads).[49] Most observers agree that geothermal energy will not be a significant source until after 1985. For the year 2000, estimates of geothermal energy potential range widely, from 40,000-800,000 Mw (1.2-24.0 quads).[50]

**Bioconversion.** It has been estimated that some 5-10 percent of our demand for electricity could be supplied from urban solid waste when burned in combination with other fuels. Experimentation is already underway on the use of algae and vegetable matter (e.g., trees) as sources of fuel. Algae can be harvested easily in water, and processed through a furnace to yield several hundred barrels of substitute oil per acre per year. If commercially sound, this could prove to be a limitless source for future energy. Indeed, many types of land and marine forms could be developed to convert organic matter into energy sources. This prospect may be enhanced if the waste production from the growing of food can be utilized for bioconversion.

According to the Energy Research and Development Administration, the use of waste materials could provide up to 2.5 quads of energy (1.2 MBPD of oil equivalent) by 1985, while the use of terrestrial and marine biomass could produce up to 2 quads of energy (0.9 MBPD of oil equivalent).[51] These estimates are much larger than those of the FEA Task Force on Solar Energy, which puts the potential for urban solid waste at only 0.65 quads (0.3 MBPD) and for biomass at 0.16 quads (75,000 BPD).[52]

**Hydropower.** Hydropower accounts for some 4 percent of the total energy generated in the United States. Although only about one-third of the nation's hydropower potential has been harnessed,[53] most of the sites suitable for power dams and greater hydroelectricity generation have been utilized. Therefore, only marginal increases in hydropower generation from the current level of 3 quads are expected.

**Electric Power.** Electric utilities are basically consumers of primary fuels; however, the electricity they generate competes with primary fuels in various end-uses. Nearly 30 percent of the nation's primary energy is now converted into electricity for end-use, compared to about 20 percent twenty years ago.[54] The electric utilities form an integral part of the nation's energy picture, especially considering the large amount of capital that will be required to expand their activities over the coming decade.

Electric utilities can convert many different types of fuels into electricity. In general, they tend to utilize oil, coal, hydropower, and nuclear power for meeting their base load demands and natural gas turbines for covering the peak loads of each day and week. Overall generating capacity must cover both the base load, the peak loads and have a reserve margin in case of breakdowns or unexpected increases in demand. Most of the time, therefore, generating capacity is considerably underutilized. Currently, gas provides 19 percent of our electricity; oil, 19 percent; coal, 49 percent; nuclear power, 7 percent; and hydropower, 6 percent.

As the nation's demand for electricity continues to grow—the past rate was some 7 percent a year—the need for decisions now on the expansion of capacity becomes more urgent. Lead times are very long. In the past, there have been delays in finding appropriate sites for nuclear power plants and in getting construction approvals from the public authorities.

Moreover, despite the nation's huge coal reserves, there was a shift from coal to oil-burning plants during the 1969-73 period. Until 1969, coal's share in the total fuels used by the electric utilities was relatively stable. Through the mid-1960s, the rapid expansion in gas-fueled generators was at the expense of oil and hydropower. This shift was largely the result of the economic expansion in the Southwest and in California, as well as the controlled price of natural gas. Since 1969, there has been a shift back to oil, and away from coal, due to oil's environmental advantages and the eased import policy for residual fuel on the East Coast. Natural gas has declined in relative terms, although there was no conversion to gas.

Environmental regulations, especially those governing sulfur dioxide emissions, have encouraged utilities to convert from high sulfur coal to cleaner oil. Efforts to control these emissions, such as stack gas scrubbing, have so far proved to be very costly and their effectiveness is in dispute. The utilities have been reluctant to undertake the heavy investment in pollution control equipment, especially at a time when they find it hard to raise capital for maintaining and expanding their generating capacity.

By 1985, coal-fired power plants could more than double their installed capacity, from 150 Gwe to some 330 Gwe, according to the National Academy of Engineering.[55] Of this increase, only 20 Gwe would be due to conversions from oil-fired plants. An additional 20 Gwe of capacity may be obtained from conversion of natural gas-fired plants to intermediate-BTU gas made from coal. However capacity of oil and gas-fired plants could decline due to reconversions back to coal and the diversion of oil and gas to uses where these fuels cannot be replaced by nuclear energy or coal.

*How to Set Production Priorities*

Whatever the size of a national energy program, decisions must be made implicitly or explicitly as to its composition—those combinations of various energy sources that promise to give us the desired level of production. The composition is directly related to the scale. The greater the scale, the less the leeway for changes in the mix of energy sources. If our 1985 production target is 118 quads of energy, equivalent to the potential achievable level, we would have to utilize each possible energy source to its fullest potential—and hope that the assumptions which we have made that are supposed to bring output to the top of each range of estimates can be realized. On the other hand, if our objective involves the production of less energy, we would have more flexibility in selecting a desirable mix of energy sources.

Within any program, there are critical decisions on the criteria for setting priorities among the competing energy sources. There are many overlapping possibilities:

**How important should economic criteria be?** There are two factors in relying on economic criteria as a means of setting priorities between alternative energy sources and as a means of evaluating the desirability of the different degrees of energy development programs.

One function helps determine whether we should give highest priority to the development of those energy sources that have—or promise to have—the lowest cost per BTU of energy produced. What other considerations, such as a desire for quick results, would justify our modifying or nullifying the influence of costs?

There are many practical difficulties in depending on costs as an allocator of our energy investment efforts. For one thing, we do not have reliable cost estimates, especially in those cases where new technologies have to be developed. For another, costs vary widely *within* any one energy source so that it may not be meaningful to discuss average cost estimates between sources. Variations reflect the size of operations, the location and degree of accessibility of the coal or oil, the type of technology to be used, and the physical characteristics of the energy itself (high or low sulfur coal, high or low BTU gas, heavy or light crude oil).

Without a substantial improvement in our knowledge of comparative costs, it is difficult to use economic criteria. The problem is, what is better? Should costs be disregarded in favor of technical criteria or environmental criteria? Should we depend on "seat-of-the-pants" judgment? Or should a major effort be made to estimate costs *before* we commit ourselves to large investments? Large offshore deposits may be less expensive to develop than many onshore reserves, except offshore Alaska. Geothermal energy appears cheaper than solar. Hydroelectricity is cheap, but the sites are virtually all committed now or blocked by environmentalists. Nuclear plants take longer than fossil fuel and cost more to build, but their power is cheaper. Do we build on such knowledge or do we disregard costs in making energy investment decisions?

A second important function of economic criteria is to assess the economic aspect of alternative energy programs, an issue discussed earlier. If we had more reliable cost data, we would be in a better position to evaluate the capital costs required for these programs by 1985. Unfortunately, we really do not know, with any precision, how much the alternative energy development programs will cost. Efforts have been made to estimate total capital costs of various proposed programs. The FEA, in its *Project Independence Report*, presents five estimates–including two of its own–which range from $367-$457 billion (1973 dollars) over the 1975-85 period.[56] They exclude investment in infrastructure (other than transportation and electric transmission), in supplier industries and in long-range R&D. The highest estimate is from the National Academy of Engineering, which estimated a range of $490-$610 billion for the eleven-year period 1974-85. Moreover, the Academy found that by adding not readily identified infrastructure (railroad, storage facilities) the total cost of its suggested program (49.2 MBPD by 1985) could total nearly $700 billion, excluding investments that will not pay off until after 1985.[57]

When all costs are totaled, they could reach $1 trillion dollars in 1973 dollars–and perhaps more because, as other programs have demonstrated, total costs typically exceed early estimates. Will this be excessive in terms of our other national priorities? Can it be accommodated? Must the nation undertake it, because the risks of not doing it are more costly?

Some energy sources involve more employment opportunities after the construction phase than others–coal more than nuclear power, especially when needs for transportation facilities are considered. How much of an influence should job creation have on investment decisions?

**How important should environmental criteria be?** Energy production and use generally have negative impacts on the environment. Should we set priorities based on environmental impacts, including the banning of those activities that threaten serious damage—surface mining in the arid West, emissions from fossil fuel plants, the possibility of nuclear accidents? How much priority should be given to the correction of potentially adverse environmental impacts before they occur? To cleaning up after environmental problems occur? How do we define "acceptable environmental safeguards" in approving energy investments?

Each energy source has its own impact on the health of people and the environment, as the following list of potential damages indicates.

*Oil*

1. Spillage, resulting from oil drilling
2. Ocean pollution
3. Emissions into air during refining
4. Pipelines may affect land environment, especially in the permafrost regions of Alaska
5. Outer continental shelf: highest risks in the Gulf of Alaska, due to storm and seismic conditions

*Natural Gas*

1. Similar drilling problems as those of oil
2. Danger of shipping and storing liquefied natural gas

*Coal: Underground Mines*

1. Acid mine drainage leading to downstream pollution
2. Piling and storage of waste materials
3. Subsidence of land over shafts
4. Mine safety and black lung disease

*Coal: Surface Mines*

1. Degradation of immediate and surrounding land
2. Lack of rainfall in the West limits reclamation possibilities; possibility of erosion
3. Damage of aquifers would reduce water supplies
4. Acid mine drainage
5. Disruption of rural and other nonindustrial communities—"boom and bust" problems

*Coal: Air Pollution*

1. Easing of emission standards could add to air pollution

*Nuclear*

1. Possibility of radioactive emissions caused by leaks, or accidents during the transportation, reprocessing, storage, and disposal of nuclear fuels; possibility of irremediable damage
2. Waste heat discharge
3. Danger of sabotage, theft, bombing or blackmail by terrorists

4. Although not under U.S. control, worldwide proliferation of nuclear power plants increases the spread of nuclear military capabilities, thus creating additional risks for mankind over the next quarter-century and beyond
5. Development of the fast breeder reactor would increase the amounts of toxic and highly radioactive plutonium that would be produced and shipped around the country

*Coal Gasification*

1. $SO_2$ emissions associated with the burning of high-sulfur coals will be reduced by their conversion to a low-sulfur gas
2. Strip mining of coal creates problems of land degradation
3. Gasification plants might usurp limited water resources
4. Thermal pollution
5. Disposal of coal ash

*Coal Liquefaction*

1. Noxious air emissions, including $NO_X$ and CO and particulate matter
2. Solid waste disposal
3. Disposal of waste water
4. May require an influx of people and associated facilities into sparsely populated areas
5. Thermal emissions

*Oil Shale*

1. Huge volume of waste requires disposal
2. Mining would scar the land; need for reclamation
3. Would monopolize limited water resources
4. Would require an influx of people and associated facilities to sparsely populated areas

*Solar Energy*

1. Large number of collectors could be a form of visual pollution; extensive land use

*Geothermal Energy*

1. Hot water fields produce toxic and saline liquid wastes, creating a disposal problem
2. Subsidence of land
3. Thermal effluents
4. Noise and smell

*Bioconversion*

1. May take away land that could be used for growing food or for recreation

*Hydropower*

1. Diversion of rivers, flooding of lands
2. Seepage could raise water tables
3. Collapse of dams

*Generation of Electricity*

1. Relaxation of Clean Air Act will increase air pollutants, especially particulates and sulfur dioxide

2. Steam-electrical power plants release thermal discharges, affecting surrounding waters
3. Disposal of wastes from stack gas cleaners

These diverse impacts, affecting the air, the waters, the land, and possibly influencing human health and the quality of our lives, present us with a host of critical issues. Three of the most pressing and most difficult issues to resolve appear to be the following:

1. *Should we press forward with the conversion of electric power plants to coal?*

*Argument for Action.* Coal is our most plentiful fossil fuel. Conversion of oil-burning plants to coal-fueled plants can be accomplished within reasonable costs and time. The lead time for alternatives—nuclear plants, new offshore oil, coal gasification—is much longer and the capital investment higher.

The energy shortage necessitates the conversion. The use of high-sulfur coal should be permitted at places and during periods where the climatic conditions prevent damage to the health of the population. In addition, cleaning of stack gases can eliminate sulfur and other pollutants.

*Argument Against Action.* The great accomplishments of environmental legislation must not be compromised. Coal mining creates environmental problems. A flexible policy of coal usage is apt to be misused. Burning coal will generate small particulates, which cannot be precipitated by known methods, as well as sulfur.

2. *Should we press forward with nuclear reactors?*

*Argument for Action.* Nuclear reactors are clean, safe, and the only proven way to expand energy supplies in the long run. Worries about their safety have been exaggerated. Additionally, other countries are pushing ahead in this area and can leave the United States behind, both in technology and perhaps in the generation of nuclear power itself.

*Argument Against Action.* The major argument centers on the possible danger of radioactivity due to accidents or sabotage. There is also concern that nuclear technology and nuclear materials will become available to terrorists or potential enemies—even though the United States no longer has the ability to contain nuclear knowledge and materials that are now available throughout the world.

3. *Should we press forward with oil drilling?*

*Argument for Action.* New deposits are available which, in the short run, increase energy supplies. Moreover, research will minimize any adverse environmental impacts.

*Argument Against Action.* The size of the environmental hazard is hard to estimate and the effects may become irreversible, especially in hostile environments such as Alaska, the Arctic, and the outer-continental shelf.

**Should we concentrate on only a few promising energy sources, or try to develop all potential sources of energy?** Some people believe nuclear energy is the energy of the future and thus should receive highest priority. Indeed, the R&D budget of the federal government emphasizes nuclear reactors (two-thirds of the nuclear budget is devoted to the fast breeder reactor and some criticize the concentration of this effort). Others would like the nation to develop a concerted energy program around coal, of which we have vast reserves. Other energy sources also have their spokesmen pressing the case for strong federal assistance.

The issue is whether any one or two sources should be selected now, or whether it is in the best interest of the nation to keep its options open by more or less supporting all sources until we are more certain of their relative merits.

**Should we be concerned with an energy production program that will give us the quickest results or one that fits best into a strategy for 1985-2000 and beyond?** During the next several years, the economies of the free world will be especially vulnerable to potential shortages of energy. Do we want to accelerate the development of our domestic oil and gas resources, despite possible dangers of depletion and the resulting prospect of increased dependence in future years on imports and on currently unproven technologies, such as synthetic fuels? Or do we want to stretch out our domestic oil and gas supplies, reserving them for transportation and petrochemical uses, until the new technologies are more proven? Do we want to accelerate the use of coal in electric generating plants, even though this may delay nuclear installations? Or vice-versa? Or try to do both?

How can we be flexible enough in our investment decisions so that we can adjust the choices as we go along? Will it be easier to commit ourselves now to an extensive energy program and cut back later if not all the efforts are needed, or will it be better to begin with a less costly program and add to it if the need arises? How much priority should we give now to keeping open our technological options after 1985? Some technological possibilities, such as *in situ* processing of oil shale and coal liquefaction, have not yet been adequately tested. How much dependence should we place on them?

**Should we concentrate on the expansion of supplies of those particular fuels that are likely to be in short supply?** As we have seen, oil and natural gas are the two fuels which face us with the prospect of depletion. Should we concentrate our efforts on the search for additional deposits—onshore and offshore? Should we accelerate or slow down the development of these deposits? Should we accelerate the development of oil and gas and utilize liquefied natural gas to supplement dwindling domestic supplies, regardless of cost?

*How Do We Expand Energy Production?*

Numerous public policies can help to increase the domestic production of the various energy sources. In deciding on how much help is desirable, we face the basic choice:

Price-oriented policies

*or*

Direct public involvement.

Market advocates believe that we should depend mainly on the price mechanism to increase our energy output. The expectation of high prices and profits will encourage producers to invest in the development and production of the various energy sources. Through price and profit, supply will seek to reach demand.

According to this viewpoint, the most desirable government programs would be those that enable prices to give adequate incentives to private business. This could involve the following measures:

1. the easing or removal of price controls on oil and natural gas production, whether new or old
2. the further easing or removal of state regulations on permitted production levels
3. the accelerated leasing or sale of federal fuel-bearing lands (offshore oil and gas, coal, shale) to private development, including the Naval Petroleum Reserves
4. the streamlining of licensing and approval procedures, especially for nuclear power plants
5. the streamlining of regulatory procedures on rate-making for utilities to permit earlier reflection of increased costs and ensure reasonable rates of return so as to facilitate raising needed capital
6. the establishment of a stable and consistent energy (and environmental) policy, so that businessmen can plan ahead and justify large investments
7. the development of programs to deal with the negative impacts of reliance on prices, especially the resulting inequities.

The alternative choice, direct public involvement, is based partly on skepticism about the strength of the price elasticity of energy supply—whether higher prices will by themselves call forth increased production. The energy sector is one of high business risk. Lead times are very long. The National Academy of Engineering estimated that, from approval to production, it takes two to four years to develop a surface coal mine, three to five years for an underground coal mine, nine to ten years for a nuclear power plant, and three to ten years to obtain oil and gas from new fields.[58] New technologies may have to be developed—coal liquefaction, conversion of marine biomass, *in situ* processing of coal and oil shale. Scale requirements often call for very large and indivisible production units. All these factors make for heavy capital outlays and involve high business risk. The concern is that price alone may not compensate for these risks—or may not be permitted to rise high enough and over a long enough time period.

There is also the point of view that since the government is already so heavily involved in all phases of the energy industry, it is just not realistic to concentrate on price effects. The extent and direction of public policies are the crucial factors. The need is to ensure that the already considerable direct government involvement is made consistent with increased production.

Advocacy of direct public involvement leads to two more choices:

Support the private sector

*or*

Restrict or replace the private sector.

The first alternative is based on the view that the private sector is more efficient than the public sector and that its healthy development is crucial to the continuation of our free enterprise economy. Accordingly, the following policies would be recommended:

1. tax credits, subsidies and other special allowances to private energy companies, especially those in the high-risk areas of energy development
2. support for private R&D, through funding assistance and/or through the joint construction of pilot plants and demonstration projects; support might be especially directed to those R&D projects that promise payouts after 1985
3. import restraints (tariffs, quotas) in order to protect the large investments required from competition of lower cost foreign fuels
4. manpower training programs to help ensure that the nation has the engineers, miners, construction workers and other personnel needed to undertake the desired energy development program.

The alternative of restricting or replacing the private sector is based largely on the view that energy development is too large and important a matter to be left to private industry. The public interest is considered so great that it can only be met by further regulation of private companies or by direct public operations, jointly or alone, in exploration, production, refining, and importing. This viewpoint is fostered by the belief that the private oil companies benefited unduly at the public expense from the 1973-74 oil crisis and that, therefore, higher prices or more public support for their activities are not justified.

Those opposed to more restrictions on the private companies, including the establishment of public operating entities, disagree that the oil companies benefited excessively and stress that the private sector, with appropriate incentives is more likely to help the nation achieve its energy objectives than are governmental entities. They also point to the great costs of public bureaucracies and the inefficiencies that tend to surround governmental operations. The nationalized industries of other nations have not necessarily benefited the consumers, but often have blunted their ability to complain about prices and services.

## V. Strategies: Critical Conservation Choices

### *How Much Energy Can Be Conserved?*

There are two basic ways to conserve energy: (1) do with less and (2) use energy more efficiently. Examples of the first approach include lower thermostat settings in winter, less frequent airline service, and more car pools. There are costs involved, such as less comfort, less service, and less privacy. The more efficient uses of energy would include insulating attics and reducing the horsepower of automobiles. These, too, involve a financial cost.

There is general agreement that the largest energy savings can come from the industrial and transportation sectors. Potentially large savings can also be obtained by the use of more efficient heating and cooling equipment in residences.

Many observers believe that there is much energy waste that can be eliminated from the American way of life with little adverse effect. But there is a critical issue in who is to determine what is "waste." To many people, "waste" is what someone else is using. What one person may regard as waste, another may consider a necessity—an electric garage door opener, a second car, frost-free refrigerators.

When the price of oil was low, Americans bought a lot of energy-using goods and services. American businesses selected a host of energy-intensive industrial processes. They were not profligate to do so. This was a wise course of action under the circumstances—an optimal use of resources considering the low energy prices. It was also encouraged by the high costs of labor, which are continuing. Indeed, one of the rationales for steadily increasing wages has been the continuous increase in the "productivity" of American labor. But it is additional machines, energy, and technology which make greater labor productivity possible, not simply the individual worker's efforts.

Adjustment to a higher price means cutting back on lower priority uses of energy—or making "waste" more expensive. This is already happening in homes, businesses, and municipalities. People are turning to smaller and more energy-efficient automobiles. Companies are beginning to advertise the energy efficiencies of their consumer products—this is becoming as important a sales feature as style and convenience. Companies are developing "energy budgets" as a tool in keeping energy costs down. In these ways, the "marginal" demands for energy are being reduced voluntarily under the stimulus of higher prices.

In recommending programs to reduce energy use, it is important to remember that energy is just one element in our lives. We must be wary of proposals designed to maximize just its efficiency or minimize just its cost. Should we encourage eating out in restaurants because this would give a 25 percent energy savings compared to cooking at home? Should we encourage the use of microwave ovens because they are so energy efficient, though their price is double that of other ovens? Should we ban color TV sets or station wagons or auto airconditioners because of the extra energy they use? Should industry discard energy-intensive equipment and processes in favor of more costly, but less energy-intensive substitutes? Do we really want to go back to more reliance on direct human and animal labor—back to pushcarts and horse-drawn wagons? Clearly, the benefits to be obtained by conservation efforts must be related to all the costs involved, including the impact on our living standards.

We must also be aware of how the trade-off between prices and other means of restricting energy demand may especially affect the poor, the aged and the small businessman. Compensatory assistance may be required to achieve an efficient energy conservation program to assure popular support. Special programs may be required to minimize unemployment resulting from cutbacks in energy demand.

Over the 1950-70 period, energy demand has increased at an annual rate of 3.4 percent; if it were to continue at this rate, demand would rise from 75 quads (35.4 million barrels per day of oil equivalent) in 1973 to some 116 quads (54.7 million barrels per day) by 1985.[59] This figure is roughly comparable to that projected by studies made before the October 1973 oil embargo and subsequent price hike. For example, a U.S. Department of Interior study published in December 1972 on "U.S. Energy Through the Year 2000" projected U.S. energy consumption in 1985 at 116.6 quads.

The quadrupling of world oil prices by the OPEC countries has made such projections obsolete. Higher oil and other energy prices can be expected to curb the growth in U.S. energy demand, although the extent and timing of this impact cannot be determined with any certainty. The Department of Commerce Technical Advisory Board believes that the increased prices alone will reduce energy demand in 1985 by 12-16 percent below the 125 quads (59 MBPD) that it otherwise projects for 1985.[60] This would bring demand down to 105-110 quads (49.6-51.9 MBPD); using the base of 116 quads, demand would be reduced to 97-102 quads (45.8-48.1 MBPD). If public conservation measures were also implemented, domestic energy consumption could be reduced even further.

Tables I-7 and I-8 summarize the potential energy savings that various sources have calculated. "Potential energy savings" represents the amount of energy savings that is considered feasible by 1985, with heavy weight given to the technical and institutional factors and only marginal consideration to the economic and environmental factors. Because the data on savings have been derived from diverse sources, they do not always conform to this definition. Therefore, the figures should be regarded as approximations rather than "hard" numbers. The wide range of the estimates also indicates the use of divergent assumptions.

It is important to stress that the savings in Tables I-7 and I-8 represent reductions in energy use from what might have been had consumption continued its pre-1973 growth trend. Although the past growth is no longer relevant for projection purposes, it is useful as a benchmark against which we can judge other future alternatives, and especially the effect of the price increase and proposed policy measures.

Total potential savings (gross) of energy by 1985 are estimated at a range of 14.2-24.2 quads (6.7-11.4 million barrels per day of oil equivalent). A critical choice is how much of this potential savings we would actually want to realize. This, in turn, depends on which of the four types of self-reliance we seek to pursue. The more ambitious our objectives, the more we may have to depend upon ways to reduce energy demand. The more that domestic energy production can be increased, the less we need to rely on energy savings to meet our overall energy objectives (and vice-versa).

The following suggest, in somewhat more specific terms, the ways in which energy can be conserved.

**Residential Energy Use.** Residential use of energy totaled 16.3 quadrillion BTUs (7.7 MBPD) in 1973, accounting for some 22 percent of the nation's total energy consumption. Before the jump in world oil prices, it was estimated that

**Table I-7**
**Estimates of Total Potential Energy Savings by 1985**

| | (quads of BTUs) | MBPD |
|---|---|---|
| a. Federal Energy Administration–($11 oil) | 14.2 | 6.7 |
| ($ 7 oil) | 16.8 | 7.9 |
| b. Ford Foundation | 24.2 | 11.4 |
| c. Office of Emergency Preparedness | 24.0 | 11.3 |
| d. National Academy of Engineering | 17.0-19.0 | 8.0-9.0 |
| e. Energy and Environmental Analysis, Inc.[a] | 19.8 | 9.3 |

Note: Table I-8 presents the range of estimates for achievable savings, by major sectors of savings.

[a]Study commissioned by the Commission on Critical Choices for Americans.

**Table I-8**
**Estimates of Potential Energy Savings by Use Sector**
(units–quads of BTUs)

| Sector | Energy Consumption–'73[a] | Energy Consumption–'85 Historical Growth[a] | Range of Estimates/ Potential Savings–'85[b] | Energy Consumption–'85 Based on Maximum Potential Savings |
|---|---|---|---|---|
| Residential | 16.3 | 22.9 | 2.2- 5.2 | 17.7- 20.7 |
| Commercial | 10.4 | 15.1 | 0.6- 1.4 | 13.7- 14.5 |
| Industrial | 29.5 | 52.0 | 5.9-10.2 | 41.8- 46.1 |
| Transportation[c] | 18.8 | 26.0 | 3.1- 7.4 | 18.6- 22.9 |
| Electric Utilities | (19.2) | (37.5) | (0.9-21.5) | (34.0- 36.6) |
| Total: (quads) | 75.0 | 116.0 | 14.2-24.2[d] | 91.8-101.8 |
| Total: (MBPD) | 35.4 | 54.8 | 6.7-11.4 | 43.3- 48.0 |

[a]Ford Foundation, *A Time to Choose* (Cambridge, Mass.: Ballinger Publishing Company, 1974).
[b]FEA, Ford Foundation, Energy and Environmental Analysis, Inc.
[c]Data on consumption and savings included in above energy sectors.
[d]Range from table I-7.

the historical growth rate in residential energy demand would have produced an energy consumption level in 1985 of some 23 quads (10.8 MBPD).[61] This can be reduced in the following ways:

*Insulation.* Improved ceiling insulation in single family homes can reduce considerably the use of energy for space heating. Insulation of floors, walls, and attics, the use of storm windows and weather stripping, and the caulking of cracks help keep heat within the house during the winter and cooled air within the house during the summer. Better insulation of hot water heaters and pipes further conserves energy. Mobile homes, in particular, could benefit from more insulation. All in all, insulation could account for up to one-third of total residential energy savings.

*Heating/Cooling Equipment.* Some types of heating equipment are more energy efficient than others. Gas heaters and heat pumps, for instance, use less energy than electric resistance heaters. Heat pumps are reverse airconditioners; by cooling the outdoors, they provide heat for the indoors. They alone could account for nearly one-half of total residential energy savings. Room airconditioners also show widely varying energy efficiencies. Substitution of the more energy-efficient heating and cooling equipment and a reduction in the installation of oversize heating and cooling systems would lead to a net energy saving. Proper operation and maintenance, including regular tune-ups, would also help.

*Housing Design.* Some types of housing design are more energy-efficient than others. Orientation toward the sun can cut down on space heating requirements during winter months for houses in the northern regions. Rooms with cathedral ceilings, large window areas, and excess ventilation tend to require more heating than others. Area thermostats provide more control over both heating use and use of central airconditioners than does one thermostat for the entire house. The installation of individual meters in multifamily dwellings would provide more incentives for individual households to curb energy demand.

*Appliances.* There is wide variation in energy efficiency of household appliances. Use and development of more efficient models could cut total energy use without affecting service. The replacement of gas pilot lights by electric igniters would reduce the energy needed for stoves and clothes dryers, which are used only briefly each day or week. Improved oven and refrigeration insulation would also help, as would "power-saving" switches on refrigerators, dishwashers and airconditioners.

*Conservation Ethic.* Additional savings can accrue if people observe a conservation ethic in the home: turn off unnecessary lights, shut outside doors, unplug "instant" TV sets, turn down the thermostat during the winter days and especially at night, close fireplace flues when not in use, use the lowest watt bulbs that are necessary or fluorescent lights, set hot water heaters at the lowest acceptable temperatures, fix hot water leaks, use only full loads in dishwashers, clothes washers, and dryers, use pressure cookers, use regular–not frost-free–refrigerators and freezers. Much can be accomplished by teaching the conservation ethic in schools.

**Commercial Energy Use.** The commercial consumption of energy came to 10.4 quads (4.9 MBPD) in 1973, some 14 percent of the nation's total energy consumption. If it were to continue at its past rate, it would reach some 15 quads (7.1 MBPD) in 1985. The increased price of energy and the use of public measures can reduce this somewhat.

*Space Heating.* Most of the measures suggested for residences also apply to commercial buildings, especially the use of heat pumps, adequate insulation and caulking, lower thermostat settings in the winter and higher ones in the summer, and the proper maintenance of heating/cooling systems. In the long run, heat pumps are expected to account for most of the commercial sector's savings.

*Lighting Levels.* Many buildings use illumination more for "show" than for function. Bulbs can be removed or wattage lowered without affecting visibility. Conversion from incandescent to fluorescent lighting would also save energy. The decentralization of switch controls would enable workers to illuminate only that section of a high-rise office building they are using at night, and not the entire floor–or floors.

*More Selective Building Materials.* Up to now, the selection of building materials by architects and engineers has generally ignored energy considerations. Some materials, such as aluminum, require much more energy to produce than others. Some materials, such as glass, are poor insulators. More consideration of these properties in selecting construction materials could help reduce energy consumption.

**Industrial Energy Use.** Industry uses more energy than any other sector. Industrial energy consumption of 29.5 quads (13.9 MBPD) in 1973 accounted for nearly 40 percent of the nation's total usage. Before the price rise, industrial energy demand in 1985 was projected at 52 quads (24.5 MBPD). This can be reduced significantly, as the following measures indicate, although at the cost of some capital investment and possibly some unemployment.

*Industrial Processes.* Some processes are more energy-efficient than others. For example, Alcoa has reportedly developed a process that reduces the energy requirements in production of aluminum by 30 percent. Technological development in other industries can also be expected to lower the energy-intensiveness of output, especially where energy costs represent a large share of total product costs. Improved processes could account for nearly half of total industrial savings.

*Heat Recuperators.* Much of the process heat is dissipated in exhaust gases and in materials in process. The use of recuperators could recover part of this wasted energy, lowering overall fuel consumption some 20-25 percent.

*Recycled Material.* Use by industry of recycled materials, especially such metals as aluminum and copper, requires less energy per unit of output than does the extraction and refining of virgin materials. Energy would be saved if products were designed to encourage resource recovery and, particularly, were made more durable. The reclaiming of waste oil would be a direct help.

*Process Steam.* Almost half of the energy used by industry goes to generate "process steam"–hot steam applied in a variety of processes. This steam is generated in a wasteful way. The major part of the energy is used to evaporate water for which cheap energy sources could be utilized–solar energy or waste heat. Furthermore, the "spent" process steam may be utilized in the local generation of electricity and space heating. These efforts may cut in half current fuel requirements.

**Energy Use in Transportation.** Transportation is the second largest user of energy, consuming 18.8 (8.9 MBPD) in 1973–some 25 percent of the national total. With eight out of ten American households owning at least one car and three out of ten, at least two cars,[62] this sector absorbed some 60 percent of all the petroleum consumed in the United States. If energy prices had not increased, energy use in transportation might have increased to 26 quads (12.3 MBPD) by 1985. However, the higher prices and public policies may slow down or even halt this growth.

*Shift in Modes.* Trains, buses, and mass transit facilities are much more energy efficient modes of transport than automobiles and airplanes. Mini-buses and jitneys are also energy efficient. A shift of people and freight to these more efficient modes would lead to a net savings of energy. So, too, would more walking and more use of bicycles.

*Load Factors.* Many automobiles transport only the driver, no passengers. Airplanes, buses, and trains also contain many unoccupied seats. A fuller utilization of these transport facilities–an increase in their load factors–would bring a net energy savings.

*More Efficient Transport Facilities.* Substantial energy savings can be achieved through the design, construction, and use of more energy efficient transport facilities. Key measures in reversing the trend of declining fuel economy of automobiles would include increased use of smaller—and hence lighter—cars, more efficient transmissions and accessories, and use of radial tires. The automobile can become a more efficient converter of gasoline into vehicle miles by reduced speeds, proper vehicle maintenance (tune-ups, tire pressure), a shift away from automatic transmissions, and less power-consuming accessories, especially reduced provision and use of airconditioners. The use of efficient transport facilities could account for most of the total transportation savings of energy. A national transportation policy that used each mode in its appropriate application and related modes to each other in a balanced manner, that eliminated duplication and unnecessary service could produce great savings and better transport.

**Conversion to Electricity.** The electric utility industry consumed some 19.2 quads (9.1 MBPD) of primary fuels in 1973 (this figure is included in the totals of the sections on residential, commercial, industrial, and transportation energy use), which was reduced to below 18 quads (8.5 MBPD) in 1974. (This may reflect the impact of higher prices.) If prices had not increased and past demand trends had been maintained, the 1985 consumption of primary fuels by the electricity-generating industry would have nearly doubled to 37.5 quads (17.7 MBPD). However, there is potential for savings. Of the 19.2 quads (9.1 MBPD) of primary fuels consumed in 1973, only 6.4 quads (3.0 MBPD) were actually converted to electricity—an efficiency rate of 33 percent. The rest were lost as heat during the generation, transmission, and distribution stages.

Measures which could raise this efficiency rate would conserve on the use of primary fuels. Potentially useful would be the smoothing out of the daily demand cycle, which would reduce the need to use inefficient generating equipment during peak periods. Higher charges on the use of electricity during peak periods might help, as would the more effective utilization of exhaust heat.

### *How to Set Conservation Priorities*

The most critical issue in determining where to conserve energy is deciding if conservation is crucial to our overall energy program. To the extent that the price mechanism is used to curb demand, it may not be necessary, outside of equity considerations, to be concerned with where the cuts will be made. Private individuals and companies, as well as municipalities, will make their own adjustments to price signals—and in ways each determines is best for it. Only if the price mechanism is regarded as inadequate, does the question of where to conserve energy become a policy issue. Even then, the real issue is how much and where to conserve *beyond* what the already increased price of energy will achieve.

If we decide to supplement (or supplant) the price mechanism with public policies to promote energy conservation, we confront a number of important strategic choices in setting priorities.

1. *Should we concentrate on those sources that have the largest potential for saving energy, or should we be concerned with all sources?*

Three areas of energy savings would provide one-half of the nation's achievable savings:

a. More efficient industrial processes
b. More efficient transport facilities
c. Use of heat recuperators.

Should public policy be concentrated here, or is it more desirable from an equity and public participation point-of-view to spread the burden to all areas of potential energy savings?

2. *Should we concentrate on those conservation measures that have the smallest negative impacts on the economy?*

To what extent should we let economics–costs–help determine the most desirable combination of conservation measures? Estimates of capital costs are very rough and are subject to wide variation based on differing assumptions. There are few benchmark studies to give us reasonable confidence in the capital requirements of the various conservation measures. The ratio of potential savings to capital costs is itself not very meaningful, since some investments–such as insulation–should produce energy savings for decades to come. Moreover, as already indicated, social costs need to be added to economic costs in order to get a mere relevant cost calculation.

Nevertheless, we do know that some sources of energy savings involve no capital costs at all. This could be an important consideration if other aspects of an energy self-reliance program involve heavy capital costs. Examples of these sources are:

a. Conservation ethic
b. Reduce decorative lighting
c. Increase transport load factors.

In addition, it is possible to determine those conservation activities that will involve large capital expenditures. These include:

a. More efficient transport facilities
b. More efficient conversions to electricity
c. Use of heat recuperators
d. More efficient generation of process steam.

Another important consideration is the maintenance or operating costs associated with specific conservation measures. These could play a significant role in determining the economic feasibility of energy-efficient industrial and transportation processes.

A reduction in the growth of energy consumption, due either to prices or public policies, may have a negative impact on overall economic growth and employment. At least over the next several years, specific sectors of the economy will be affected, either positively or negatively, by various conservation measures. For example:

*Increased Sales and Employment*
a. Manufacturers of small cars
b. Servicemen who tune-up home heating/cooling systems
c. Manufacturers and installers of insulation material, storm windows/doors
d. Heavy construction and building trades for retrofitting power plants, boilers, pumps
e. Manufacturers of electric igniters for gas stoves
f. Civil servants who evaluate and set standards and who check on compliance.

*Lower Sales and Employment*
a. Producers of large automobiles
b. Producers of incandescent light bulbs
c. Producers of nonthermopane glass.

This raises a key question: how to persuade those people who benefit to compensate those adversely affected by policies that are in the national interest. The fiscal system is, in some ways, designed to effect such transfers, with those people and businesses experiencing higher incomes being subject to higher taxes. The market place also encourages a transfer of resources from less profitable to more profitable activities. A critical choice is whether the market place and our current fiscal system perform this function effectively or whether—and what—public interventions may be desirable.

3. *Should we concentrate on conservation measures which have the largest positive impact (or smallest negative impact) on the environment?*

The more energy that can be saved, the less the need to produce energy from domestic sources, which can relieve some of the environmental problems associated with energy production. At the same time, we must ensure that the reverse does not happen: efforts to improve the environment may require increased energy usage. Thus far, this has tended to be the rule.

Considered especially desirable are such measures as:

a. Adopting a conservation ethic
b. Using recycled materials
c. Reducing the use of the automobile
d. Encouraging more efficient conversions to electricity
e. Using heat recuperators
f. Stimulating better generation of process steam.

4. *Should we concentrate on conservation measures which have the least negative impact on the quality of life?*

Some conservation measures would impair some people's quality of life, directly or indirectly, by cutting back on demand or by raising prices. Those affected, therefore, can be expected to oppose mandatory regulations promoting such measures as a shift in transport modes, attempts to increase transport load factors, and adoption of a conservation ethic.

5. *Should we concentrate on conservation measures which are more workable and, hence, promise to bring the quickest results?*

If conservation is regarded as essential until domestic energy production can be expanded sufficiently, we might want to favor those measures which, from a practical point of view, promise the largest, near-term results. This is a time when the country remains especially vulnerable to another oil embargo. Among the quick measures are the following:

a. Conservation ethic
b. Reduction in decorative lighting
c. Improved transport load factors
d. Selective insulation.

6. *Should we concentrate on measures that conserve particular fuels?*

Oil and natural gas are the two fuels that are in particularly short supply. Should we focus a conservation program on those activities that use these fuels? Oil would be most affected by another embargo. To preserve our supplies, should we give high priority to energy conservation measures in the transportation sector, where the possibilities of substituting for petroleum are the most limited?

With respect to natural gas, which is already in short supply, should we eliminate present price controls and regulations to seek reduced use through price? Should we begin to reserve natural gas for industrial and petrochemical use and discourage its use for domestic heating and electricity generation?

7. *Should we concentrate on conservation measures that interfere least with the private sector?*

Some measures, such as fuel standards on automobiles and insulation standards on new homes, may have a considerable impact on private business decisions. Other measures will have a less significant influence on the public-private sector relationship. How much relevance should be given to this aspect in evaluating specific conservation measures?

*How to Conserve Energy*

As the previous section indicates, the critical choice in determining how to conserve energy is:

Depend on Prices

*or*

Depend on Nonprice Programs.

Only if the price mechanism is rejected as inadequate or otherwise unacceptable do nonprice measures become relevant. There are a number of different policy measures, involving regulations and incentives, for reaching whatever level of potential savings is considered desirable. These enhance the effect of past price increases in reducing energy demand. The following are some of these major policies. They are organized in categories, which may be helpful in assessing their relative desirability.

*Support Private Sector*

1. Sponsor R&D efforts in:
   a. Industrial processes
   b. Conversion to nonfossil fuels
   c. Heat recuperators.

The government could accelerate R&D in conservation technology through financial support of private R&D and the joint undertaking of demonstration projects.

2. Tax credits or subsidies for:
   a. Manufacture and use of insulation material

b. Better housing design
c. More efficient transport facilities
d. Conversion to nonfossil energy sources.

To stimulate the effect of the price mechanism in encouraging conservation, the government might institute a series of special tax credits and subsidies.

*Intervene in Private Sector Decisions*

3. Ban certain usage, for example:
    a. Use of autos in express bus lanes and in specified downtown areas
    b. Use of outdoor lights, including advertising signs.
4. Rationing.

Such steps should save energy, but they may adversely affect the quality of life. Ways will be found to get around the bans, necessitating adequate policing. Gray and black markets inevitably develop.

5. Encourage energy-efficiency standards for:
    a. Insulation levels
    b. Heating/cooling equipment
    c. Appliances
    d. Lighting
    e. Housing design
    f. Industrial processes
    g. Automobile fuel economy.

Before mandatory standards can be set, we need a strong factual basis for determining energy-efficiency levels. Proposed mandatory levels must themselves be subject to a cost-benefit analysis to ensure that the energy saving is worth the increased financial outlays and other costs.

6. Tax on usage:
    a. Of autos, tax based on weight or fuel economy
    b. Of autos, tolls based on number of passengers
    c. A BTU tax on energy-intensive products.

Rather than prevent the purchase of a gas-guzzling automobile, this policy would make it more expensive to do so. Additionally, taxes can be used to internalize social and environmental costs; this has long been advocated by environmentalists, who hold that polluters and ultimately the consumers should bear the cost of the pollution that is generated. Such action may help promote the efficient use of energy.

*Support Consumers*

7. Require labeling of the energy efficiencies of:
   a. Heating/cooling equipment
   b. Appliances
   c. Automobiles.

Through such labeling, the consumer would be able to compare the relative energy efficiencies of different products, and thus have a better basis than at present for making a selection.

8. Public education:
   a. Conservation ethic
   b. All residential uses of energy.

More public knowledge about how to save energy and the use of life-cycle costing in assessing such measures as insulation would encourage the savings of energy.

## VI. Strategies: Critical Standby Choices

The third type of general strategy for meeting our energy self-reliance objective is the creation of standby facilities and arrangements that will enable this country to withstand the effects of temporary supply disruptions. The more oil that we can store domestically, the more shut-in production capacities we can call upon. The more emergency regulations that are on the books, such as rationing and other ways of enforcing energy conservation, the less vulnerable will our economy be to another oil embargo. The storage option can be used by itself or as a supplement to those other types of self-reliance that involve a certain level of imports. Indeed, the very existence of a stockpile might deter producing countries from withholding supplies from the United States.

From a timing point of view, storage could help supplement the short-run effect of an energy conservation program, until we are able to expand significantly domestic energy production. However, stockpile programs would do little to deal with the other and more long-run possible energy objectives, the replacement of our depleting petroleum resources.

If we decide to utilize the storage option, we still must wend our way through a number of critical choices. The first concerns how much stored oil is adequate. A stockpile equivalent to 90 days of imports? 180 days? A full year? Do we want to cover ourselves against imports from all foreign suppliers, or only from "unstable" sources? The problem is that sources which appear stable today, may be unstable later. Moreover, loss of freedom of the seas may have quite dramatic consequences.

There is no one answer as to an adequate level of stockpile protection. The National Petroleum Council believes that it is sufficient to have a national security storage program of 500 million barrels of produced crude oil, of which at least one-third is low in sulfur content.[63] The Council believes that only 3 million BPD are likely to be embargoed out of imports estimated at approximately 8 MBPD annually during the 1980s. Considering the fact that U.S. companies maintain working inventories and that crude oil and products would be in transit to the United States at the time of supply interruption, the Council estimates the supply coverage of the 500 million barrels to be more than six months.

The size of an oil storage program would depend largely on the costs involved, the use of other insurance policies, and the time frame for reaching the target level. Bohi and Russell have estimated that the annual storage cost of a six-month supply of projected insecure (Arab) imports in 1985 (2-8 million barrels per day) would range from \$0.7-\$3.8 billion, based on \$10 per barrel oil.[64] They also estimate that the annual cost of standby capacity to cover such insecure imports at between \$3.0-\$13.1 billion. A combination policy of ninety-days storage plus standby capacity could cost from \$1.2-\$5.8 billion a year, or some \$12-\$58 billion over the 1975-85 period, according to varying assumptions on oil import levels.

The National Petroleum Council estimates that the cost of storage in salt domes could approximate \$0.60-\$0.85 per barrel in caverns that can hold more than 100 million barrels each. Thus, the storage cost for a stockpile of 730 million barrels (2 million barrels per day for one year) would come to \$0.4-\$0.6 billion. Cost of storage in steel tanks above the ground ranges from \$3.80-\$7.00 a barrel, depending on location and other factors.[65] The storage cost for a 730 million barrel stockpile would come to \$2.8-\$5.1 billion. At a price of \$10 a barrel, the purchase price of 730 million barrels would come to \$7.3 billion, bringing the total capital cost to \$7.7-\$7.9 billion (in salt domes) or \$10.1-\$12.4 billion (in steel tanks).

For a ten-year period, the FEA has estimated that the cost of a 1.5 billion barrel stockpile level could come to \$26 billion. The cost of the 1.0 billion barrel stockpile level called for in the proposed Energy Independence Act of 1975 (Title I) is estimated at \$17 billion.[66]

The NPC recommends the development of the Naval Petroleum Reserve at Elk Hills as the basis for an oil storage program. Production costs are relatively low, estimated at \$1.50-\$2.00 per barrel. Total storage costs for facilities and fill are estimated at \$3.50-\$4.85 per barrel, or \$1,750-\$2,425 million for a 500 million barrel stockpile.[67]

All these cost estimates—from Bohi and Russell, the FEA, and the NPC—indicate that storage of 500 million-1 billion barrels of oil would be a much less expensive strategy than programs to expand domestic energy output or to conserve energy.

The issue is not only how adequate is such a level of stockpiling and for how long, but how can we most effectively obtain the oil that is to be stockpiled. We face another critical choice. Either we accelerate our purchases of foreign oil and thereby put upward pressure on world oil prices and strengthen the financial power and influence of the OPEC countries, or we gradually build up stocks from our own sources over a period of years in order to minimize the chances of these developments—but at the cost of less energy security in the intervening years until the stockpile can be completed. Even the development of Elk Hills, recommended by the NPC, would involve six to seven years of production at the maximum efficient rate before a 500 million barrel storage system could be completed.[68] This includes some three years for environmental studies and engineering evaluations before the storage fill can begin.

The international financial considerations would argue for a gradual increase in oil stocks, especially if imports serve as fill, directly or indirectly. More direct national security considerations would argue for immediate action. The latter position is also shared by those who view the stockpile as a means for protecting the nation in the short run, together with conservation measures, until our effort to expand domestic production can show results.

Stockpiling is not the only form of an economic insurance policy we can take out. The use of "shut-in" capacity is, in effect, a means of conserving domestic oil output for (possible) future use. It would require the development and maintenance of appropriate infrastructure, particularly pipelines, so that we are effectively prepared for an emergency. Since production could not start up immediately—it might take up to six months in certain cases—a policy of "shut-in" capacity might be most effective when combined with storage capabilities.

Because most locations for developing a shut-in capacity are far from consuming areas, an emergency situation could bring serious regional shortages if we depend only on shut-in facilities. However, the main drawback is that the more we shut-in production capacity to meet future emergencies, the less oil is available to meet current consumption levels—hence, the greater would be our current reliance on imports. Additionally, the development of significant shut-in capacity could prove to be very costly.

Another similar measure would be the formulation, in advance, of legislation that would be activated at any time when energy shortages, for whatever reason, were threatening our national interest. Such legislation might include mandatory conservation measures, such as gasoline rationing, lowered speed limits, and office lighting restrictions. The Energy Supply and Environmental Coordination Act of 1974 does authorize the government to direct those power plants that burn oil and gas to convert to coal and to require new power plants to utilize coal as their primary fuel source.

Where oil is stored will be determined mainly by cost and locational considerations. Oil can be stored in salt domes, large numbers of which are situated on the Gulf Coast in Texas and Louisiana. Many are close to existing pipelines and, as we have seen, costs are relatively low. Alternatively, crude and refined oil could be stored above ground at some cost in steel tanks, closer to places of use. Other possibilities include surplus oil tankers and abandoned mines.

To implement a storage program, the government would have to finance, or underwrite the financing of, appropriate storage facilities and establish policies on the acquisition and disposal of the stored oil. Government financial support could be needed in the construction of loading facilities and pipelines and in the maintenance of shut-in capacities. Contingency regulations might have to be prepared on how to cope with another supply shortage, including mandatory allocation arrangements.

To encourage storage by private producers—enlarged inventory accumulations—federal price ceilings on oil and natural gas may have to be revised. Some assurance against price freezes during any future supply disruptions may also be required. State controls on maximum production levels may have to be modified.

## VII. Conclusions

Americans are still seeking a long-range energy policy. Considerable uncertainties about the basic issues involved and the directions in which to proceed have so far prevented effective action. As a result, we are more vulnerable today to Arab oil pressures than at the time of the oil embargo.

Much of the uncertainty stems from the fact that this nation is caught in a series of interrelated dilemmas, each requiring us, either consciously or otherwise, to make a critical choice. The following are some of these critical choices. It should be noted at the outset that for most choices there are compromise positions between the extremes presented. Even so, where the line is drawn can make a crucial difference, and looking at choices from the viewpoint of extreme positions may help us better understand this difference.

### *Energy Program or No Energy Program*

Those advocating a major domestic energy program are vitally concerned that our increasing dependence on foreign oil will jeopardize the national security interests of this country by exposing us to continuing political pressures from the oil exporting countries. They are also concerned about the economic and political implications, at home and abroad, or large payments for foreign oil.

Those wary of a major energy program believe that market forces will work to curb the monopoly power of OPEC. Higher oil prices are already encouraging enlarged worldwide activity in oil exploration and development, which will lead to a growing world surplus of energy. High prices are encouraging people and businesses to find ways to use less energy. Thus, no major new policies are needed.

### *Complete or Limited Self-Reliance*

Among those who believe that a domestic energy program is needed are some who advocate that the objective of such a program should be to reduce our net energy imports to zero and even achieve net energy exports. Only in these ways would we be sure to protect the United States against excessive foreign influence.

Those in favor of more limited types of self-reliance believe that we can develop an energy program that will adequately protect ourselves against imports. Moreover, they are concerned about the economic and environmental costs implied by the size of an energy program to achieve complete self-reliance.

### *Production, Conservation, or Storage*

Those advocates of energy programs geared to expanding the domestic production of energy regard this as the fundamental means for us to meet our long-range energy requirements. Using existing technologies, we can probably develop sufficient energy measures to carry us through the year 2000; for the period thereafter, new technological breakthroughs will be required. On the other hand, energy conservation and storage offer only short-run benefits.

Those supporting conservation argue that much energy is wasted in our society. Over time and with appropriate programs, this waste can be reduced without significantly affecting economic growth or the quality of life. Moreover, many conservation measures can bring results relatively soon, while the expansion of energy production generally involves long lead times.

Advocates for enlarged storage facilities believe that this could give us adequate protection against any foreseeable oil embargo in the future. It could involve much less cost than energy production or conservation programs.

### *Private or Public Efforts*

Those who believe that the private sector can efficiently bring about the expansion of energy output argue that we should relax those public policies and regulations that threaten to curb private energy investment. Moreover, new public initiatives should be limited to ways that support private energy activity.

Advocates of more public involvement believe that the energy sector is too important for the country to be left to private decision-making. Because of the concentrated structure of the industry and the inability of the individual oil companies to bargain effectively with OPEC, the national interest requires that the government get further involved. Some also believe that the private companies benefited unduly from the oil embargo.

*Prices or Nonprice Measures*

There are those who argue that prices should form the cornerstone of our energy policy, just as they have a central position in our market economy. Although price elasticities may be limited in the short run, they could prove significant in long-run efforts to increase supply and reduce demand.

Advocates of nonprice measures, such as setting energy efficiency standards on automobiles and appliances and rationing scarce energy supplies, argue that these can have a more immediate and more direct impact than price-related measures. Also, they are less obviously inflationary.

*High Price or Low Price Objectives*

Those supporting high energy prices believe they are needed to encouarge the exploration and drilling for domestic oil and gas, as well as for investment in alternative energy sources. Unless businessmen can expect to make a profit over and above their costs, they will get out of the energy business. High prices help encourage the expectation of an adequate rate of return. Low prices in the future could jeopardize new energy investment.

Advocates of low energy prices believe that the world will face an increasing energy glut over the next several years which will force world prices down. The United States should encourage and prepare for this development since it will enable our economy and society to benefit once again from low cost energy and it will reduce our payments for foreign oil–provided the volume of oil imports can be held in check.

*Break OPEC or Live with OPEC*

Many of our domestic and international economic problems stem from the actions of OPEC. Therefore, some advocate that we should devote considerable effort to making OPEC less effective, now and in the future. Possible courses of action include the development of a domestic alternative to foreign oil, encouraging the development abroad of non-OPEC sources of oil, and making special bilateral arrangements with individual OPEC members guaranteeing access to our market. A system of bidding for the right to export oil to the United States might also help.

Others, however, are skeptical that OPEC will break up. They believe that new oil exporters, like Britain, may well join OPEC and that it is in the self-interest of each OPEC member not to make special arrangements on price in exchange for access. Accordingly, the United States should concentrate on ways to live with OPEC and, hopefully, through the establishment of mutual interests, encourage responsible action in the future by the oil cartel.

### *National or International Approach*

There are those who believe that the United States must first get its own energy house in order before undertaking international arrangements. This will strengthen the U.S. bargaining position in international energy negotiations and will not divert us from the task of becoming self-reliant in energy. Only after we provide for ourselves, can we begin to help others.

Advocates of a more immediate international approach cite the fact that energy is a worldwide problem, affecting most of our allies much more severely than our own country. Its solution, therefore, requires a multinational effort. Indeed, the national interest could be more affected by what happens to our allies than by what happens just to us.

### *Energy Objectives and Other National Objectives*

Our efforts to achieve energy objectives may at times conflict with our economic, environmental and social objectives. Trade-offs are required, which could cause us to reduce some of our energy objectives.

Each choice will, of course, have its own consequences, which must be taken into account in evaluating the relative desirability of the various alternatives. Among the major consequences are the following:

1. A program to expand domestic energy production could lead to inflation and other distortions of economic resources, to environmental problems and to an expanded influence of the public sector over our lives.
2. An energy conservation program could reduce the quality of life of many people.
3. The lack of programs to develop and conserve our energy supplies could threaten the national security and the leadership role of the United States.

In examining the specific issues regarding which domestic sources of energy should be expanded and which areas of energy conservation should be encouraged, it is helpful to utilize cost-benefit approaches. To do so adequately, however, requires a much better quantitative knowledge of both costs and benefits than we now have. Major gaps in our knowledge, especially about capital costs, need to be closed.

Moreover, specific measures cannot be evaluated in isolation from an overall energy program. Some measures may be useful because they can have an immediate impact, others because of their medium-range impact through 1985, and a few for their potential contribution beyond the year 2000. This time dimension is important when we consider such crucial issues as whether to slow down or accelerate the exploitation of our depleting oil and gas reserves.

Numerous choices have been set out in this report. They affect the shape and direction of a national energy program. On one issue, however, we have no choice—the *need to choose now* what kind of energy program we want. We will make this choice either consciously or unconsciously. Up to now, the latter method has tended to predominate, with the result that we are more dependent than ever on foreign oil. It would be far better to choose with an understanding of the implications of our choices and an appreciation of the trade-offs involved. Only then is there hope that specific energy measures will be consistent with one another and supportive of our national energy objectives.

## Notes

1. Federal Energy Administration, *Project Independence Report* (Washington, D.C.: Government Printing Office, November 1974), p. 39.

2. National Petroleum Council, *Energy Preparedness for Interruption of Petroleum Imports into the United States* (September 1974), p. 59.

3. Federal Energy Administration, *Monthly Energy Review* (Washington, D.C.: Government Printing Office, September 1975), p. 18.

4. Ibid.

5. Federal Energy Administration, Office of Economic Impact, *The Economic Impact of the Oil Embargo on the American Economy* (Washington, D.C.: Government Printing Office, August 8, 1974), pp. 5-6.

6. Paul MacAvoy, "The Separate Control of Quantity and Price—State and Federal Regulations in the Energy Industries," in Volume III of Carnegie-Rochester Conference Series, to be published by North Holland (Rotterdam), as a supplement to the *Journal of Monetary Economics*, July 1976.

7. Ibid.

8. National Academy of Sciences, *Mineral Resources and the Environment* (Washington, D.C., February 1975), p. 81.

9. John D. Moody and Robert E. Geiger, "Petroleum Resources: How Much Oil and Where," *Technology Review* 77, 5 (March-April 1975): 5. © Alumni Association of MIT.

10. Ibid., p. 4.

11. *Mineral Resources and the Environment*, p. 98.

12. Ibid., p. 112.

13. Ibid., p. 98.

14. Percentage based on figures in *Mineral Resources and the Environment*, p. 98.

15. U.S. Department of the Interior, *Geological Estimates of Undiscovered Recoverable Oil and Gas Resources in the United States*, Geological Survey Circular 725 (Washington, D.C., 1975), p. 34. Identified reserves are that part of economically recoverable resources that has been discovered.

16. John W. Duane and Michael A. Karnitz, "Domestic Gas Resources and Future Production Rates," *Power Engineering* (January 1975).

17. USGS Circular 725, p. 46.

18. Ford Foundation, *A Time to Choose* (Cambridge, Mass.: Ballinger Publishing Company, 1974), p. 136.

19. *U.S. Energy Prospects: An Engineering Viewpoint* (Washington, D.C., 1974), p. 98.

20. Edward Teller, "Energy–A Plan for Action," in *Power & Security*, Edward Teller, Hans Mark, and John S. Foster, Jr., Critical Choices for Americans, Vol. IV (Lexington, Mass.: Lexington Books, D.C. Heath and Company, 1976), p. 9.

21. Hans H. Landsberg, "Low-Cost, Abundant Energy: Paradise Lost?" *Science* (April 19, 1975): 250.

22. Ibid., pp. 11-25.

23. *Project Independence Report*, p. 83.

24. *Mineral Resources and the Environment*, p. 91.

25. Ibid.

26. *Project Independence Report*, p. 81.

27. Computed from *Project Independence Report*, Appendix AI.

28. Federal Energy Administration, *Project Independence Blueprint*, Final Task Force Report on Natural Gas (November 1974), p. I-10.

29. *Circular 725,* p. 34. Measured reserves contribute that part of the identified resources that can be economically extracted using known technology and whose amount can be substantiated by geological evidence and engineering measurements. Inferred reserves are those eventually to be added to known fields through extensions and revisions.

30. Ibid., p. 4.

31. *Project Independence Blueprint*, p. IV-19.

32. Reported by Dr. Thomas Stauffer, "Natural Gas Supply," *Energy Self-Sufficiency: How Much and How Soon?* (McLean, Virginia: The Mitre Corporation, March 1975), p. 173.

33. Federal Energy Administration, *Project Independence Summary*, p. 48.

34. Stauffer, "Natural Gas Supply," p. 174.

35. Federal Energy Administration, *Project Independence Blueprint*, Final Task Force Report on Coal (November 1974), p. 4.

36. Landsberg, "Low-Cost, Abundant Energy," p. 248.

37. *Project Independence Report*, p. 185.

38. FEA, *Monthly Energy Review*, pp. 43-44.

39. S. William Gouse, "Research on Coal and Synthetic Fuels," *Energy Self-Sufficiency: How Much and How Soon?* (McLean, Virginia: The Mitre Corporation, 1975), pp. 39-47.

40. *U.S. Energy Prospects: An Engineering Viewpoint*, p. 71.

41. *Project Independence Report*, p. 129.

42. Ibid., p. 72.

43. *U.S. Energy Prospects: An Engineering Viewpoint*, p. 73.

44. Energy Research and Development Administration, *A National Plan for Energy Research, Development and Demonstration: Creating Energy Choices for the Future* (1975), Vol. I, p. VIII-2.

45. Edward Teller, "Energy–A Plan for Action," *Power & Security*, p. 69.

46. Federal Energy Administration, *Project Independence Blueprint*, Final Task Force Report on Solar Energy, p. I-7.

47. Ibid.

48. ERDA, *A National Plan for Energy Research*, p. II-3. There are four kinds of geothermal resources: dry steam, hot water (wet steam and brine fields), geopressured zones, and hot, dry rock formations.

49. Federal Energy Administration, *Project Independence Blueprint*, Final Task Force Report on Geothermal Energy (November 1974), p. I-4.

50. "ERDA Sees Bright Future: Solar Energy Reconsidered," *Science* 189 (August 15, 1975): 539.

51. ERDA, *A National Plan for Energy Research*, p. VIII-5-6.

52. Ibid., pp. V-17, 20, 25.

53. *Science* (April 19, 1974), p. 382.

54. Louis H. Roddis, Jr., "Electric Power Generation and Distribution," *Energy Self-Sufficiency: How Much and How Soon?* (McLean, Virginia: The Mitre Corporation, 1975), p. 187.

55. *U.S. Energy Prospects: An Engineering Viewpoint*, p. 54.

56. *Project Independence Report*, p. 282.

57. *U.S. Energy Prospects: An Engineering Viewpoint*, pp. 98, 99, 130.

58. Ibid., p. 92.

59. *A Time to Choose*, pp. 20-21.

60. Ibid., pp. 51-53.

61. Data on energy consumption in this and other chapters are based on the Ford Foundation's *A Time to Choose*.

62. *Automotive Facts and Figures*, Annual Yearbook of the American Automobile Association (1974).

63. National Petroleum Council, *Petroleum Storage for National Security* (NPC, 1975), pp. 8-10.

64. Douglas Bohi and Milton Russell, *U.S. Energy Policy: Alternatives for Security* (Johns Hopkins University Press for Resources for the Future, Inc., 1975), p. 98.

65. National Petroleum Council, "Emergency Preparedness for Interruption of Petroleum Imports Into the United States" (NPC, September 1974), p. 14.

66. *Project Independence Report*, p. 384.

67. *Petroleum Storage for National Security*, pp. 14-15.

68. Ibid., p. 12.

# II Report of Panel II: Food, Health, World Population, and Quality of Life

## Introduction

In the darker past of human experience, the Horsemen of the Apocalypse—famine, war, pestilence, and plague—may have been the inevitable means of balancing food and population. In our age, the challenge is to conquer hunger through human compassion and intelligence.

At present, the world, and especially the developing world, exists on a very thin margin. The resources and the knowledge exist to increase world food production many times above present levels. However, a sustained, long-term effort will be required to achieve this increase, especially in view of still high rates of population growth.

*Now* is the propitious time to act decisively to improve the world food situation, not only because we *can* do something, but, more importantly, because we *must* do something. One might even go so far as to say that probably the existence of our civilization and certainly the nature of it is at stake. The world food outlook is in the hands of those who will live to enjoy the benefits or suffer the consequences of the response which they, themselves, mount.

Over the past few years, many conferences were held and various reports were written on world agriculture and on its interrelations with population growth and world health levels. These evaluations were occasioned in part by the poor crops of 1972 and 1974, which reduced world food stocks to dangerously low levels and caused world food prices to rise beyond the reach of millions of already undernourished people. Even the United States, traditionally a leader in crop yields and food output, could not escape the effects of production shortfalls in other countries. Moreover, the United States suffered a severe shortfall in its own production levels in 1974, with grain output down 38 million tons (almost 6 percent lower than the previous year) and soybean output down over 300 million bushels (over 20 percent lower than 1973).

There is little doubt that the experience of the past few years emphasizes an upward trend in world food demand due to rising populations and higher incomes. Minor fluctuations in grain production in populous countries that have insufficient grain reserves will place considerable strain on the modest grain reserves held by the surplus producing nations. In spite of the promising successes of the "Green Revolution" and the optimism which it spawned, it is now all too apparent that new efforts and new food and population policies must be forthcoming if the expected six to eight billion people of the world are to be adequately fed by the year 2000.

Recognizing these doubts about the future, Panel II's charge has been to examine the critical choices facing the United States in its response to the precarious world food situation. The objective is to help determine the key options for the United States in light of its own long-run self-interest, its preeminent position as a food producer, its role as an international leader, and its deeply held humanitarian traditions.

The report incorporates many of the findings coming out of the recent discussions on world food, health, and population, and few of the data are original. But what appears to be lacking up to now in much of the discussions, and what this report seeks to accomplish, is an explicit consideration of the alternative objectives that could guide specific U.S. international food policies.

## I. Critical Choices

World food production has increased over the past thirty years. Unfortunately, the expanding world population and continuing unequal distribution of output (both among nations and within nations) has led to considerable individual deprivation. In the developing countries, food production has barely kept ahead of expanding demand and in some of these countries has lagged far behind.

While there are many ways in which further increases in world food production may be accomplished, by the year 2000 a world population of six to eight billion is expected, compared to four billion at present. With such a population explosion, some people doubt whether a widespread food crisis can be averted. If such a crisis does occur, the people of the United States cannot expect to escape its deep impact.

One basic choice that has to be made is whether our long-term interests can best be pursued through domestic agricultural policies geared to the long-term interest of the entire world or whether—and to what extent—our interests should be designed more specifically to improve the U.S. bargaining position with other countries. The use of food as a bargaining weapon includes efforts to link food exports to energy or raw materials imports or efforts to limit our food shipments to friendly and peaceful countries. This policy might also include restricting our food sales to those countries which have a real economic need for our food and do not desire it just to further their own political ends—e.g., by reexporting it on favorable terms to other countries.

If we decide, for economic, political, or ideological reasons, that it is in our own self-interest to help the less developed countries, without using food as a bargaining weapon, we face critical choices on how this objective can best be achieved. There are three alternative strategies:

A. Continue current U.S. agricultural policies and practices, making only marginal changes
B. Encourage more U.S. food aid abroad, with major efforts devoted to rapid development of our domestic capabilities to expand the volume and quality of our food assistance
C. Work with the less developed countries to expand their own food output.

### *Strategy A: Continue Current U.S. Agricultural Policies and Practices, Making Only Marginal Changes*

This choice would have the United States undertake no major new initiatives, domestically or internationally, in its international food policies. It is based on one or more of three alleged reasons.

First, the problems of food and population are heavily influenced by traditional social values and attitudes and by conservative political institutions. There is little chance of major change, even if we knew what to do from a technical and economic point of view. No miraculous, all-encompassing cures can be expected. Thus, there is very little more that the United States can effectively do than it is already doing.

Second, our efforts may prove to be counterproductive. Our past experience with large shipments of food aid to certain less developed countries has shown how in some cases they reduced the incentives and the urgency to develop local agriculture. The transfer of our capital-intensive food technology to the less developed countries, has at times, aggravated already high levels of rural unemployment and underemployment. Our arguments for birth control have been resented. In the 1974 Bucharest Conference, our attempts to help were called "Neocolonialism."

Third, the production shortfalls of 1972 and 1974 were due mainly to temporary factors. The fundamental trend is still for food production to exceed population growth, as it did in the 1950s and 1960s. There is faith in the workings of market forces to bring this about. High food prices already are resulting in higher food production around the world; high fertilizer prices have encouraged investment in new fertilizer capacity, and high grain prices are reducing the volume of grains used for livestock feed. Therefore, no new policy initiatives are required for the restoration of a favorable balance between the world demand and world supply of food.

Behind these reasons for the continuation of current policies is a belief that the United States should assume minimal responsibility for the state of foreign agriculture or population changes. These sensitive areas are matters of national sovereignty. We could be drawn unduly into conflicts with other countries in negotiations over the terms of aid or conditions for other forms of assistance.

Continuation of current policies would *not* mean no assistance for developing countries. Domestic grain stocks would still have to be rebuilt in order to cover possible domestic deficiencies and to permit the continued export of surplus products for hard currencies, although possibly with soft repayment terms. Some food aid would continue to be given outright. The distinction between humanitarian and foreign policy objectives in the allocation of food shipments would still have to be more clearly defined. Exports of grain would be carefully controlled to ensure that they are in the U.S. national interest and do not disrupt the U.S. domestic economy. Technical and capital assistance in food production to developing countries would continue at about the present levels. U.S. domestic food production would continue to receive approximately the same kind of support as at present.

If the above strategy is rejected—if the reasons justifying it are judged to be inaccurate and if it is believed that the United States does have a positive responsibility for the state of world food—there are two alternative levels of response: concentrate on food distribution from the developed to the developing countries (Strategy B) *or* concentrate on food production in the developing countries to enable them to feed themselves (Strategy C).

### *Strategy B: Encourage More U.S. Food Aid Abroad, with Major Efforts Devoted to Rapid Development of Our Domestic Capabilities to Expand the Volume and Quality of Our Food Assistance*

This strategy gives major emphasis to the expansion of U.S. food output, as a precondition to a considerably enlarged transfer of food assistance abroad. Reliance on this strategy, however, involves a number of potential difficulties:

1. In the next twenty-five years, world population will increase by approximately three billion people. Of this increase, 90 percent is expected to occur in developing countries. The burden of feeding these people would be so great that in all likelihood the United States could not carry a considerable percentage of it—certainly not for any length of time.

2. The strategy of expanding food deliveries may reduce pressures and incentives in recipient countries to expand their own food production.

3. Greatly increased food production may have adverse environmental consequences in the United States and other food exporting countries.

4. The program may not be viable without extensive government intervention in both the producing and consuming countries.

On the other hand, one must consider that:

1. An expanded food and health aid program may relieve much suffering, at least in the short run.

2. In case of catastrophic harvests and mass starvation, it would be immoral for the United States to withhold food and health aid.

If this alternative of emphasizing the need to distribute food from the developed to the less developed countries is accepted, a series of other choices then have to be made:

1. To what extent should the United States undertake an assistance program alone or as part of a multinational effort?

2. To what extent should food stocks be accumulated on a national basis or as part of an internationally managed system? How much grain should be stored? Where should the grain be acquired and how should it be distributed? Who controls and who pays for acquisition and maintenance? Where should the food stocks be located–in producing or in consuming countries?

3. Are we willing to accept a large dependence by other countries on us for their food supplies? Are we willing to commit ourselves to providing for them in times of shortage? How do we limit dependence?

4. To what extent should we be concerned about the impact of food aid on the agricultural development of the recipient country? What can be done to prevent potentially adverse impacts? Should food aid be considered a substitute for other forms of aid?

5. To what extent should food aid be conditional upon the recipient governments adopting effective policies to control their population growth rates? Should the United States provide more technical and financial assistance to foreign population control programs?

6. To what extent should the dietary habits of Americans be altered so that more grains can be made available to the less developed countries?

7. To what extent should we be concerned about the impact of health care on population growth and on economic prospects?

### *Strategy C: Work with the Less Developed Countries to Expand Their Own Food Output*

This alternative strategy (which is not altogether exclusive of Strategy B) is based on the premise that the United States and other developed countries do not have the capability to feed the world indefinitely. The less developed countries can feed themselves if they have capital and technical assistance *and* if they have the will to make needed policy and institutional changes. Therefore, while some food aid might be needed for a limited period, the United States should emphasize the provision of substantial capital and technical assistance and the continued access to the markets of the developed countries for those low income countries which are firmly committed to agriculture and health development.

This strategy concentrates on the production of food in the developing countries, while including distributional improvements as a short-run necessity. The benefits of this approach to the low income countries could be substantial. Agriculture typically provides approximately three-fourths of total employment and one-half of gross national product. A thriving agriculture increases national nutrition and health levels and provides an engine of growth for the rest of the economy.

A thriving agricultural sector can make an important contribution to overall economic growth. In England, the agricultural revolution preceded and made possible the industrial revolution. In the United States, it was agricultural development that stimulated industrial progress. As the world population continues to expand, and as the search for economic growth intensifies, the benefits of agricultural development are potentially as significant for the less developed countries as they once were, and still are, for many of today's industrial countries.

Domestically, the objective of this choice would be to assure adequate supplies of food at reasonable prices for the internal market and to permit the United States to make an appropriate contribution to world supply. The United States may also try, through bilateral and multilateral trade negotiations, to speed improvements in the agricultural policies of other developed countries, especially where their policies impede expansion of U.S. exports to foreign markets or slow the agricultural development of poor nations. It would seek reciprocal action by others for trade policies that will increase the agricultural exports of some less developed countries.

The United States would significantly increase its financial and technical assistance to countries seeking to improve their own agricultural production capabilities. Food aid would be given after careful assessment that the recipients will not reduce efforts to develop their own agricultural sectors.

Technical assistance would be offered on a wide range of activities, especially on storage and agricultural research. The United States could contribute to the latter in three primary ways. First, it could continue to be a major financial contributor to the international agricultural institutes organized under the Consultative Group for International Agricultural Research, as well as to other internationally-oriented domestic research institutions which have yet to attract international funding. Second, it could promote the linkages of U.S. research institutions to the international research institutes by funding research in a series of "frontier" activities which have international as well as domestic production implications. Finally, either directly through the U.S. government's own staff (which may have to be strengthened significantly) or by financing private or public organizations established for this purpose, the United States could provide technical assistance to national research and production programs in developing countries.

Improvement in nutrition and health will, in their initial impact, increase life expectancies and hence enlarge the size of the populations in the less developed countries. However, a healthier population will be better able to maintain itself than an undernourished, though smaller, one. The United States can help by seeking ways of strengthening medical research capabilities within the less developed countries. It can help train local personnel and utilize mass media techniques to make people aware of what they can do to improve their own health. Overall, the United States can try to switch the emphasis on health care from the care of categorical diseases to the institutionalization of local resources to deal with health-related matters.

The selection of this alternative would also necessitate a number of other decisions:

1. To what extent should agricultural assistance (finances, research, manpower training) be conditional upon the adoption by the host government of policies to strengthen the agricultural sector (removal of price controls on food, more local expenditures on agricultural infrastructure)?

2. To what extent should the United States provide assistance alone, or in concert with other developed nations? Should the United States take the lead in multinational arrangements, considering its leading position in agriculture? Should the United States work only through the existing international institutions?

3. To what extent should the United States encourage the less developed countries to adopt the objective of food self-sufficiency despite the economic burden this may place on some countries and despite possibly adverse impacts on world trade?

### *Other Choices*

Apart from choosing the basic critical strategy, a series of other important choices need to be made. Particular attention should be given to the choices which apply to food production around the world, in both the United States and other surplus food producing countries, and in the deficit regions. These choices include the following:

1. How much effort should be given to the production of food from the seas? To capture fishing versus the farming of the oceans? To fresh water versus salt water farming?

2. How much effort should be given to weather prediction (to minimize adverse effects of droughts or hurricanes) and weather modification (for the

purpose of better food production by the redistribution of rainfall over land and sea)?

3. How much effort should be given to reducing dependence on current pesticides—through the development of more specific, more rapidly decomposing varieties or through the breeding of pest-resistant varieties of plants?

4. How much effort should be given to advanced research on agricultural programs, recognizing that research findings may take a quarter of a century or more before they can make a significant contribution?

These choices have international implications and any implementation may well involve international cooperation. Americans alone cannot determine the outcome. But it is a critical choice for Americans as to where to place the emphasis and how great an effort to make toward a resolution of these issues.

## II. Pressures On The Demand For Food

World population and income growth are putting continuing pressures on world food availabilities. An estimated 400 to 500 million people, or 10 percent of the world's population, were suffering an absolute shortage of calories or severe malnutrition in 1970 (see table II-1). If anything, the situation has deteriorated since then because of the extensive crop shortfalls in 1972 and 1974. These shortfalls in a few key regions underscored how slim the margin has become between the supply and demand for food.

The year 1972 was the first time during the past two decades when food production actually declined on a global basis. The Soviet Union unexpectedly made large purchases in the world grain market. Dollar prices rose rapidly and food reserves were reduced. Some relief was provided in 1973 by relatively favorable food production worldwide. However, the energy crisis erupted at year-end and since then, it has proven to be especially injurious to those less developed countries that must import large amounts of the much higher priced foreign oil. Moreover, food production was again disappointing in 1974, especially in North America and the Soviet Union as well as in some of the developing countries. As a result, widespread hunger persists in many parts of the world, reserve stocks are at the lowest levels in twenty years, and the confidence of many observers in the world's ability to handle its short-term as well as its long-term food problems has been shaken.

The problem of a world trying to feed itself is the combined result of:

1. Continuing high birthrates in many countries
2. Lower infant mortality and higher life expectancy
3. A resultant increase in population growth rates—requiring only thirty-five years for world population to double
4. Increasing consumption of more and higher quality food by people in the developed countries

**Table II-1**
**Estimated Number of People with Insufficient Protein/Energy Supply, 1970**

| Region | Population (billions) | Percent of Population Below Lower Limit | Number Below Lower Limit (millions) |
|---|---|---|---|
| Developed regions[a] | 1.07 | 3 | 28 |
| Developing regions (excluding Asian centrally planned economies)[b] | 1.75 | 25 | 434 |
| Latin America | 0.28 | 13 | 36 |
| Far East | 1.02 | 30 | 301 |
| Near East | 0.17 | 18 | 30 |
| Africa | 0.28 | 25 | 67 |
| World (excluding Asian centrally planned economies) | 2.83 | 16 | 462 |

Source: U.N., Assessment of the World Food Situation, Rome, 1974, p. 66.

[a]*Developed regions* includes thirty-three major countries located primarily in Europe and North America but also Australia, Israel, Japan, New Zealand, South Africa, and the USSR.

[b]*Asian centrally planned economies* includes The People's Republic of China, Democratic People's Republic of Korea (North), Mongolia, and Democratic Republic of Vietnam (North).

5. Recurring shortfalls in crop production in the Soviet Union, Eastern Europe, and China, and increasing use of imports to cover these shortfalls
6. Failure to bring under cultivation arable regions of the world which have the potential of providing food surpluses above needs
7. Public policies which act to discourage food production.

*Population Pressures on the World Food Supply*

There has actually been an increase in world food production over the last twenty years. Between 1954 and 1973, world food production increased by an average of 2.8 percent annually. Furthermore, food production has increased at approximately the same percentage rates in both the developing and the developed group of countries over this period. In the developed countries, population has been increasing at 1.1 percent annually. However, the annual rate of population increase in the developing countries has been over twice as high. As a result, the developed countries now produce more than 40 percent more food per person than in 1954, while the developing countries produce less than 10 percent more food per person (see Table II-2 and Figure II-1).

The current population burst is unprecedented in human experience. The highest growth rate in history is being multiplied annually against the highest population base ever. The impact is to add 8,000 persons to the world population in an hour, 76 million in a year. These absolute figures will grow even if the growth rate remains steady. The less developed countries contain some 70 percent of the world's population and account for some 86 percent of the annual increase.

Population grows exponentially, in the way that compound interest accumulates. A population increase of 2.0 percent, the present world rate, doubles the total population size in thirty-five years. The 2.5 percent growth rate of the developing nations doubles population in only twenty-eight years. World food production is barely keeping pace with these population increases. The population growth rate in developed countries, in contrast, is only about 1.0 percent, producing a population doubling time of 70 years. Europe has the lowest continental growth of 0.4 percent (see Figure II-2).

People in the less developed countries typically spend 50 percent or more of their income on food, compared with only about 20 percent for those in developed countries. This overall demand for food is determined both by population and by incomes. As incomes rise in the less developed countries, there is an increased demand for grain for direct consumption. As incomes rise in the developed countries, the increased demand for grain is indirect, via more consumption of meat products.

Of the world's total population, two-thirds live in the developing lands, which have the highest birthrates. Indeed, the birthrate provides a rough definition of

**Indices of World Population and Food Production[a]**

(1961-65 = 100) – units

| Calendar Year | World | Food Production | | Developed Countries | Food Production | | Developing Countries | Food Production | |
|---|---|---|---|---|---|---|---|---|---|
| | Population | Total | Per Capita | Population | Total | Per Capita | Population | Total | Per Capita |
| 1954 | 84.2 | 77 | 91 | 89.1 | 77 | 86 | 80.6 | 77 | 96 |
| 1955 | 85.7 | 80 | 93 | 90.3 | 81 | 90 | 81.5 | 78 | 95 |
| 1956 | 87.3 | 84 | 96 | 91.5 | 85 | 93 | 84.4 | 82 | 97 |
| 1957 | 89.0 | 85 | 96 | 92.7 | 86 | 93 | 86.3 | 83 | 96 |
| 1958 | 90.7 | 90 | 99 | 93.9 | 91 | 97 | 88.4 | 87 | 98 |
| 1959 | 92.4 | 91 | 98 | 95.1 | 92 | 97 | 90.5 | 89 | 98 |
| 1960 | 94.2 | 94 | 100 | 96.3 | 96 | 100 | 92.8 | 92 | 99 |
| 1961 | 96.1 | 95 | 99 | 97.5 | 95 | 97 | 95.1 | 94 | 99 |
| 1962 | 98.0 | 98 | 100 | 98.9 | 98 | 99 | 97.5 | 97 | 100 |
| 1963 | 100.0 | 100 | 100 | 100.1 | 99 | 99 | 99.9 | 100 | 100 |
| 1964 | 101.9 | 103 | 101 | 101.2 | 103 | 102 | 102.4 | 104 | 102 |
| 1965 | 103.9 | 104 | 100 | 102.3 | 104 | 102 | 105.0 | 104 | 99 |
| 1966 | 105.9 | 109 | 103 | 103.4 | 111 | 107 | 107.7 | 106 | 98 |
| 1967 | 107.9 | 114 | 106 | 104.3 | 115 | 110 | 110.4 | 111 | 101 |
| 1968 | 109.9 | 118 | 107 | 105.3 | 119 | 113 | 113.2 | 115 | 102 |
| 1969 | 112.0 | 118 | 105 | 106.3 | 117 | 110 | 116.1 | 121 | 104 |
| 1970 | 114.2 | 121 | 106 | 107.3 | 119 | 111 | 119.0 | 126 | 106 |
| 1971 | 116.4 | 126 | 108 | 108.3 | 125 | 115 | 122.1 | 128 | 105 |
| 1972 | 118.7 | 124 | 104 | 109.3 | 124 | 113 | 125.3 | 125 | 100 |
| 1973 | 120.9 | 133 | 110 | 110.2 | 133 | 121 | 128.5 | 132 | 103 |

Source: U.S. Department of Agriculture, *The World Food Situation and the Prospects to 1985*, Economic Research Service, U.S. Department of Agriculture, Foreign Agricultural Economic Report No. 98, Washington, D.C., December 1974, p. 2.

Note: The USDA definition of developed countries includes the same countries covered by the FAO definition given in table II-1.

The USDA definition of developing countries includes those countries which FAO includes in developing regions, also excludes the Asian centrally planned economies (see table II-1).

[a]World excluding Communist Asia.

Index: 1961-65 = 100

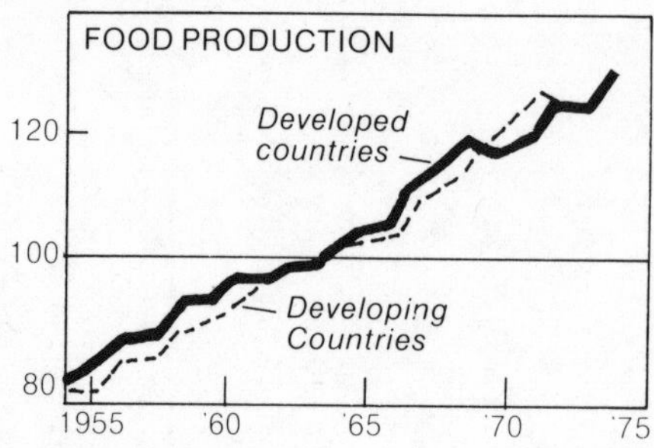


Food production has grown steadily over the past two decades. Growth in the developing countries has roughly paralleled that in the developed countries.

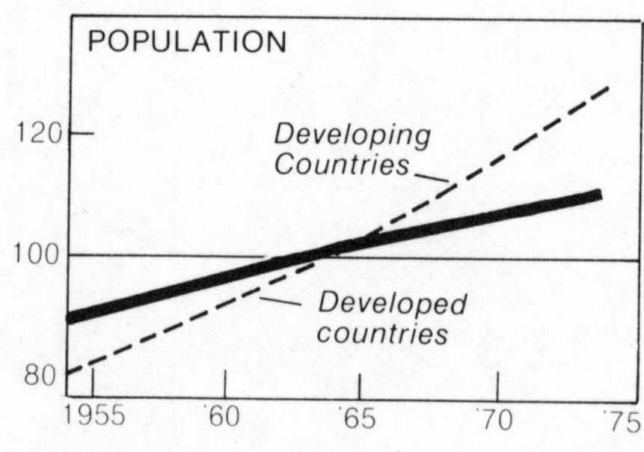


Population has grown much faster in the developing countries.

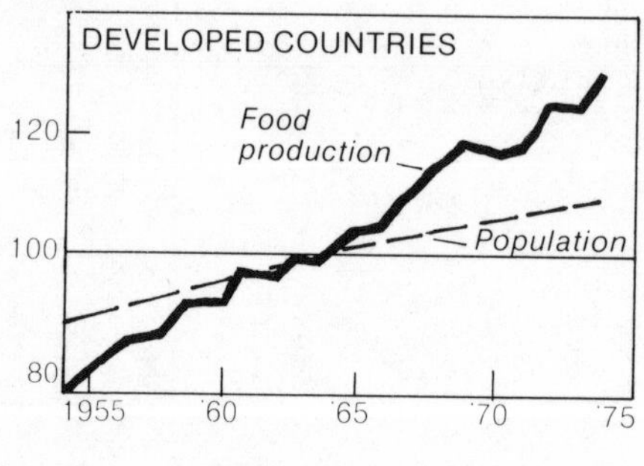


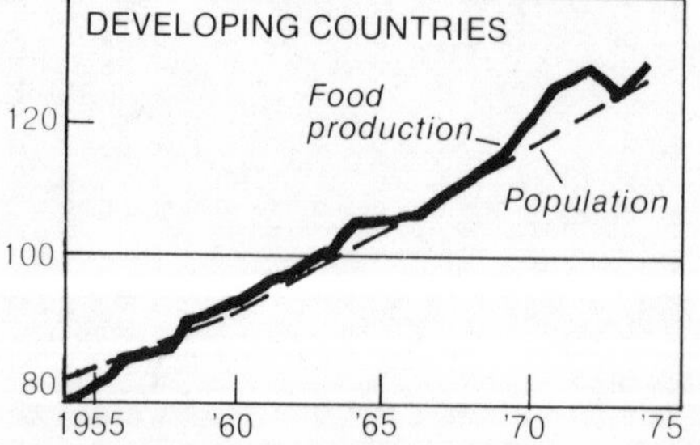


Peoples of the developed and developing country groups have not fared equally from the roughly equal growth in food production. In the developed countries production has increased much faster than population, boosting production per capita. In the developing countries, population gains have absorbed nearly all of the production increase; production per capita has improved only slightly.

Data exclude Communist Asia

Source: U.S. Department of Agriculture, *The World Food Situation and the Prospects to 1985*, Economic Research Service, U.S. Department of Agriculture, Foreign Agricultural Economic Report No. 98, Washington, D.C., December 1974, page 13.

Source: U.S. Department of Agriculture, *The World Food Situation and the Prospects to 1985*, Economic Research Service, U.S. Department of Agriculture, Foreign Agricultural Economic Report No. 98, Washington, D.C., December 1974, p. 13.

**Figure II-1.** Food Production and Population, Developed and Developing Countries

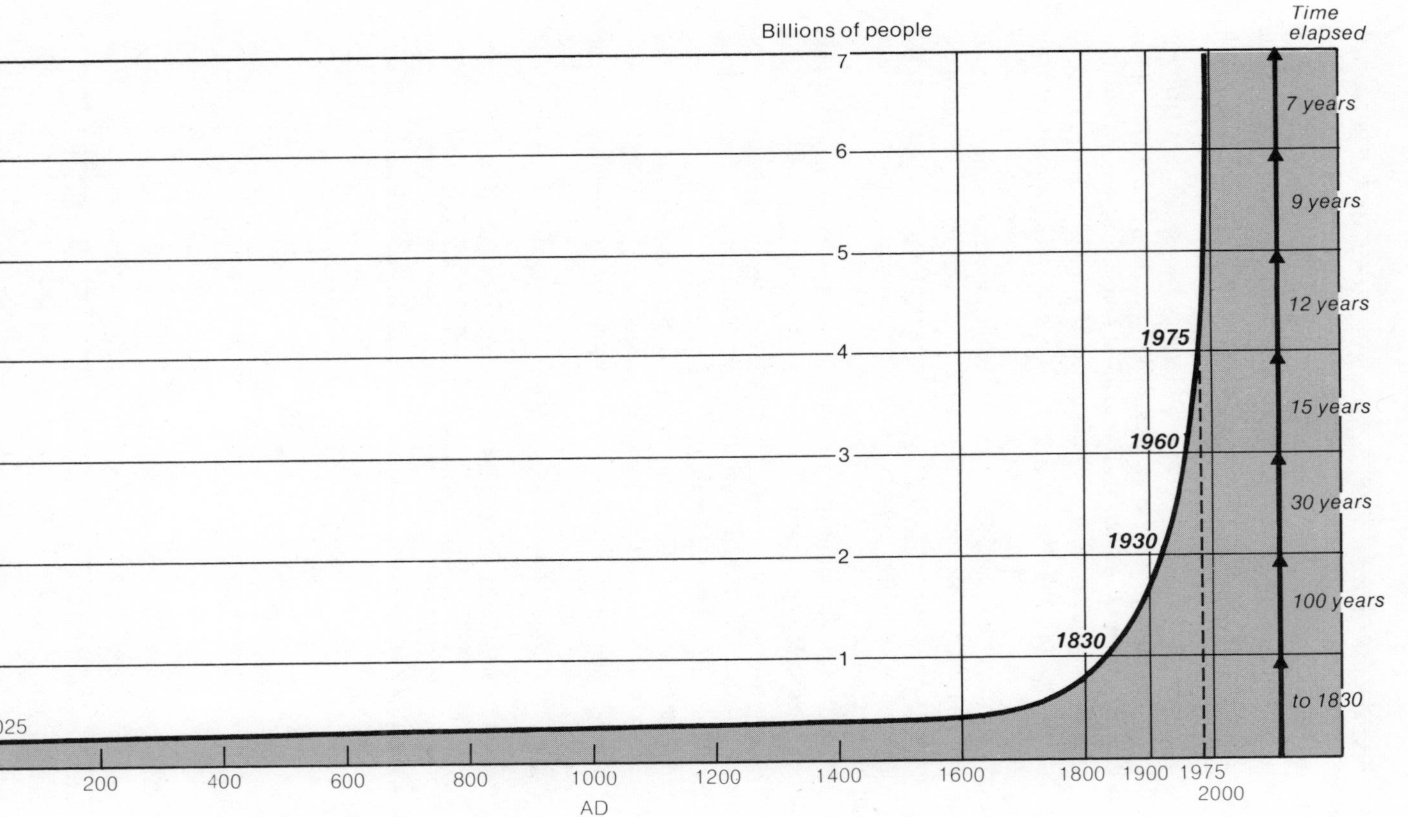


Source: U.S. Department of State.

**Figure II-2.** The World's Population Growth Past and Projected (*If* present rate of growth continues)

"developing" and "developed," since there are few less developed countries with birthrates under 30 per 1,000 and no developed countries with birthrates above that figure. Low productivity economies, high illiteracy, a low percentage of children in school, and few medical facilities—these are the factors that are more likely to lead to high fertility. Each of these problems is related to the others and can only be resolved by broad action on all fronts.

Some examples of the swift growth of developing nations: Between 1970 and 1985, the population of India has been projected to rise from 547 million to 808 million; Pakistan, from 60 million to 101 million; Bangladesh, from 51 million to 123 million; Indonesia, from 116 million to 184 million; Brazil, from 93 million to 146 million; and Mexico, from 51 million to 84 million (see Table II-3).

A characteristic of less developed countries is the large proportion of young persons, who are not yet productive and hence dependent on the efforts of the rest of the work force for their support. In some countries, such as Egypt, the youth dependence population (those fifteen years old and younger) is nearly one-half of the total.

The efforts thus far of national, international, and private agencies to reduce birthrates in the developing countries have been only partially successful. Among the population giants, only the People's Republic of China appears to be reducing its birthrate substantially. On the Indian subcontinent, reductions have been minimal, despite continued attempts.

The United States has a critical stake in the race between world food supplies and population, whether for selfish or selfless reasons.

1. The rising world food demand presents economic opportunities for the

**Table II-3**
**Population and Population Growth Rates**

| | Population[a] (million) | Population Growth Rate – % |
|---|---|---|
| Africa | 362 | 2.8 |
| East Asia | 1,332 | 1.8 |
| South Asia | 984 | 2.4 |
| Europe | 465 | 0.5 |
| Latin America | 323 | 2.8 |
| Northern America | 236 | 0.6 |
| Oceania | 21 | 1.4 |
| Soviet Union | 254 | 0.9 |
| World Total | 3,978 | 1.8 |

Source: U.S. Agency for International Development.

[a]Estimates for mid-1975.

highly productive U.S. agricultural sector. The United States is the world's largest food producer and exporter. In order to earn foreign exchange to pay for our imports, we are highly dependent on these agricultural exports. Over the past two decades, food exports have contributed over 20 percent of the income earned from all exports; in 1973, food exports rose to over $17 billion, or about 26 percent of the total (see Table II-4).

2. World food supplies influence food prices, including those paid by U.S. consumers. For example, a very poor grain crop prompted the Soviet Union to purchase a full quarter of the 1972 grain production of the United States, which contributed to a large drawdown of U.S. reserves. Also, the decline in anchovy harvests off the west coast of Peru in 1971 increased the demand in Europe for U.S. soybeans, an alternative livestock feed. These external developments contributed to rising food prices and general inflation in the United States.

**Table II-4**
**Value of U.S. Exports, 1955 to 1973**
(millions of dollars) units

| | | Agricultural Exports | | | |
|---|---|---|---|---|---|
| Calendar Year | Total Exports | Commercial | Government Programs | Total | Agricultural Share of Total U.S. Exports (Percent) |
| 1955 | $15,419 | $ 2,081 | $1,118 | $ 3,199 | 20.7 |
| 1956 | 18,940 | 2,459 | 1,711 | 4,170 | 22.0 |
| 1957 | 20,671 | 2,970 | 1,536 | 4,506 | 21.8 |
| 1958 | 17,745 | 2,622 | 1,233 | 3,855 | 21.7 |
| 1959 | 17,451 | 2,747 | 1,208 | 3,955 | 22.7 |
| 1960 | 20,375 | 3,371 | 1,461 | 4,832 | 23.7 |
| 1961 | 20,754 | 3,541 | 1,483 | 5,024 | 24.2 |
| 1962 | 21,031 | 3,555 | 1,479 | 5,034 | 23.5 |
| 1963 | 23,062 | 4,064 | 1,520 | 5,584 | 24.2 |
| 1964 | 26,156 | 4,704 | 1,644 | 6,348 | 24.3 |
| 1965 | 27,135 | 4,880 | 1,349 | 6,229 | 23.0 |
| 1966 | 29,884 | 5,528 | 1,353 | 6,881 | 23.0 |
| 1967 | 31,142 | 5,118 | 1,262 | 6,380 | 20.5 |
| 1968 | 34,199 | 5,039 | 1,189 | 8,228 | 18.2 |
| 1969 | 37,462 | 4,918 | 1,018 | 5,936 | 15.8 |
| 1970 | 42,590 | 6,226 | 1,033 | 7,259 | 17.0 |
| 1971 | 43,492 | 6,624 | 1,069 | 7,693 | 17.7 |
| 1972 | 48,876 | 8,248 | 1,153 | 9,401 | 19.2 |
| 1973 | 69,121 | 16,814 | 863 | 12,677 | 25.6 |

Source: *U.S. Foreign Agricultural Trade Statistical Report, Calendar Year: 1973* (Washington, D.C.: U.S. Department of Agriculture, 1974).

3. The tragedy of millions of people threatened with death by starvation challenges the humanitarian impulses of the American character. From the European relief efforts of World War I under Herbert Hoover, through the Marshall Plan in the 1950s and the Indian famine relief efforts in the 1960s, to virtually every disaster afflicting the world in recent times, a ready American response in food aid has become virtually axiomatic.

4. Finally, and perhaps most importantly, the availability of adequate food at reasonable prices is basic to the political stability of nations, whether they be developing or developed. The United States is the major surplus country to provide food in times of production shortfalls in other countries. It also is the primary supplier of technical knowledge and finances to assist developing countries in strengthening their own food production programs. This situation gives the United States both tremendous power and immense responsibility in deciding how to use its food, knowledge, and finances to build a more stable future world.

### *Health Pressures on Population Growth*

The relationship of health and medical care to population growth is inextricably involved in the issue of whether the less developed countries will be able to provide adequate food supplies for their people. Health care improvements have an initial impact on reducing death rates and have thereby been a factor contributing to the increase and high rate of population growth typical of many less developed countries. However, the hope is that birthrates will also come down—a cycle that has already occurred in the industrial countries.

In many poor, agrarian societies, surviving children are looked upon as a source of labor and as a form of social security for parents in their old age. In societies with high infant mortality, having numerous children provides a degree of insurance that enough sons will survive to maturity to fulfill their filial duties. But as infant mortality rates decline, this incentive to have more children is weakened.

To be sure, as Figure II-3 indicates, there is still considerable scope for reducing infant mortality rates. Throughout the underdeveloped world, the major source of sickness and death in the five and under age group is the pneumonia-diarrhea complex. This disease group accounted for an estimated 750 million cases of gastritis, 125-350 million of pneumonia, 90 million of measles, 70 million of whooping cough, and 50 million of dysentery in an average year. Infants and the elderly are dying of severe colds and stomach disorders because inadequate diets have weakened their resistance.

Sufficient and balanced food supplies would go a long way toward reducing malnourishment, which directly and indirectly contributes to susceptibility to disease and to high mortality rates. Moreover, a healthier population is more

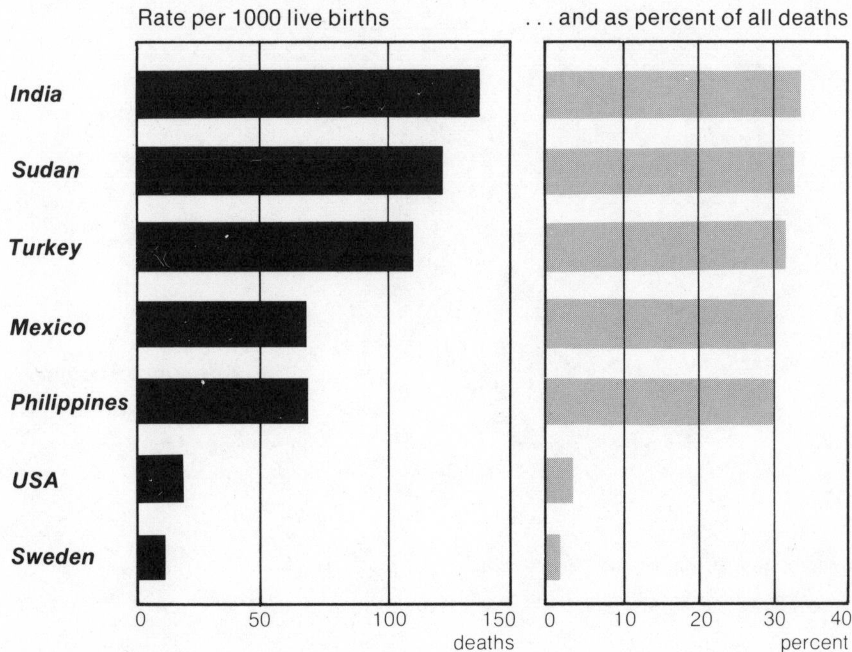


Source: *1975 World Population Data Sheet*, Population Reference Bureau, Inc., Washington, D.C.

**Figure II-3.** Infant Mortality, Selected Nations

productive and hence better able to feed itself. Thus, increased food is needed to improve health, while improved health is needed to give more food. This cycle of malnourishment is estimated by the United Nations to encompass some 460 million people.

Because countries are poor, their health care resources are often very limited. Annual expenditure for all health services in the developing countries ranges around $1.00 per person, compared to $440 per person in the United States (see Figure II-4).

Simple, relatively inexpensive, long-available preventive medical techniques such as vaccinations are grossly underused in the poorer nations. Although most children have now been vaccinated against smallpox, limited use is being made of vaccinations against diphtheria, tetanus, and polio. Measles vaccination is nearly unheard of, though measles is a serious cause of deaths among children in these nations.

The poorer nations are desperately short of medical personnel (see Figure II-5). Many world areas are served by one doctor per 20,000 or even 30,000 population. The United Nations recommended standard is 1 doctor per 10,000.

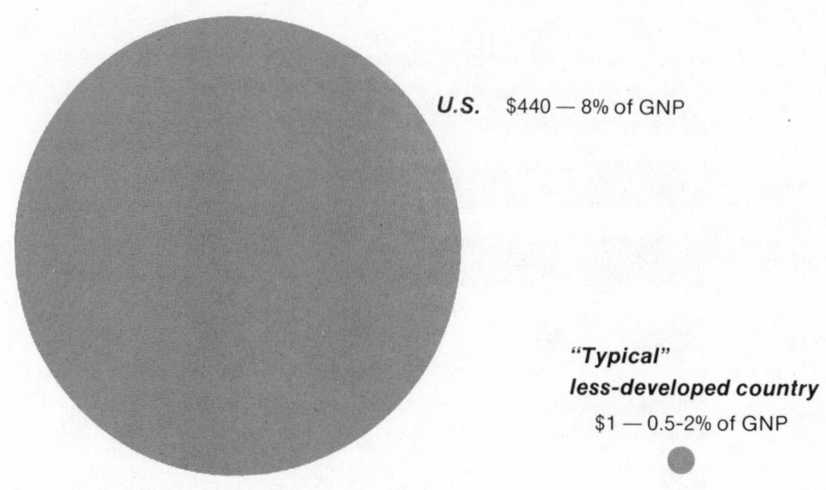


Source: Rockefeller Foundation estimates.

**Figure II-4.** Per Capita Health Service Expenditures

In the United States, the ratio is one doctor per 600 persons. To reach the standard recommended by the United Nations would require training an additional 3.5 million doctors, at a cost of at least $100 billion.

Uneven distribution of medical personnel aggravates an already unsatisfactory medical care environment. In some countries, most of the doctors live in the capital city, which contains only a fraction of these countries' total populations.

For all their desperate health needs, these countries suffer a severe drain of medical personnel to Western nations. The Philippines, Thailand, India, and Taiwan have medical training programs that amount to export industries. Colombia, which has been graduating 600 new doctors a year to serve its population of 22 million, has been losing 60 to 80 physicians a year to the United States.

Infant mortality rates will be lowered and family planning will become more socially desirable as the total environment of the poorer nations improves. The greatest cause of childhood deaths among the poorer nations, the pneumonia-diarrhea complex, cannot be combated by medical treatment alone. High infant mortality rates will yield most quickly to public health efforts, purer water supplies, better waste disposal, improved diets, and wider use of immunization. The great advances in reducing mortality rates and in extending lifespans have occurred when public health measures are intensively applied. It is in the field of public health that new technology tends to be more important even in individual health care.

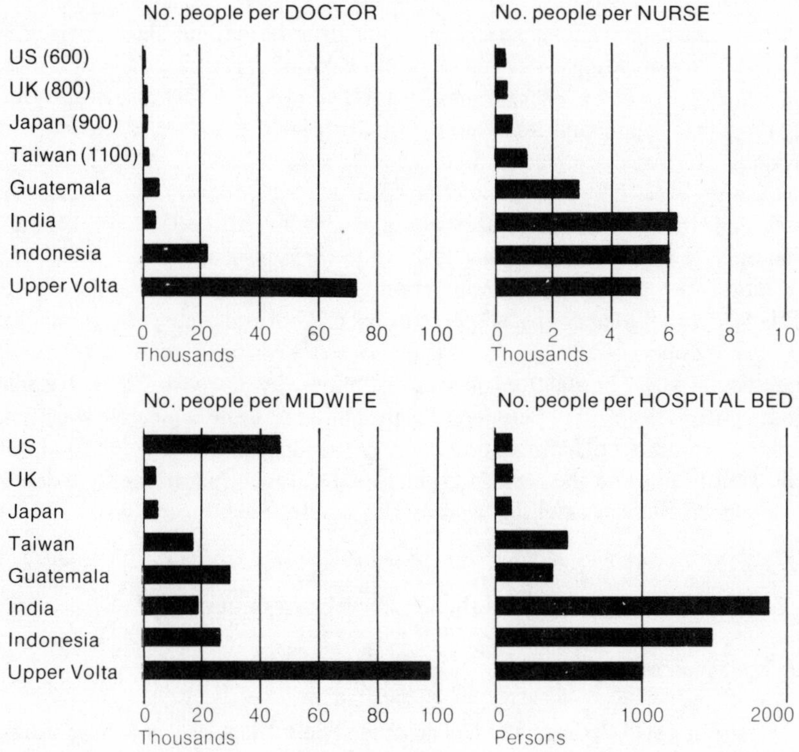


Source: Dorothy Nortman, "Population and Family Planning Programs: A Factbook," Reports on Population/Family Planning No. 2, 7th ed. (New York: The Population Council, October 1975), tables 3 and 4.

**Figure II-5.** Health Care Services in Relation to Population

Insufficient attention has been accorded to health conditions as a precondition to economic development. Yet, widespread economic growth cannot occur in a pesthole. In Africa, for example, the prevalence of river blindness (onchocerosis) has severely inhibited the economic development of the fertile Volta River area. The World Bank organized a consortium of agencies to eradicate the disease as an indispensable first step in development of the area. Such recognition of the indispensability of a sound health base for economic development is all too rare.

Rising economic prospects, assisted by improved health conditions, can produce a social climate in which families do not feel compelled to have the large numbers of children characteristic of poor societies.

If a significant change in the population trend in the poorer nations is to be achieved, the demographic pattern and the disease pattern must be seen as inseparable, representing, in effect, opposite sides of the same coin. An assured food supply, a reduced infant mortality rate, good health services, educational and economic opportunities–overall, an acceptable standard of living–will provide the strongest motivation for smaller families.

However, even if model population control policies were adopted in the poorer countries today, the impact would be distant. In the United States, for instance, once population growth gets down to the replacement level, it will take fifty more years to get to zero population growth–during which time the U.S. population would increase by 40 percent. Even if birthrates are reduced rapidly, the large number of the young already in less developed countries virtually guarantees a world population of over six billion by the year 2000. Without serious controls, a world population of eight billion or more is possible sometime thereafter, which would put enormous pressure on the demand for food and would greatly increase the need to expand food output–in both the food-deficit less-developed countries and the food-surplus developed countries.

## III. Food Production Potential of the Less Developed Countries

### *Past Performance*

In the previous two decades, the less developed countries as a whole have shown encouraging gains in crop yields and in total food production. From the period 1948-1952 to 1966-1970, they increased grain production by 78 percent, to 378 million tons. About half of this increase was due to higher yields. In the same period, the developed countries increased grain production by 61 percent, although this lower rate partly reflects policy restraints to avoid further accumulation of surplus stocks.

Increased fertilizer supplies, available at lower costs due to dramatic changes in production technology, account for part of the higher grain yields experienced by the less developed countries. World fertilizer consumption doubled in the 1950s and it has tripled again since then.

New technologies also have contributed to gains in grain yields and overall food production. In Mexico, the joint Rockefeller Foundation-Mexican government team developed high-yielding dwarf wheats, which matured sooner than indigenous wheats and more than doubled their yields. In the Philippines, the International Rice Research Institute successfully developed high-yielding dwarf rice varieties. In 1973, over 80 million acres were planted to the high-yielding rices and wheats in the developing countries, compared to practically none in 1965. A fifth of the rice area and a third of the wheat area in non-Communist Asia are now sown with the new varieties. (The dramatic uptrend for Asia and North Africa is shown in Figure II-6.)

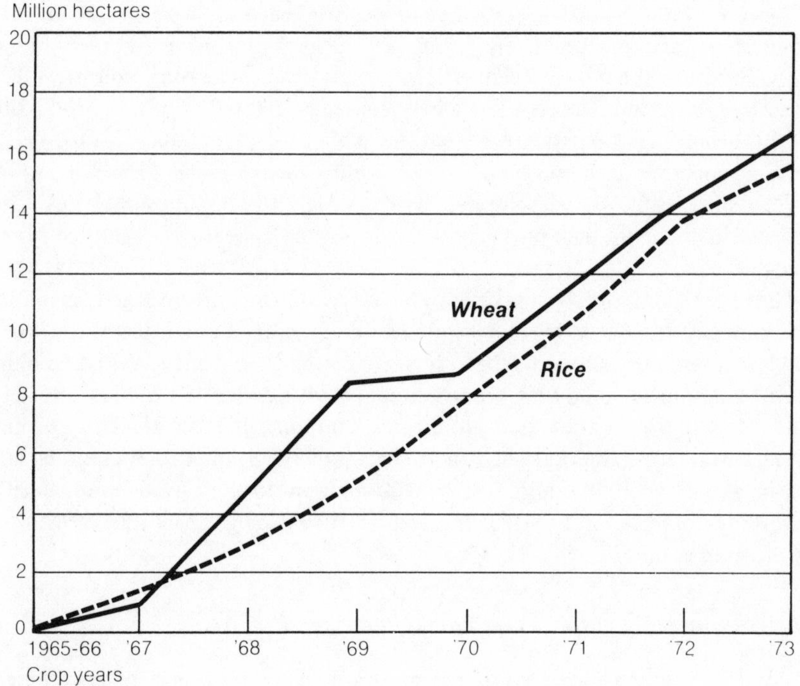


Source: U.S. Department of Agriculture, *The World Food Situation and the Prospects to 1985*, Economic Research Service, U.S. Department of Agriculture, Foreign Agricultural Economic Report No. 98, Washington, D.C., December 1974, p. 67.

**Figure II-6.** Estimated High-Yield Wheat and Rice Area: Asia and North Africa, 1965-66 to 1972-73 (Excluding Communist Nations)

However, very large yield gaps still remain. There are 131 countries for which corn yield figures were reported by FAO (the Food and Agricultural Organization) in 1972. The highest average country yield reported was over 7 tons per hectare (for New Zealand, which has a small area); the U.S. average was over 6 tons per hectare. But the world average was only 2.8 tons per hectare. Over 100 countries, most of which produce corn for human consumption rather than for animal feed, have yields below the world average; 81 of these countries have yields below 1.5 tons per hectare, which is one-half of the world average and one-fourth of the U.S. average. Much the same picture holds for the other food crops. As a result, while the developing countries have approximately the same area in cereal production as the developed countries, they produce only little more than half as much grain.

Among the developing countries there has been a wide range in food production performance. There have been several real success stories, but in many countries there have been little per capita gains and some countries have actually lost ground. However, as we have already pointed out, food production on the average has barely exceeded the high rate of population growth. In addition, incomes have continued to rise, adding further to the total demand for food. As a result, the developing world, which was a substantial net food exporter in the early part of this century, is now an increasingly significant food importer.

Gross cereal imports by the developing market economies averaged 33 million tons annually for the 1969-71 period. The Preparatory Committee of the World Food Conference estimates that, if recent trends continue, the developing market economies could have a gross annual cereals deficit of 85 million tons by 1985, almost three times their gross cereals imports in 1969-71. This estimate assumes normal production conditions. In a good year, the deficit could be less, but in a bad year, it could rise to 100 million tons or even more. Such a magnitude could seriously strain the projected financing capabilities of many of the affected countries.

### *Factors Influencing Future Food Production*

If world population increases to the generally estimated range of six to eight billion people by year 2000, and if world demand for food continues to grow in line with rising incomes, then the present output of food grain will at least have to be doubled in order to feed this population. Livestock and other protein sources must also be more than doubled. The rest of this chapter examines some of the ways in which the food output of the less developed countries themselves can be expanded.

**Land Availability.** On a worldwide basis, soils capable of producing food under good management are not yet in short supply. In 1967, the Panel on the World Food Supply of the President's Science Advisory Committee classified the land area of the world according to soil type, amplitude of the seasonal variation in temperature, and the amount and seasonal distribution of precipitation. They concluded that 3.2 billion hectares, or 24 percent of the total ice-free land surface of the earth, was potentially arable, that is, it included soils considered to be cultivatable and acceptably productive of food crops adapted to the environment. All arable land was considered to have potential for grazing and, where not too dry, for forestry. The average level of technology required was assumed to be equivalent of the average level of U.S. agricultural technology. It was recognized that some potentially arable soils would need irrigation, drainage, stone removal, clearing of trees, or other measures, the costs of which would not be excessive in relation to anticipated returns.

Only 1.4 billion hectares, or 44 percent of the potentially arable land in the world, are currently being cultivated. Both Africa and South America have less than 20 percent of their potentially arable land under cultivation; even Asia has some land yet available to bring into productive use. The use of multiple cropping has an immediate potential for extending the effective land base in densely populated areas by an additional 800 million hectares without a need for additional water development. Another 28 percent of the land area of the earth is estimated to have some grazing potential, even though it is not considered to be potentially arable.

The state of technology is one of the major reasons why much of the potentially arable land is not being cultivated. The tsetse fly keeps cattle away from large areas of Africa. Too little is known about the soils, climate, crop varieties, and farming systems in the Amazon or Congo basins. Much the same is true of the Sudan and the Mekong basin. However, research already carried out on such areas as the Campo Cerrados in Brazil, the Llanos in Colombia and Venezuela, and the Southern Cone in Argentina, Uruguay, and Chile can have immediate payoffs in improving the productivity of these lands. The Campo Cerrados, which was not considered to be productive land twenty years ago, is now being rapidly developed for crops.

The new, yet to be developed lands are generally located in inhospitable areas where population densities are low. They also lack the transport, the industries, and the institutions essential for a successful, sustained agricultural development. Substantial capital investment will be required to bring these lands into cultivation—estimated by the Preparatory Committee of the World Food Conference to total up to $30 billion to add 6 to 7 million hectares a year by 1985.

Despite the fact that throughout the world there are large unutilized and underutilized areas of arable land and that some portion of this will be brought into production, it is unlikely that additions to areas under cultivation over the next ten years will grow much faster than they have during the past ten years. The costs of land development are high and the returns are generally low. Therefore, increases in yields will most likely continue to account for the major portion of increases in future food production.

**Water Supply.** The limited availability of water resources is probably the most significant long-run constraint on future world food production. However, there is substantial scope for new development of supplementary irrigation, especially in sub-Saharan Africa, Latin America, and even in parts of Asia. More importantly, much more efficient use can be made of the irrigation facilities already developed. The Panel on the World Food Supply of the President's Science Advisory Committee estimated that, if irrigation potential could be fully developed for double and triple cropping, the gross cropped area of the world could be increased to the equivalent of five times that now under cultivation.

Large investments also will be required to develop our water resources fully. The Preparatory Committee of the World Food Conference estimated that renovating 46 million hectares of existing irrigated areas, which are in need of overhauling, would cost $21 billion; irrigating an additional 23 million hectares under new programs envisaged to be feasible between now and 1985, would cost an additional $38 billion.

In the early 1960s, development of the centrifugal compressor technology in ammonia production practically halved the cost of nitrogen fertilizer. Research was reoriented to show the advantages of using more fertilizer on traditional varieties of cereals. The Food and Agricultural Organization (FAO) organized thousands of fertilizer demonstration projects throughout the world. Credit facilities were expanded. Fertilizer distribution systems were improved. The development of cereal grain varieties that were responsive to fertilizer and were high yielding brought on new demands for chemical nutrients. Worldwide consumption of chemical fertilizers has increased sevenfold since 1950. The sheer increase in volume has meant that fertilizer is now being used on millions of small farmers' fields to produce food crops.

In the mid-1960s, there was a surge in the construction of new fertilizer plants in order to take advantage of an expected huge increase in demand. The actual demand, however, fell below expectations. The market became saturated and prices dropped. Because of the resulting low profits, the traditional exporters–North America, Western Europe, and Japan–closed inefficient plants and built few new ones after 1968. On a worldwide basis, planned production capacity continued to grow ahead of demand, but most of the new construction was in the Soviet Union, Eastern Europe, and some of the low-income countries. Because of their high domestic needs, the long lead-times in construction, and serious inefficiencies in plant operation in these countries, new production was slow in becoming available to the world market. The glut quickly changed to a shortage. The shortage was compounded for the less developed countries when they were outbid for available fertilizer supplies by the developed countries, which had superior purchasing power.

Then, in 1973, the oil embargo curtailed supplies of petroleum, one of the elements in the production of nitrogen fertilizer, and considerably higher petroleum prices followed. From 1972 to 1974, the world price of nitrogen fertilizers rose from 11 cents to 25 cents a pound, reflecting the hike in oil prices charged by the OPEC (Organization of Petroleum Exporting Countries) cartel.

The changes in price and availability of fertilizer have placed hardships on the food production plans of many developing countries. The diversion of available fertilizer supplies to the developed countries also tends to work against efforts to increase *total* world food production. Fertilizer gives a progressively smaller incremental return to production as levels of use are increased. In India, for instance, a pound of fertilizer can produce 10 to 15 additional pounds of grain. But in the United States, which is already a heavy user of fertilizer, an additional pound of fertilizer produces perhaps only five additional pounds of grain (see Table II-5).

The current world fertilizer shortage reflects a lack of investments. Capital spending of as much as $100 billion in fertilizer production plants, raw material production facilities, transport and storage facilities, and distribution facilities could be required to meet estimated fertilizer demands over the next ten years. There are encouraging signs that much of this investment is beginning to be undertaken. Private firms are responding to the profit motive; there is now an unprecedented surge in fertilizer plant construction. The fertilizer supply may thus be in balance with demand over the long run, although the market can be expected to continue to be plagued with recurring short-run shortages and surpluses as producers overbuild and then are forced to adjust. There are also important technological opportunities, especially the new methods of "fixing" nitrogen, which could expand supply considerably—even if natural gas supplies begin to recede.

**Environment.** There is evidence that even at existing levels of output, agriculture in both developed and low-income countries is generating considerable environmental stresses in some places. For example, wind and water erosion, loss of habitat, desertification, and destruction of soil fertility are occurring in some areas where land was once relatively abundant. In the more intensely cultivated areas, environmental problems can result from the relatively heavy use of fertilizers and pesticides and, where irrigation is used, from increasing soil and water salinity and the spread of water-borne diseases.

Erosion is eating into arable lands in the Indian subcontinent, the Middle East, the Caribbean, Central America, and the Andean countries. Over the past few years, human and livestock population along the sub-Saharan fringe have increased rapidly. This population pressure has led to overgrazing and the denudation of the land. This is a major reason why the Sahara Desert is estimated to be edging southward in some places by several miles per year.

**Table II-5**
**Corn-Yield Gains from Successive Fertilizer Applications[a]**

| Additional Nitrogen Applied | Average Gain in Corn Yield Per Pound of Nitrogen Applied |
|---|---|
| First 40 pounds | 27 pounds |
| Second 40 pounds | 14 pounds |
| Third 40 pounds | 9 pounds |
| Fourth 40 pounds | 4 pounds |
| Fifth 40 pounds | 1 pound |

Source: U.S. Department of Agriculture.

[a]Data from Iowa, 1964.

Clearing land in the Himalayan foothills in order to plant more crops has contributed to increasing flooding in India and Pakistan. Cutting trees on the Javan slopes has rapidly increased the level of silting in the irrigation channels that are so vital to Indonesia's agricultural production. Slash and burn techniques in South America are exposing substantial areas of land to deterioration and soil erosion. These activities are causing several million acres to be lost to cultivation each year. Unless major changes occur, these stresses are likely to worsen in the future.

**Climate.** Since the early decades of this century, a warming trend had set in around the globe, with annual average temperatures rising to a maximum in the 1940s. From the 1940s to the present, there has been a cooling trend, most clearly noticeable in the Northern Hemisphere. However, annual average temperatures are still higher than the averages of the past few centuries.

It is not certain whether the decline in the Northern Hemisphere temperature will continue; it may halt or reverse itself. However, temperature change per se is not the most serious potential climatic threat to food production. There is a possibility that, associated with the temperature changes, there will be increased climatic variability, which may result in some of the following conditions, varying from region to region:

1. Changes in temporal and geographical distribution of precipitation
2. Shorter crop-growing seasons in lands in the higher latitudes
3. Cooler temperatures during crop-growing seasons in some regions.

Some effects of such climatic changes would be beneficial to agriculture and others would be detrimental; the net effect, for the whole world or for any particular region, is not known.

There are three possible responses to this potential problem: agricultural research, improved weather prediction, and weather modification.

The adequacy of current research efforts on food yields that are based on a stable climate may have to be reviewed in the light of the possibly greater climatic fluctuations that may occur in the future. Of particular importance would be research on enhanced crop tolerance to drought, on tolerance to saline soils for some locations, and on the increasingly efficient use of water, which will be in diminishing supply in some important regions regardless of future climate patterns. The development of seeds of crop varieties with short growth periods could prove to be especially useful.

Steady progress is being made in the field of weather prediction. In recent years, the prospects have become more hopeful, partly because of the use of weather satellites and partly because of the application of fast electronic computers. With the help of weather satellites, we are for the first time in a position to obtain a global picture of the weather. The use of the electronic computers opens up the development which will permit predicting weather with some reliability for one day, five days, or longer. Both these developments have particularly important implications for world food production.

Weather modifications may become a useful technique for increasing food production as a consequence in part of improved weather prediction. Careful weather prediction extending over increasing periods of time should demonstrate in detail the generally known fact that atmospheric phenomena are full of instabilities. These instabilities, or "trigger effects," magnify small original causes into big eventual results. These instabilities may set a limit to the time span for practical weather prediction. In attempting weather prediction over increasing periods, one may discover the nature and opportunity for such trigger effects. By the use of these triggers, weather modification may, in the end, become possible.

**Energy Requirements.** The recent energy crisis has focused attention on the importance of energy sources for continued agricultural development. Oil and gas are used as inputs for the production of chemical fertilizers, which are needed to raise or even maintain crop yields. These energy sources are also needed to fuel the irrigation pumps, the tractors and other farm machinery and the transport equipment needed to get the harvest to market. Because of their tight foreign exchange position, the very low-income countries generally have suffered considerably from high oil prices. The cost of oil imports alone for the developing countries rose from $3.7 billion in 1972 to some $15 billion in 1974.

The use of energy in agricultural production has increased because economic incentives have encouraged it. However, the efficiency of fossil fuel energy conversion to food appears to be decreasing, especially for the United States, which is producing at increasingly higher levels of output and where the marginal contributions of all production inputs are lower. However, the low-income countries have not yet reached the levels of energy consumption of the United States or other developed countries. In some of the labor-abundant countries, multiple cropping or "gardening" techniques require relatively low fossil fuel inputs. Phased dosages of fertilizers have been shown to have significant nutrient economies. If petroleum products remain at their presently high price levels or go higher or if long-term supply availabilities cannot be assured, the new economic considerations may require a reexamination of production practices for the future.

**Research.** There are numerous ways to close the yield gap. Much can be done to improve yields by applying more water, using water more effectively and using more fertilizer. However, closing the yield gap is complex; it requires basic answers to the problems of climate, environment, energy, and the use of new lands. Major efforts are needed to attract the investments required to open the new lands for farming, to develop the irrigation facilities, and to produce the fertilizer.

While much new research is now underway, the status of research on the basic food crops for the tropics and subtropics still has to be considered very inadequate, with the exception of wheat and rice grown under controlled irrigated conditions. This should not be too surprising; there hardly has been time to develop fundamental information, much less get it applied. Internationalized research efforts for the tropics and subtropics in rice date only to the early 1960s, wheat and maize to the late 1960s, and the other food crops to only the last two to three years.

Establishment of a three-component, interlocking international agricultural research system whose respective foci of activity are based on comparative advantage in manpower, resources, and location gives reason for confidence that new varieties and practices will be developed that will increase the productivity of the new lands and narrow the yield gap for the major food crops.

The first and basic component is the national research and production systems of the developing countries. To be widely adopted, agricultural technology has to be tailored to every crop, every season, every region, every nation; it has to take into account a multitude of strains of insects and diseases, different soils, varying rainfall patterns, and differing consumer preferences. At a minimum, every nation or group of nations must develop a system to implement operational research at the farm level in order to allow selection of experimental lines of the major food crops and the adaptation of farming methods to the environment in which the varieties and practices are to be used. Countries with greater quantities and qualities of scientific personnel may, in addition, want to carry out their own plant breeding programs in order to concentrate on the specific problems of their countries. This is probably the weakest component in the system at present.

The second, newest component is the international agricultural research institutes. These assist developing countries in solving more difficult problems by developing basic lines of crops, training personnel, arranging useful cooperation among nations, and backstopping national programs in other needed ways. They began with the International Rice Research Institute (IRRI), established in the Philippines in 1963. Now a total of eight institutes are funded under sponsorship of the Consultative Group of International Agricultural Research. More are currently on the drawing boards (see Table II-6). Several other institutions of an international nature cooperate closely with these centers. This system now covers most of the major food crops and animals, and extends to most of the geographical areas of the developing world.

The third, probably least exploited component, is the research programs in developed countries. Laboratories and research centers in the advanced countries can play a much needed supportive role in carrying out research which is (1) of both a fundamental and applied nature, or (2) which is outside of the commodity, cropping systems orientation of the international institutes, or (3) which is beyond the capability or not considered a high-priority use of scarce

**Table II-6**

**The Developing International Agricultural Institute Network and the World's Major Food Crops**

PRESENT INTERNATIONAL INSTITUTES (Operational and Planned)[a]

| Center | Commodities | First Year Funded | Location | Agroclimatic Area Served |
|---|---|---|---|---|
| *Operational* | | | | |
| IRRI–The International Rice Research Institute | Rice, multiple cropping | 1960 | Philippines | Rainfed and irrigated areas–subtropical/tropical |
| CIMMYT–The International Maize and Wheat Improvement Center | Wheat, maize, barley, triticale | 1966 | Mexico | Rainfed and irrigated–temperate/tropical |
| IITA–The International Institute of Tropical Agriculture | Corn, rice, cowpeas, soybeans, lima beans, root and tuber crops, and farming systems | 1968 | Nigeria | Rainfed and irrigated low tropics |
| CIAT–The International Center of Tropical Agriculture | Beans (*Ph. vulgaris*), corn, rice, cassava, beef and forages, and swine | 1969 | Colombia | Rainfed and irrigated tropics–1000 meters to sea level |
| CIP–The International Potato Center | Potatoes | 1972 | Peru | Rainfed and irrigated areas–temperate to tropical |
| ICRISAT–The International Crops Research Institute for the Semi-Arid Tropics | Sorghum, millets, peanuts, chickpeas, and pigeon peas | 1972 | India | Semi-arid tropics |
| ILRAD–The International Laboratory for Research on Animal Diseases | Blood diseases of cattle | 1974 | Kenya | Mainly semi-arid tropic |
| ILCA–The International Livestock Centre for Africa | Cattle production | 1974 | Africa | Humid to dry tropics |
| *In Planning Stage* | | | | |
| ICARDA–The International Center for Agricultural Research in Dry Areas | Wheat, barley, lentils, broad beans, oilseeds, cotton, and sheep farming | – | Lebanon | Mediterranean |

Source: *International Research in Agriculture*, Consultative Group on International Agricultural Research, New York, 1974.

[a]CGIAR-sponsored. The Asian Vegetable Research and Development Center (AVRDC) in Taiwan and the Arid Lands Agricultural Development Program (ALAD) are international in character but are not now in the CGIAR group.

scientific resources in the developing countries. There remain numerous promising potentials for improving production through new technology now in the research and development phases.

**Waste.** Despite numerous attempts, we still do not really know how much food waste actually occurs. Wastage occurs at every stage, from the time a crop emerges from the ground until its eventual destruction either as food, feed, or industrial product. There is loss at the farm, in transportation and distribution channels, in storage, and in food preparation and consumption. In many countries, livestock serve as scavengers, collecting lost, unused, spoiled or surplus food, in this way sponging up the otherwise "wasted" resource and storing it in animal tissue to be consumed later. The pig is used as an especially efficient scavenger in many countries throughout the developing world. In modern agricultural societies, the scavenger role of animals has all but disappeared. Estimates of waste in storage range from 5 to 10 percent in the United States and could average as much as 25 percent of the total food supply for the world as a whole. Additional waste outside of storage–due to rot, insects, rodents, birds, and other pests–may total at least this amount. Control of even part of these losses may be the fastest and least costly way of substantially increasing the food available to people who live close to subsistence levels.

Major attention must be directed at reducing losses due to pests and diseases. As science has engineered new plant types and altered their growing environment, plant protection has figured as an essential component of the high-yield package. However, the narrow gene bases of the new grain varieties and their widespread use can now place food staples of whole nations in jeopardy. Attack by a new or newly lethal pest or disease organism against which plants have no adequate defense can severely damage or even wipe out the large-scale plantings now devoted to a single or a few closely related varieties. Modern plant protection has to be as ingenious and persistent as the plant enemies which exhibit astonishing resilience in the face of perennial attempts to destroy or disarm them.

A major aspect of plant protection is chemical control of insect pests. New research is being carried out to develop pesticides that attack only the target insect and do not harm other species or remain in the environment.

Progress is also being made in insect control through the use of pheromones (insect communication media, chiefly sex attractants). Investigators have made considerable progress toward identification and synthesis of the chemicals used by various insects to signal readiness to mate, to warn of danger, or to mark out trails. These compounds can be applied to key locations to disrupt normal patterns of insect reproduction, foraging and nesting, and the like, in order to reduce populations. Sex or danger signals can be used to bait traps so that large numbers of insects can be poisoned. This technique is also useful for monitoring population size as a guide in applying chemical pesticides at appropriate times, thus reducing the total load of chemicals applied to a crop.

Juvenile hormones, anti-juvenile hormones, and hormone mimics have been used experimentally to disrupt insect development at different stages of their life cycles, either killing or sterilizing them.

One of the major tools of plant protection—and one that holds the greatest promise for the low-income farmer who cannot buy agricultural chemicals—is the development of crop varieties that have built-in resistence. Plant pathologists and geneticists are currently aiming at so-called horizontal, or generalized, resistence in all the major food crops. Their objective is to incorporate into a single crop variety those genes needed for resistence to a number of pests and pathogens, as contrasted with single-gene resistence to one plant enemy.

The recent unprecedented movement of germ plasm around the world and the widespread introduction of new crop varieties have revealed the existence of previously unknown pathogens as well as unsuspected virulence in familiar ones. Investigations have proven further that differences in temperatures and other environmental factors can influence the amount of damage done by a pathogen in a given situation. Prediction, monitoring, and control of ravages of pests and diseases are also essential weapons of plant protection strategy. The need for international reporting, communications, quarantine enforcement, and development of models for predicting the spread of disease is widely recognized.

Plant pathologists and entomologists are not counting on any one of these approaches to do the job alone. Their aim is to achieve integrated strategies based on a combination of methods, which can be used in comprehensive plant protection programs.

Major efforts must also be made in improving the distribution systems and in providing pest- and disease-free storage. Inadequate storage facilities, in addition to causing losses in food available for consumption, force the growers to sell their crops at low prices soon after harvest, thereby making it difficult for them to earn an above-subsistence income and also meet their financial obligations. Small container methods utilizing the principle of minimizing the oxygen in stored grains are one way of reducing losses by small farmers.

**Livestock.** Livestock—cattle, water buffalo, swine, chickens, goats, and others—play an important supplementary nutritional role in providing protein, energy, vitamins, and minerals in diets of people in developing countries. Demand for animal products in the developing countries can be expected to increase in the future as living standards improve. Furthermore, animals in developing countries provide a major source of on-farm energy to produce food grains. They play many other roles, including providing a major means of savings.

In contrast to the practices in developed countries, animal production in the developing countries is generally carried out in minimum competition with human beings for food; that is, the animals are grazed or are largely fed waste products. Even though these restricted diets limit the possibilities for growth, actual production is far below potential. Disease is widespread, reproduction rates are low, and weight gains are slow. There obviously is much scope for improvement.

**Aquaculture and Fisheries.** The important potential contribution of aquatic proteins to world human nutrition appears to be little understood by decision-makers. Doubling the world capture fisheries harvest of aquatic animals and a tenfold increase in aquaculture production could be achieved before the end of the century; yet, there are few adequate plans to realize the potential and no significant commitment by the United States or most other nations.

There exists a considerable unrealized potential to increase food production from living aquatic resources. At present, fish provide 14 percent of the world consumption of animal protein, with this percentage varying down to less than 1 percent in some landlocked countries. Coastal developing nations already use living aquatic resources for significant percentages of their high-grade animal proteins, particularly in Southeast Asia where capture fisheries and aquaculture account for more than 60 percent of protein consumption. It is fortunate that many of the developing countries, which are heavily dependent on aquatic animals to provide high quality protein, also possess significant potential to increase production of these resources.

With respect to capture fisheries, the present world yield is about 65 million metric tons per year. The maximum potential world harvest is estimated at about double this amount, with most of the unexploited stocks existing in the waters of or adjacent to developing countries. Direct human consumption of fish (which accounts for about 75 percent of the total catch) has increased annually by 4 percent over the past twenty years. At this rate, it is clear that the demand for fish will surpass the natural resource of the world's oceans and lakes well before the end of the century. If the increasing demands for fish protein are to be met, significant increases in the fish production from aquaculture must be attained.

Present world production from aquaculture is approximately 6 million metric tons per year, or less than 10 percent of the yield from capture fisheries. However, the potential for significantly increasing production from aquaculture is quite promising. In many parts of the developing world, particularly Southeast Asia, aquatic organisms have been successfully cultured for centuries. In these countries, herbivorous species such as mullet and milkfish are cultured in brackish water ponds. Such techniques utilize naturally occurring foods and lead to the production of human food at relatively low costs. Moreover, if methods are developed which allow for routine production of juveniles of these species, the acreage of coastal wetlands devoted to aquaculture could be greatly increased.

There is a direct link between aquaculture and capture fisheries. In Southeast Asia, for example, pond production of mullet and milkfish depends on obtaining a supply of juveniles from natural stocks. As aquaculture expands, more and more juveniles are taken and thus the natural fishery may be imperiled. Consequently, a large and dependable supply of cultured "seed" is a prime necessity for increased aquaculture production.

To realize the potential of aquatic foods requires better understanding of the life processes of the most important species, and improvement in the technology of both aquaculture and capture fisheries. For the less developed nations, improvement is needed especially in pond and estuarine-enclosure forms of aquaculture. The infrastructure to service aquatic food production also needs drastic improvement, and extension services and manpower training are clear requirements.

Most needed, however, is a commitment to the goal of maximizing aquatic food production. The United States is in an ideal position to lead an international effort by applying its scientific and technical skills to both its own requirements and those of the less developed world. U.S. aquaculture already is making a contribution, even with no strong federal policy and support. An International Center for Living Aquatic Resources Management has been established in Hawaii. With a clear and forceful policy, backed by a relatively modest commitment of resources, aquatic protein production can achieve a vital role in world food production while contributing to the American economy and the domestic supply of high quality aquatic foods.

**Government Policy.** Availability of physical resources and development of the knowledge to exploit them is not, by itself, enough. The key to achievement of large production gains is to promote interaction, that is, the total output from the use of several inputs simultaneously and in the proper combinations. This takes a great deal of planning and effective implementation by governments and by farmers to put the proper combinations to use.

Farmers in the low-income countries *will* increase individual agricultural production if they *can*—if a technology is made available to them, including access to the required production inputs that will significantly increase their incomes. The new wheat varieties spread across northern India at a faster rate than hybrid corn was adopted in the U.S. midwest when it was first introduced. Furthermore, governments *can* increase national agricultural production if they *will*. Much experience has been gained in organizing successful national food production programs. A number of nations, including India, Pakistan, the Philippines, and Mexico, all taking advantage of the new high-yielding varieties, have demonstrated the results that a concerted national effort can produce in terms of increased yields.

Schemes like the Puebla Project in Mexico, begun in 1967 to assist small subsistence farmers in a rainfed area, provide evidence that increased food production can be obtained simultaneously with increased income for small farmers and rural laborers. This latter point is important because policymakers must recognize that the problem is not just to produce more food, but also to do so in such a way that the food is distributed to a wide group of people. Therefore, one cannot consider agricultural production in isolation from more general economic development, which has as a goal the distribution of, as well as the total gain in, income.

As yet, few governments have made the policy commitments necessary to fulfill the constructive role they can play in stimulating agricultural development. The reasons for this state of affairs are complex. In large part, however, they stem from greater concern with other priorities, especially the objective of keeping food prices down in an effort to combat domestic inflation or otherwise restrain the cost of living. Such an objective has been implemented by policies to control wholesale and retail prices and to establish public monopolies to purchase domestic and imported grains at low prices.

These policies have, unfortunately, tended to weaken the domestic agricultural base by reducing the incentive for growers to invest, to use modern methods and new technologies, and to sell more food. The impact has been to reduce the volume of domestic food output as well as the portion of that which enters legitimate markets. The net result often is the creation of serious economic dislocations, including the inflationary pressures these policies were originally designed to prevent.

In more general terms, a number of less developed countries have given such a high priority to industrialization that they have even been willing to sacrifice an already efficient agricultural system to this end. Argentina is a classic case in point. This unfortunate tendency to equate economic development with industrialization has prompted some governments to discriminate against agriculture, not only in pricing policies but in many other ways, especially the allocation of funds to finance production and agricultural R&D. Other governments have preferred to sacrifice their agricultural sector for the sake of political ideology.

## IV. Food Availabilities from the United States

We have seen that food production in the less developed countries, while making some progress, is still not up to the level of the needs of these countries. This situation became painfully obvious during the crop shortfalls in 1972 and 1974, when the world had to rely heavily on the surpluses of the major exporting countries. It is necessary, therefore, to examine the potential for the United States, the world's premier agricultural producer and exporter, to supply increasing amounts of food to the food deficit areas of the world.

### *The North American Breadbasket*

The production of food in the United States is one of the world's great development success stories. Early production increases, based on expansion of land under cultivation as the nation's people moved westward, were replaced with rising yields beginning in the late 1930s and early 1940s. The United States today is self-sufficient in the production of most major food crops and is also a major exporter of wheat, rice, feedgrains (corn, sorghum, millets, oats, and barley) and oilseeds (soybeans and peanuts). It accounts for approximately 30 percent of all food commodities shipped in international trade, including approximately (1974-75 projections) 25 percent of the rice, almost 40 percent of the wheat, 50 percent of feedgrains, and over 90 percent of the soybeans (see Figure II-7). Along with Canada, another major exporter, the United States today produces as large a share of the world's exportable surplus of grains as the Middle East does of oil. A significant portion of these exports has been utilized for humanitarian rather than commercial purposes. Billions of dollars worth of food have been either given to other countries or provided at low prices or through low interest loans.

This nation's ascent to the position of the world's major food exporter has, of course, been accompanied by the relative decline in exports of other regions. Between 1934-38 and 1973, Latin America, Eastern Europe and the Soviet Union, Africa and Asia all turned from being net grain exporters to becoming net grain importers. North America, during this period, went from a slight export position to the dominant export position—from average net exports of 5 million metric tons of grains in 1934-38 to 88 million metric tons in 1973 (see Table II-7).

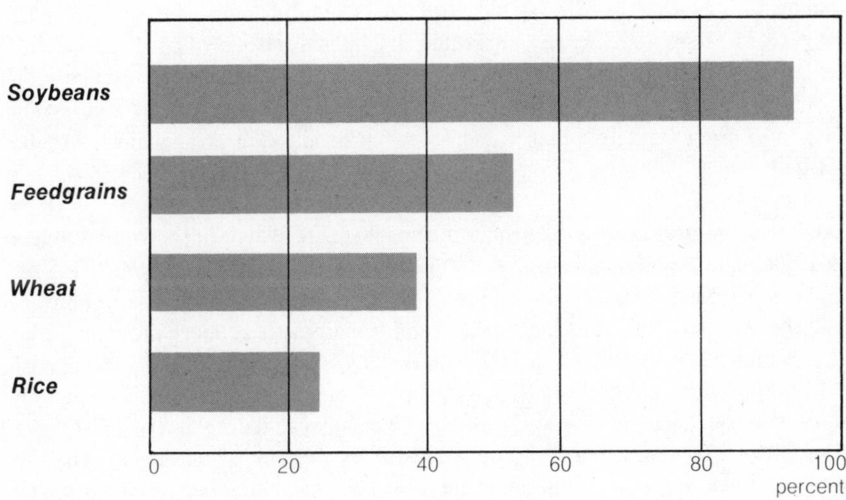


Source: U.S. Department of Agriculture.

**Figure II-7.** Principal U.S. Food Exports as a Percentage of World Food Exports (1974-75 projected)

**Table II-7**
**The Changing Pattern of World Grain Trade**
(million metric tons) units

| Region | 1934-1938 | 1948-1952 | 1960 | 1966 | 1973[a] (prel.) |
|---|---|---|---|---|---|
| North America | +5[b] | +23 | +39 | +59 | +88 |
| Latin America | +9 | + 1 | 0 | + 5 | – 4 |
| Western Europe | –24[b] | –22 | –25 | –27 | –21 |
| Eastern Europe & Soviet Union | +5 | – | 0 | – 4 | –27 |
| Africa | +1 | 0 | – 2 | – 7 | – 4 |
| Asia | +2 | – 6 | –17 | –34 | –39 |
| Australia & New Zealand | +3 | + 3 | + 6 | + 8 | + 7 |

Source: Brown & Eckholm, *By Bread Alone*, Published for the Overseas Development Council, Praeger Publishers, 1974, p. 61. Reprinted with permission.

[a]Fiscal year.

[b](plus-net exports; minus-net imports)

## *Influences on Future Food Availabilities*

There is still considerable room for further increases in U.S. food production. Studies by the U.S. Department of Agriculture (USDA), for instance, estimate that an all-out effort by 1985 could produce 315 million tons of feedgrains (over 50 percent above 1973 levels), including 9.1 billion bushels of corn (up over 60 percent), 2.2 billion bushels of soybeans (up almost 40 percent), and 2.3 billion bushels of wheat (up 35 percent from 1973). The following factors will largely determine the extent to which these potential production gains will actually be realized.

**Land Use.** Approximately 322 million acres were cultivated in the United States in 1974, up considerably from the 289 million acres cultivated in 1972. This expansion reflected such economic incentives as wheat selling for $5 per bushel and the release of all areas set aside under government support programs. The 322 million acres cultivated in 1974 contrasts with the record one-year high of 359 million acres planted in 1929. It is a point of concern that over 160 million acres, the equivalent of roughly one-half of our harvested cropland in 1974, have gone out of farming since the late 1880s. This process is continuing. On the average, a net of 1.25 million acres are lost each year. Some 2.5 million acres of farmed land are converted to other uses–highways, houses, and shopping centers, as well as grass and trees. This is only partially offset by the development of nearly 1.25 million acres of new cropland each year.

There are approximately 300 million acres of Class I, II, and III lands still out of cultivation (areas which are considered potentially available for production).

Some of this land is forested and, to maintain productivity, not all of it should be cropped continuously. At present relationships between farm prices and costs, economic incentives have not been adequate to bring much of this land into production. Some of the land is either held out of production or underutilized because of speculative intentions. However, cultivation and development of as much of this land as is possible is a very important objective if we are to slow the declining availability of agricultural land, the basic resource on which our food supply is dependent. This may require a comprehensive, nationwide land use and development policy.

**Research.** A strong federal, state, and private research system has been a key to the large production gains achieved in the United States, especially since the late 1930s. In fact, this contribution has been the result of sustained efforts extending back to the Morrill Act of 1862, which established the land grant colleges.

Production efficiency of U.S. agriculture, as measured by increases in yields of crops or in feed-to-product conversion ratios in animals, in some cases appears to have slowed in recent years. While there are numerous causes for this decline, the research system may be a primary cause. There has been a trend away from public support for crop production research in the traditional U.S. agricultural research establishments. Federal support for the State Agricultural Experiment Stations system has fallen behind that required to keep up with inflation. New demands to increase research efforts in the areas of environment and rural development have been added. Among the twenty-one national problems warranting greater research and development efforts as reported by the National Science Board of the National Science Foundation in 1973, food production was not listed.

Increasing criticisms are being directed at both the administration and the focus of agricultural research. In particular, some feel that too much attention is being paid to routine duplicative research of a marginal nature as opposed to pursuing "frontier" types of research, which must be carried out to support the high agricultural growth rates needed in the future, whether in the United States or in the developing countries. Numerous promising potentials exist for improving production through research of a "frontier" nature.

The high-yielding varieties of wheat and rice were developed by manipulating natural cross-breeding and selection mechanisms to restructure plant types and introduce genes for disease resistance, fertilizer responsiveness, early maturity, day-length insensitivity, high-lysine levels, and other desirable traits. The concept of breeding crops to specification (called biological engineering) leads logically to the idea of crossing unrelated species to achieve superior plants never found in nature. A number of useful crosses have been made between different species of the same genera. A much rarer occurrence is a cross between different genera. Triticale, a hybrid of wheat and rye, represents one such cross that has been successful. Although it is still under intense study, triticale clearly can be of great commercial value.

Breeders are now attempting to cross wheat with barley and with oats and to cross barley with rye. One technique utilizes chemical immunosuppressants of the kind used on animals and human beings to prevent rejection of transplanted tissues and organs in order to prepare female parent plants for pollination. Another radical approach to biological engineering is development of new crop varieties and strains by artificially fusing the somatic (or body) cells of plants that are too genetically different to mate. Crosses between selected parent plants that have superior traits—resistance to disease, the ability to fix atmospheric nitrogen in association with soil bacteria, tolerance to cold or heat or drought, for example—could conceivably result in hardier, higher-yielding, more nutritious crops than have yet been evolved by nature or engineered by man. Fertile hybrids already have been developed by each of these techniques.

Symbiotic and nonsymbiotic fixation of atmospheric nitrogen by soil bacteria has been an object of scientific research for years, but a marked drop in interest occurred around the mid-1960s, when nitrogen fertilizer could be cheaply manufactured. Recently, the research focus has returned to search for means of exploiting this phenomenon for the alleviation of food and fertilizer shortages. The high-input, high-yield technologies based on new crop varieties are most important for those nations of the developing world where agricultural land is becoming scarce, and those are precisely the nations where the cost of fertilizer is becoming prohibitive. In these circumstances, plants that can manufacture their own fertilizer out of air have a distinct advantage.

The earth's atmosphere is 78 percent gaseous nitrogen, giving about 30,000 tons over each acre of land, but only a few species of plants are able to tap this nutrient source. Nitrogen-fixing soil bacteria live both independently and in association with certain plants, chiefly (but not exclusively) the legumes. Scientists are searching for ways of extending the range of host plants, and some work is being done on use of free-living forms of nitrogen-fixing organisms. More intensive exploitation of the legumes for this purpose is also under active investigation. Another possibility being explored is crossing legume species with nonlegumes through unconventional plant-breeding techniques, such as cell and tissue culture.

The foregoing examples of "frontier" type research (wide crosses and nitrogen fixation) do not begin to exhaust the list of the many promising opportunities which exist. Previously some of the new strategies for pest control were mentioned. Other possibilities include increasing the photosynthetic efficiency and inhibiting photorespiration of plants genetically, physically, and chemically; water and fertilizer management (trickle irrigation, foliar application, and timely placement of materials); improved grain quality (especially amino acid balances in foodgrains); protected cultivation; carbon dioxide enrichment; multiple and intensive relay cropping (which has especially great potential for the tropics and for developing countries); plant growth regulants; treatments of plant substances, such as cotton seed meal, for human consumption; use of nonprotein nitrogen in ruminant rations; use of crop residues, animal wastes, and other methods for optimal utilization of crop acreages for livestock feeding; livestock crossbreeding; and increased fertility and disease control in livestock.

Continued support for the U.S. research system is essential, whether to counter emergencies, as was so ably demonstrated in the response to the corn blight attack in the Midwest in 1970, or to guarantee long-term high growth rates.

**Crop Vulnerability.** U.S. agriculture has enjoyed generally favorable weather over the past twenty years—that is, until the series of events which happened in 1974—spring rains which delayed some planting followed by a severe summer drought in the Midwest and then an early frost. However, just four years earlier, the U.S. Midwest was hit by a severe attack of Southern corn blight disease, which depressed production significantly. The U.S. Midwest has experienced severe droughts on approximately a twenty-year cycle. The 1974 drought fit into this pattern, although the reasons for this occurrence are not known. Southern corn blight persists in minor degrees every year, but a combination of factors, including varieties available to farmers having a too narrow germ plasm base and ideal weather conditions for spread of the disease, increased the severity of outbreak beyond normal limits. These two events underscore the fact that neither weather nor protection against pestilence can be taken for granted. The growing dependence on food exports from North America places the rest of the world in a highly vulnerable position in the event of crop failure.

**Food Prices.** The sudden rise in food prices in 1973 was a shock to consumers and temporary delight to producers. The delight proved "temporary" because production costs also rose significantly—taking away some of the attractive profits which might otherwise have resulted.

The U.S. consumer will have to get used to the fact that food prices probably will continue to be higher in the future than they were in the past. For one thing, some prices, especially those of grains, were depressed during the years immediately preceding 1972. For another, costs have risen significantly. Unless it is profitable for farmers to produce food, crops could turn out to be way below potential output, with limited surpluses available for the food-deficit countries. The only way to maintain profits and generate lower prices to consumers would be to increase productivity, not only in production, but also in the distribution and marketing ends of the business.

**Environment.** The major environmental problem related to agricultural production of thirty years ago—wind erosion, as most dramatically exemplified by the

Dust Bowl–has improved significantly. In its place, public concern has shifted to the environmental consequences of the high levels of fertilizers and pesticides now in use.

The available evidence does not demonstrate that the environmental hazards of present levels of fertilizer or pesticide use in U.S. agriculture are unacceptably high. Agricultural fertilizers generally have been found to be a minor contributor to excessive nitrate levels in water. The Illinois Pollution Control Board has determined that only about 25 percent of the phosphate in streams and lakes was attributable to agriculture; the rest comes from detergents and sewage. The evidence linking pesticide use to environmental abuse usually has been of an indirect nature. There have been a limited number of widely publicized incidents where deaths to endangered species have been related to pesticide use. However, the occasional large kills of animals and fish which have been linked to pesticide use generally have not persisted; the damaged populations generally have recovered. The EPA decisions to ban dieldrin and aldrin, two of the more highly publicized chlorinated hydrocarbons (in addition to DDT), were based on experimental evidence linking them to cancer in mice; threats to human life have not been demonstrated.

A significant portion of irrigated land is reportedly adversely affected by salinity. Of the other potential environmental threats, water erosion constitutes a recognized but manageable problem while loss of habitat, desertification, and destruction of soil fertility do not appear to be serious in the United States.

It should be noted that these conclusions are based on present levels of use. Although difficult to predict with certainty, the results could be, and probably would be, quite different if new lands were cultivated on a continuous basis or if fertilizer and pesticides were used at much higher levels than under present practices, which would be necessary to support higher levels of production. However, new practices might be developed which could minimize the deleterious impact of the increased use of fertilizers and pesticides upon the environment. This is an area which requires serious study to bring new facts to light, to establish the validity of existing knowledge, and to enable the public to weigh the trade-offs of obtaining efficiency in killing pests without doing damage to the environment.

**Structure of the Industry.** The very successful development of U.S. agriculture has in turn had a remarkable impact on the structure of the industry. Spurred originally by acute labor scarcity and a growing national demand for food and fibers, individual American farmers turned to mechanical aids to expand productivity and output–the cotton gin, the reaper, the steel plow, the thresher, the twine binder. Research and education played a major role in the development of U.S. agricultural technology, aided by the land grant colleges and agricultural extension stations. Research results were put to effective use by American farmers because they were given a financial incentive to produce more.

If anything, U.S. agriculture has been too productive, creating problems of what to do with surpluses.

Aided by such capital-intensive technological advances, U.S. agriculture has evolved into an industry where greater production has been achieved on the same land with more inputs, fewer and bigger farms, fewer farmers with greater income per farm and with higher debt and equity positions (see Tables II-8 and II-9). Government programs, the scale of operation required to achieve economies in production, and certain advantages in both the buying of inputs and the selling of commodities have all contributed to a shift in the structure of the industry in favor of "agrobusiness."

Serious questions can be raised about whether this result was inevitable. Equally serious questions have been raised about whether this process should be encouraged to continue in the future. However, the economies of large-scale production units are so compelling given today's costs and technology that only with such units are we likely to come anywhere close to our food output potential.

**Table II-8**
**Changes in U.S. Agriculture Since 1960: Farms**

Fewer and Bigger Farms[a]

| | Farms with Sales Over $20,000 Per Year (thousands) | Farms with Sales Under $20,000 Per Year (thousands) | Total Farms (thousands) |
|---|---|---|---|
| 1960 | 440 | 3,520 | 3,963 |
| 1965 | 441 | 2,915 | 3,356 |
| 1970 | 578 | 2,376 | 2,954 |
| 1972 | 695 | 2,175 | 2,870 |
| 1973 | 1,009 | 1,835 | 2,844 |
| 1974 | 1,000 | 1,800 | 2,800 |

More Inputs on Same Amount of Land[b]

| | Index of Farm Input Use (1967 = 100) | | |
|---|---|---|---|
| | Mechanical Power | Real Estate | Fertilizer |
| 1960 | 92 | 101 | 54 |
| 1965 | 95 | 101 | 80 |
| 1970 | 101 | 98 | 113 |
| 1972 | 102 | 101 | 120 |
| 1973 | 105 | 97 | 124 |
| 1974 | 106 | 101 | 128 |

Note: All figures for 1974 are estimated.

[a]Number of farms: *Farm Income Situation* (Washington, D.C.: U.S. Department of Agriculture, July 1974).

[b]*Economic Report of the President* (Washington, D.C., U.S. Government Printing Office, February 1974), p. 348.

**Table II-9**
**Changes in U.S. Agriculture Since 1960: Income**

Greater Production, Higher Debt, More Equity[a]

| | Crop Production (1967 = 100) | Livestock Production (1967 = 100) | Acres Harvested (millions) | Total Farm Debt (billions) | Farmers' Equity (billions) |
|---|---|---|---|---|---|
| 1960 | 92 | 87 | 324 | $24.8 | $178 |
| 1965 | 99 | 95 | 298 | 37.6 | 200 |
| 1970 | 101 | 105 | 293 | 58.1 | 247 |
| 1972 | 113 | 108 | 294 | 66.9 | 274 |
| 1973 | 120 | 107 | 322 | 73.7 | 310 |
| 1974 | 114 | 108 | 320 | 81.7 | 378 |

Fewer Farmers, Greater Income[b]

| | Farm Population (millions) | Average Net Farm Income (per farm) | Average Per Capita Income | |
|---|---|---|---|---|
| | | | Farm | Nonfarm |
| 1960 | 15.64 | $ 2,796 | $1,071 | $2,020 |
| 1965 | 12.36 | 3,573 | 1,668 | 2,486 |
| 1970 | 9.71 | 4,750 | 2,482 | 3,421 |
| 1972 | 9.61 | 6,150 | 3,153 | 3,876 |
| 1973 | 9.47 | 11,332 | 4,820 | 4,270 |
| 1974 | 9.30 | 10,000 | 4,290 | 4,680 |

Note: All figures for 1974 are estimated.

[a]Crop and livestock production and acres harvested: *Economic Report of the President* (Washington, D.C.: U.S. Government Printing Office, February 1974). Total farm debt and farmers' equity: *Agricultural Finance Outlook* (Washington, D.C.: U.S. Department of Agriculture, March 1974).

[b]Farm population: *Economic Report of the President* (Washington, D.C.: U.S. Government Printing Office, February 1974). Average net farm and per capita income: *Farm Income Situation* (Washington, D.C.: U.S. Department of Agriculture, July 1974).

**Hunger in America.** Hunger and malnutrition are not commonly considered to be the lot of Americans. Individual income levels have risen considerably, especially since the end of the Second World War, so that Americans today have achieved one of the highest living standards in the world. The federally-defined poverty level continues to rise and for most Americans the need to obtain adequate food is no longer a critical problem.

Despite this success, there are still pockets of poverty where segments of the population–low income minorities, the aged, the poor–do suffer from inadequate and unbalanced diets. Anemia and deficiencies of Vitamin C and protein persist among these segments. Many of these people live in rural areas and have been "left behind" by the technological change in agriculture.

The recent inflation has hit particularly hard at the food budgets of low-income American families. While the average American family spends about 16 percent of its income on food, a low-income American family is spending 44.2 percent. As consumers of all income classes seek to "spend down" to cheaper food items, the increased demand tends to force up prices even of the less expensive foods.

The food problem in the United States, in sharp contrast to that of many less developed countries, is not so much one of inadequate production, but rather one of maldistribution. Efforts are already underway to get food to those people who are hard pressed to pay for it—through food stamps and school lunch programs.

A portion of America's food supplies will continue to be allocated on a priority basis to the undernourished people of America. But if overall food production can continue to expand, there should be sufficient supplies to cover domestic requirements and help contribute to meeting the demands of the rest of the world.

**Meat Consumption.** The people of the developed countries have a high proportion of their diets in the form of meat, much of which comes from animals that have been fed with cereal grains. Because of this, the people of the developed countries consume directly and indirectly several times the amount of food grains as the people of the less developed countries. In many cases, they consume more meat than they should, based on health considerations. In a food-short world where the people of the developing countries spend a high percentage of their income on food and, due to the fact that their incomes are low, a big percentage of that food is in the form of cereal grains, many argue that meat production is a very inefficient calorie use of cereal grains. Therefore, there are frequent proposals that the public "eat one less hamburger" (or take one less drink). Some even argue that much less encouragement should be given to production of meat and animal products in the future.

Farm animals, particularly ruminants, have a unique ability to convert feeds other than cereals and oilseeds into protein for human consumption. These other feeds consist of forages, by-products, and nonprotein sources of nitrogen. In addition to the utilization of feedstuffs that would otherwise be wasted, it should also be noted that much of the grain fed to produce our beef supply is of low quality which would exclude its use for human foods. By capitalizing on this ability of the ruminant, many marginal feedstuffs are salvaged through beef cattle for conversion to highly valued and highly nutritious human food. Large portions of the world's land can be used only for grazing animals.

Even the United States, pasture and roughage provide most of the feed for livestock. However, a significant portion of the meat consumed in the Western countries is finished off with a diet which is heavily weighted with soy products and cereal grains. Normally, about three-quarters of the beef cattle receive their final several hundred pounds of weight from confined feeding. This practice has been followed because consumers prefer the taste of grain-finished meat, grain prices have been relatively low, and it has been profitable to "finish" beef with grain feed. For example, American farmers in 1971 could obtain from every dollar's worth of feedgrain, $4.15 from beef, but only $1.26 worth of cornmeal.

The recent high price of meat to consumers and the cost/price squeeze on producers in 1974 and 1975 accomplished some reductions in livestock production. Hog producers planned in the fall of 1975 to breed the fewest number of sows in ten years, the number of cattle on feed was the smallest in over six years, poultry production was cut by a tenth, and Western Europe voluntarily cut back its imports of feedgrains from the United States. The proportion of beef cattle finished on feedgrains declined to about 60 percent of the total, with a consequent reduction in demand for feedgrains and soybeans for this purpose.

However, reduced grain finishing of cattle is not, by itself, a long-term answer to the world food problem. Once grain is "released" from use in animal feed, some mechanism must be set up to transfer it to the grain deficit nations. In the longer run, if the "released" U.S. foodgrains are not sold, prices fall and incentives are weakened for U.S. farmers to produce foodgrains at maximum capacity.

There are constructive programs which could reduce the competition of animals for cereals in the future. For example, much could be done to upgrade the quality of pastures through new grasses, more fertilizer and better management. The amount of maintenance feeding could be reduced. The processing and utilization of by-products and waste production could be explored more deeply to develop nutritious animal feeds using waste products. Changes in meat grading standards have been approved which could lead to economies in the feeding of U.S. animals.

Discussion in this policy area has often been characterized by emotion rather than solid information. There is a priority need to identify the issues, sort out what is known and not known, and then develop better information and understanding as a basis on which to formulate intelligent policy.

**Grain Reserves.** In 1961, world grain reserves represented a ninety-five-day supply. These reserves gradually declined to a low point of twenty-seven days in 1974 (see Figure II-8). Much of this amount, however, represents a "pipeline" figure, that is, food which is already committed to future use but is to be replaced by new production expected shortly. Measured in terms of food available for immediate shipment to meet emergencies, the world was reduced to only a five-day reserve.

At present rates of production and utilization, global grain reserves will generally remain on the low side for the immediate future. Clearly, this paper-thin margin offers little safety to areas faced with potential famine and is also highly destabilizing to the world commodity markets.

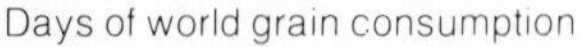


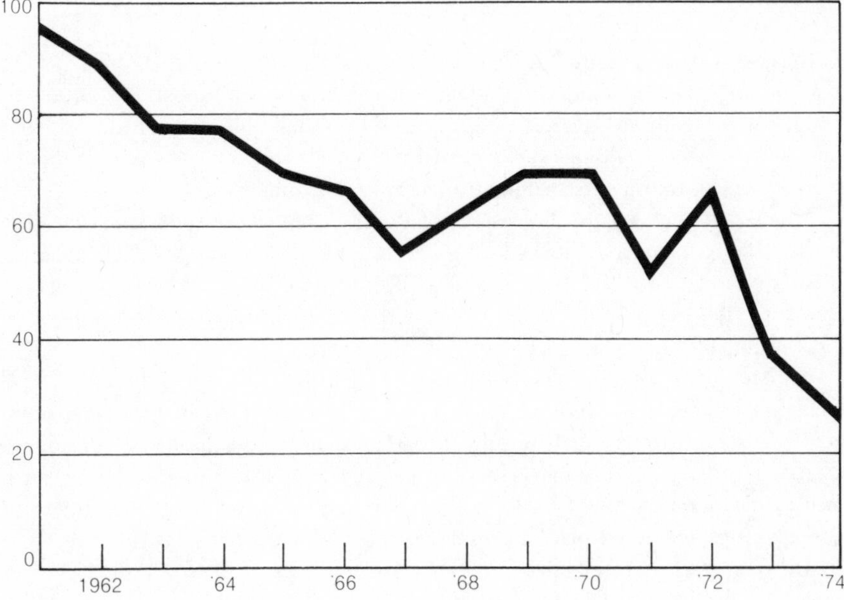


Note: "Reserves as days of grain consumption" takes into account the grain that could be produced on idled U.S. crop land as well as actual worldwide grain reserves.

Source: U.S. Department of Agriculture.

**Figure II-8.** World Grain Reserves

In the recent past, the United States was able to serve as the world's granary in times of want. This capability developed as a side effect of domestic farm policies which led to the accumulation of huge food surpluses in the 1950s and 1960s. These reserves were virtually exhausted with the massive wheat sale to the Soviet Union in 1972.

There now appears to be little domestic political inclination to rebuild these stocks. The price support system which encouraged surpluses in effect forced consumers and taxpayers to finance them, while creating the serious problem of how to dispose of the accumulated surpluses without disrupting the commodities markets.

Present discussions, therefore, are shifting to considerations of how to establish an international food reserve. The whole series of issues involving size, who finances, who holds, who has access, the rules for release, and the rules for replenishment are being intensely debated in the meetings of the World Food Council.

## V. Conclusions

Government policy until the past few years had been related primarily to maintaining farm incomes in the face of continuing surpluses. The problems today of intermittent scarcities, the need to rebuild depleted food reserves, and whether there will be sufficient food to meet the expected world population increase, require a reassessment of U.S. agricultural policy.

Americans face many choices in relation to this world food situation. The most basic choice concerns whether or not we should get involved at all in efforts to increase world food supplies. There would be three basic reasons for doing so: (1) for political or strategic purposes, (2) for economic purposes or (3) for humanitarian reasons.

If Americans should decide in favor of efforts to expand world food availabilities, we face another critical choice in how this can best be accomplished—either through distributing abroad an increasing amount of our domestic food output or through efforts to expand agriculture production abroad. While, in practice, we will likely both export food and encourage the growth of foreign crops, where we place the emphasis could make a crucial difference.

By their very nature, critical choices are not easy choices. Critical choices regarding food are especially difficult because of their life and death implications. But for this very reason, it is essential that they be consciously made. A decision to continue present policies does not enable us to escape the issue since this is as much a choice as are new policies emphasizing increased U.S. food production and distribution, or increased food production in the less developed countries. The difference is that we may be less conscious of having chosen, and of the consequences of our choice.

## Bibliography

Panel II of the Commission on Critical Choices for Americans acknowledges the following as sources for this report:

1. The Population Council and its publications, 245 Park Avenue, New York, New York.

2. The Rockefeller Foundation, 111 West 50th Street, New York, New York.

3. *1975 World Population Data Sheet*, Population Reference Bureau, Inc., Washington, D.C.

4. Dorothy Nortman, "Population and Family Planning Programs: A Factbook," Reports on Population/Family Planning No. 2, 7th edition (New York: The Population Council, October 1975).

5. Lester Brown and Erik Eckholm, *By Bread Alone*, Published for the Overseas Development Council (New York: Praeger Publishers, 1974).

6. "The People Left Behind: Rural Poverty in the United States," a Report by the President's National Advisory Commission on Rural Poverty (Washington, D.C.: Government Printing Office, May 1968).

7. *The World Food Situation and the Prospects to 1985*, Economic Research Service, U.S. Department of Agriculture, Foreign Agricultural Economic Report No. 98 (Washington, D.C.: Government Printing Office, December 1974).

8. Food and Agriculture Organization of the United Nations, *Production Yearbook*, Vol. 27 (Rome, 1973).

9. *Development and Spread of High-Yielding Varieties of Wheat and Rise in the Less Developed Nations*, U.S. Department of Agriculture, Foreign Agricultural Economic Report No. 95 (Washington, D.C.: Government Printing Office, July 1974).

10. *International Research in Agriculture*, Consultative Group on International Agricultural Research (New York, 1974).

11. *Foreign Agriculture Circular*, U.S. Department of Agriculture, Foreign Agricultural Service (Washington, D.C.: Government Printing Office, Dec. 22, 1975).

12. George Stevens, "Former Cropland in the U.S.: An Analysis of Historic Peaks in Acreage of Cropland Harvested, 1880-1969," U.S. Department of Agriculture, Manuscript, Natural Resource Economics Division.

13. *Science Indicators 1972*, National Science Board, National Science Foundation (Washington, D.C., 1973).

14. Joseph R. Barse, "Feeding Grain to Livestock in the Face of Human Hunger," Economic Research Service, U.S. Department of Agriculture.

15. Preparatory Committee of the World Food Conference, *Assessment Present Food Situation and Dimensions and Causes of Hunger and Malnutrition in the World: The Magnitude of the Food Problem in the Future and Possible Approaches to a Solution*, United Nations Economic and Social Council, May 8, 1974.

16. *The World Food Problem*, Report by the President's Science Advisory Committee, Vol. II (Washington, D.C.: Government Printing Office, May 1967).

17. *The World Food Problem: Proposals for National and International Action*, United Nations World Food Conference (Rome, November 1974).

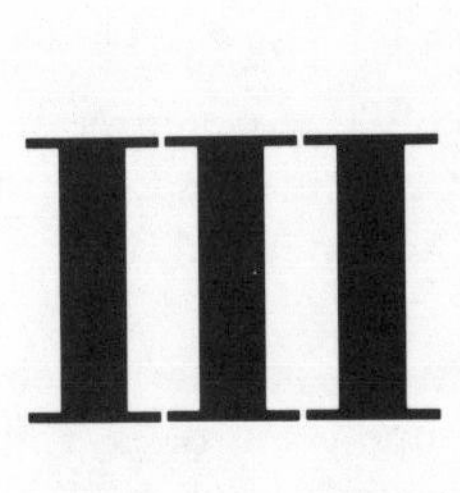

# Report of Panel III: Raw Materials, Industrial Development, Capital Formation, Employment, and World Trade

## I. Overview of Critical Choices

Some seventy years ago, Theodore Roosevelt called attention to the use and misuse of the nation's natural resources. From time to time, others have recognized the problem and called for better management of these resources. Most notable, perhaps, was the President's Materials Policy Commission Report of 1952, commonly known as the "Paley Report," which remains today the materials report by which all others are measured. This commission strongly advocated a national policy for the management of our natural resources. More recently, there was the 1973 report of the National Commission on Materials Policy that succeeded, for a brief time, in bringing the problems of raw materials into the public eye.

Traditionally, however, raw materials have not provided an issue that has gripped the public imagination. Concern instead has focused on the end-use of raw materials—the products and conveniences that form our standard of living. Only in times of specific shortages, has interest focused on the materials themselves. Yet, raw materials are the silent partner in many of the key problems affecting our daily lives. The problems of raw materials run through virtually every critical area Americans now have to contend with: the state of the domestic economy; energy and the environment; fertilizers and food; national security; the quality of life; international trade; and world economic and political security.

This report represents a gathering together of available information—not newly researched findings—that is aimed at a fuller understanding of raw materials and the choices the American people face in assuring adequate supplies.

The focus of the report is the nonenergy raw materials that are reduced to metals. Energy issues are discussed in the Commission's Panel I report (Chapter I in this volume). Although many minerals are discussed, the report concentrates on the most strategic ones.

In raw materials, we encounter two critical, and interrelated problems: (1) in the long run, how can we prevent basic supply shortages, and (2) in the short run, how can we avoid disruptions in our supplies and, failing that, how can we adjust effectively.

In considering potential long-run supply shortages, we face three critical choices. Should the United States:

1. continue to rely almost exclusively on the price mechanism and use imports to cover domestic supply deficiencies; or
2. adopt selective government policies to stimulate domestic supply and conserve on materials usage, thereby limiting dependence on imports and providing greater assurance that domestic raw materials requirements will be met; or
3. adopt major government policies to reduce dependence on imports as much as possible by accelerating the production of domestic raw materials and the conservation of scarce materials?

The first choice constitutes a market-oriented approach. It assumes that the demand and supply of minerals are sufficiently responsive to price changes to assure an adequate flow of minerals throughout the U.S. economy. Imports are not viewed as a problem, but rather as a desired response to the price mechanism.

The second choice entails somewhat greater government involvement than at present for either or both of two reasons: (1) market forces may be too slow to prevent harmful shortages; (2) a heavy reliance on imports may pose too great a risk, in terms of economic stability and national security. Accordingly, selective government programs to accelerate domestic minerals output and to conserve on minerals use would help reduce reliance on foreign sources of supply.

The third choice, to some extent representing a difference in degree from the second choice, is based on a considerable skepticism about any U.S. reliance on imports. There is concern about the ability of foreign countries to produce adequate supplies of raw materials, especially since governments have been assuming increasing control over such activities. There is also concern about whether these countries will allocate their available supplies to our market or will use them to support their own development needs. The trend toward more foreign processing and fabrication may heighten U.S. vulnerability, especially if it causes a decline in U.S. facilities for minerals processing and metals fabrication. For these reasons, it is considered necessary to maximize U.S. materials self-sufficiency, even if this means that our government must interfere significantly with market forces.

In regard to short-run supply disruptions, the United States can choose a number of different policy options, ranging from domestic rationing and stockpile programs to the development of diversified sources of supply abroad. The particular choice selected, however, would need to be related to one of the three long-run choices.

The following sections examine all these critical choices in some detail. Special consideration is given to the kinds of programs and policies needed to implement each choice and to the impact of each choice on the economy, the environment, and our foreign relations.

In setting forth these alternative choices for long- and short-term raw materials policies, the Panel realized that it could touch only the general directions of future action. Specific details needed for implementing any of these choices must, and should, be left to the decisions of industry and the government.

There are however, several themes that recur throughout this report that deserve special mention. The first is that the problems facing the materials industries are economic and political, not physical. We have been told in the recent past that the world is about to run out of many of its key materials. Geological investigations, however, indicate that this is simply not so. Management, not physical supply, is the key to any raw materials policy.

Second, we have been reminded again and again that the problems of raw materials are the problems of nearly every sector of our society. They cannot be viewed in a vacuum. Perhaps the best example of this lies in the relationship of raw materials to energy. The two interreact at virtually every stage, leading to the overriding conclusion that the United States cannot formulate an energy policy—or a raw materials policy—without taking into account one's impact upon the other.

Finally, we have seen how truly interdependent the world has become for its raw materials supplies, and how fragile that interdependence can be. In discussing a U.S. raw materials policy, we must be prepared to view its impact upon the rest of the world—not only in terms of our own national security, but in terms of the national security and economic well-being of other nations.

If the Panel, through this report, has succeeded in bringing these three points thoughtfully to the public's attention, we believe we will have made a meaningful contribution to the America of the future.

## II. A Profile of the Raw Materials Situation

In 1973 and 1974, virtually all raw materials were in short supply. This was reflected in record high prices for most metals (see Table III-1), despite large sales of a long list of U.S. stockpiled materials.

Although early 1975 saw a marked decrease in prices, future economic and/or political shortages of raw materials may once again be highly destabilizing to the

**Table III-1**
**Representative Metal Prices**
(1960 = 100) units

| | Metal | | | | | | | |
|---|---|---|---|---|---|---|---|---|
| Year | Nickel | Chromium | Aluminum | Copper | Tin | Platinum Group | Lead | Zinc |
| 1960 | 100.0 | 100.0 | 100.0 | 100.0 | 100.0 | 100.0 | 100.0 | 100.0 |
| 1961 | 109.4 | 97.1 | 98.1 | 93.1 | 111.7 | 84.0 | 91.0 | 89.2 |
| 1962 | 106.7 | 104.3 | 91.9 | 95.3 | 113.0 | 90.0 | 80.6 | 89.2 |
| 1963 | 106.7 | 104.3 | 86.9 | 95.3 | 115.0 | 100.0 | 93.2 | 92.3 |
| 1964 | 106.7 | 91.3 | 91.2 | 99.7 | 155.5 | 114.0 | 114.0 | 104.6 |
| 1965 | 105.3 | 89.8 | 94.2 | 109.0 | 175.7 | 118.0 | 133.9 | 111.5 |
| 1966 | 114.8 | 91.3 | 94.2 | 112.8 | 161.7 | 126.0 | 126.5 | 111.5 |
| 1967 | 126.9 | 94.2 | 96.2 | 119.0 | 151.3 | 142.0 | 117.2 | 106.9 |
| 1968 | 139.1 | 114.5 | 98.5 | 130.2 | 146.1 | 144.0 | 110.5 | 103.8 |
| 1969 | 172.8 | 132.6 | 104.6 | 149.2 | 162.1 | 158.0 | 124.9 | 113.1 |
| 1970 | 172.8 | 144.9 | 110.4 | 181.3 | 171.7 | 152.0 | 131.3 | 117.7 |
| 1971 | 180.0 | 160.8 | 111.5 | 162.0 | 165.0 | 146.0 | 116.2 | 123.8 |
| 1972 | 189.0 | 124.6 | 96.2 | 159.5 | 175.0 | 156.0 | 125.8 | 136.9 |
| 1973 | 206.6 | 107.2 | 97.3 | 185.3 | 224.5 | 216.0 | 136.3 | 159.2 |
| 1974 | 234.9 | 188.4 | 150.0 | 240.8 | 390.8 | 314.0 | 188.5 | 276.9 |
| 1975[a] | 274.1 | 397.0 | 152.3 | 200.3 | 344.8 | 358.0 | 180.6 | 300.8 |

Source: Calculated from U.S. Department of the Interior, Bureau of Mines, "Minerals and Materials: A Monthly Survey," November 1975.

[a]Average of six months for platinum group, eight months for tin, nine months for nickel, copper and zinc, ten months for chromium and aluminum, twelve months estimate for lead.

entire U.S. economy. Indeed, there is concern in some quarters that a return to the high economic growth rates of the 1960s could cause raw materials prices to soar once again.

### *The Nature of the Situation*

Contrary to most public opinion, the tight supplies and high prices in 1973 and 1974 did not result from a physical shortage of raw materials in the ground. Rather, they resulted from a culmination of economic factors both in the United States and throughout the world.

**The Impact of Economic Factors on the Supply of Raw Materials.** The main cause for the record high minerals prices was the concurrent economic expansion of the world's major consuming nations, which reached its peak in 1973. Strong economic growth in the United States, Europe, and Japan fueled an increased demand for all types of raw materials. Countries aggressively outbid one another for limited raw materials supplies.

The impact of increased real demand was heightened by a combination of other factors:

1. Industrial demand for inventories strengthened, in expectation both of higher prices and shortfalls in materials production.
2. The high cost of money delayed capacity expansions, as did uncertainties about the strength and duration of the sudden increase in demand.
3. The implementation of pollution control standards curtailed some operations and, by increasing costs, reduced incentives to expand production capacity.
4. Price controls stimulated domestic demand and, at the same time, encouraged the export of U.S. materials to markets where prices were not subject to controls.
5. Worldwide inflation and the devaluation of the U.S. dollar created an atmosphere which encouraged speculative flights into gold and other commodities.
6. Special production and transportation problems affected copper, aluminum, and phosphate.
7. Some producing countries attempted to raise the price of their commodities, either through holding back on exports or through increasing taxes on their mining companies, e.g., Jamaican bauxite.

Although this exact constellation of forces is unlikely to occur again, wide price swings are typical of commodity markets and could once again prove to be destabilizing to the U.S. economy.

**Not a Geological Limit.** The short supplies and high prices of metals in 1973-1974 do not signal that the world has entered the age of materials shortages—no physical shortages of raw materials exist in the world today and are not likely to exist in the foreseeable future. While a specific raw material is finite, there is no cause for concern about physical shortages because of the nature of raw materials and what they are used for.

Most metals and other materials are, to some extent, substitutes for one another. For example, aluminum, glass, paper, and plastic are substitutes for tin in cans and containers; plastics are substitutes for lead in building construction and electrical cable covering; aluminum and plastics can substitute for chromium on automobiles and nickel and zinc can substitute for chromium in plating iron and steel for corrosive-resistance purposes; aluminum can substitute for copper in some uses.

To be sure, substitution has its costs—both in terms of money and possibly altered physical properties of the end product. For many purposes and certainly in times of emergency, these costs may be tolerable.

In addition, once a metal is extracted from the ground, it is not gone forever. It is still around; the question is whether and how much of it is in usable form. Recycling can extend the economic life of some metals that have been brought to the surface and put into end use.

Contrary to popular opinion, it is not the supply in the ground, but the economic and technological considerations of getting that supply out of the ground and into production and use that determine the availability or nonavailability of raw materials.

Minerals resources can be classified in two ways—according to their economic recoverability and according to their geological availability. "Reserves" are economically recoverable materials in identified or known deposits. Nonreserve resources include deposits that cannot be economically recovered now and deposits which are geologically probable.[1] This classification can be visualized in Figure III-1.

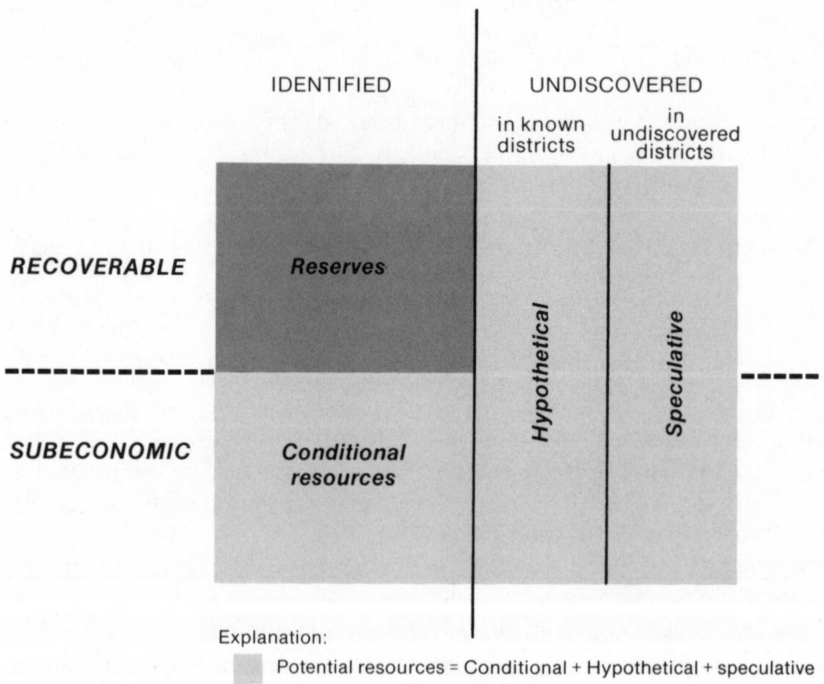


Note: Classification developed by Vincent E. McKelvy, director of the U.S. Geological Survey.

Source: *U.S. Mineral Resources*, Geological Survey Professional Report 820, U.S. Department of the Interior, p. 4.

**Figure III-1.** Classification of Minerals Resources

There is still inadequate information on the size of reserves and inadequate knowledge about long-term trends in costs per unit of new reserves, which would indicate whether discovery and exploration technology is keeping pace with the reduction in the remaining resource base. Known reserves may represent only a small fraction of total primary resources. Discovery, technological advances, and changes in economic conditions are factors which can turn potential resources into proven reserves. Discovery increases the amount of our identified resources. With improved technology, we are better able to discover deep ore bodies and to mine ores of low mineral content. With higher prices, many subeconomic resources become economically recoverable.

Higher prices not only tend to expand reserves and to increase minerals output, they also work to restrict demand. More abundant and less costly materials begin to substitute for the higher priced ores. Efforts are made to recycle products and materials in order to conserve the scarce and more costly minerals. Thus, it may be more appropriate to consider the size of domestic reserves as a flow of minerals which responds to economic forces, rather than a stock of materials in the ground.

Moreover, some state taxation systems may have the unintended effect of minimizing the size of published reserves. In those states using *ad valorem* taxes, such as Colorado, mining companies may have a tax incentive to hold back on the exploration and development of reserves. The greater their reserves, the higher the valuation of their mines upon which they are assessed, and hence, the higher their tax liabilities.

The popular view that the world's mineral resources are being rapidly depleted, advanced by the Club of Rome in its book, *The Limits to Growth,*[2] may thus be seriously misleading. The Club of Rome does not appear to give adequate attention to the importance of discovery, technological advances, and economic conditions. The opposite extreme has been stated by Professor Wilfred Beckerman of the University of London:

> At no point of time is it worth prospecting for enough to last to the end of eternity, or even some compromise period, such as a 100 million years, or even 1,000 years. New reserves are found, on the whole, as they are needed, and needs do not always rise exponentially at past rates. In fact, given the natural concentrations of the key metals in the earth's crust, as indicated by a large number of random samples, the total natural occurrence of most metals in the top mile of the earth's crust has been estimated to be about a million times as great as present known reserves. Since the latter amount to about a hundred years' supplies this means we have enough to last about one hundred million years.[3]

While this may be an excessive estimate of our ultimate metals supplies, it is clear that we are not about to run out of minerals resources.

### *U.S. Minerals Requirements to Year 2000*

It is important that we try to estimate future U.S. minerals requirements in order to assess the relative desirability of alternative raw materials strategies.

**U.S. Consumption.** Throughout the past century, the U.S. demand for all types of consumer and industrial products has shown strong growth, thus increasing our requirements for minerals. However, the *rate* of increase in the use of materials has generally been declining because of the slowing of population growth, the growing efficiency with which U.S. industry utilizes its minerals resources, and the shift of economic activity from manufacturing to services. In effect, each dollar's worth of minerals has been supporting an increasing volume of economic activity.

**U.S. Requirements.** A number of studies have attempted to estimate U.S. minerals demand through the year 2000. The more significant are shown in Table III-2.

Both the U.S. Bureau of Mines and Resources for the Future project an uneven growth trend for U.S. minerals to the year 2000. Both suggest that the rate of growth in U.S. consumption is expected to decline for chromium, aluminum, and vanadium. For other and somewhat more significant minerals, they forecast increases–iron, manganese, molybdenum, nickel, copper, tin, and zinc. There is a wide disparity in the forecast growth for lead (see Table III-3).

U.S. per capita demand for primary minerals can be expected to increase through the year 2000, as shown in Table III-4. Silicon is the only specified mineral that is expected to show a significant decline in per capita rates of growth. Moderate declines are expected for chromium and aluminum, although the absolute increase in per capita demand should be strong in both cases. All other minerals are forecast to show increased per capita growth rates. All minerals without exception, are forecast to show absolute increases in per capita levels of demand.

Although the United States will continue to be a major user of raw materials, relative to other countries, the rate of increase of demand should continue to fall below the rate of increase elsewhere in the world, as it has since the end of World War II (see Table III-5). As can be seen, the projected rate of increase in U.S. consumption is forecast to fall below that of the rest of the world for all of the minerals specified, except for molybdenum, tungsten, tin, zinc, and vanadium.

Based on its forecasts for the year 2000, the U.S. Bureau of Mines has been able to cumulate United States and world demand for the years 1972-2000 (see Table III-6).

The tabulation in Table III-6 indicates the extent to which the United States is expected to remain a major consumer of primary minerals through the year 2000. For almost all the minerals listed, except iron ore and manganese ore, the United States is forecast to account for at least one-fifth of total world consumption. And for aluminum and vanadium, the U.S. share rises to over one-third of world consumption.

It is now possible to get a rough approximation of how adequately current minerals availabilities can be expected to cover future demand. Table III-7 compares the cumulative demand for primary minerals during the 1972-2000 period with an estimate of 1972 minerals reserves—those ores that are recoverable at U.S. 1972 prices and using the 1972 level of technology.

Although the data are based on 1972 figures, they serve to highlight where U.S. policymakers might want to focus their attention. Without stepped-up discovery and technological advances, production shortfalls can be expected in the following minerals before or by the year 2000:

1. *Lead*—Insufficient Worldwide Reserves; Sufficient U.S. Reserves.
2. *Chromium, Iron, Manganese, Nickel, Aluminum, Platinum Group, Vanadium*—Sufficient Worldwide Reserves; Insufficient U.S. Reserves.
3. *Tungsten, Copper, Tin, Zinc*—Insufficient Worldwide Reserves; Insufficient U.S. Reserves.

**Influencing Materials Adequacy.** Projections of the future demand for minerals are based mainly on expected trends in national industrial growth. This, in turn, is related to population levels, income distribution, consumer spending patterns, and the availability and cost of investment capital. It is possible, however, to influence future minerals demand somewhat, without adversely affecting the pace of industrial development. This can be done by the increased recycling of scrap or waste materials, better product design, and the substitution of abundant materials for scarce ones. Similarly, technological advances in the extraction sector would make it possible to increase current reserve levels and current minerals output. Through these efforts, the projected gap between demand and supply could be prevented or at least be much less than indicated in Table III-7.

*Recycling.* The materials industry has, for the most part, developed adequate methods for reusing its own waste—the scraps, shavings and other by-products of materials-making processes. Such methods already contribute substantially to the volume of secondary materials that our economy uses. Another area of recycling is the reuse of products, such as glass bottles and paper containers, as distinct from the reuse of their materials.

Used solid items, including solid wastes, may be thought of as a reserve, much as we think of reserves of iron ore or bauxite. The less this secondary reserve is utilized, the more virgin materials we will have to mine in order to meet future minerals requirements. The potential benefit of mining this waste could be considerable.

To a certain extent, recycled materials already help satisfy part of the growing U.S. demand for minerals. Figure III-2 indicates the extent to which old scrap is currently being recycled. Over 25 percent of U.S. usage of iron, antimony, lead, and silver are currently derived from old scrap. It is this area—post-consumer products, including waste from households, office buildings and service industries—that offers the main area for increased recycling.

**Table III-2**
**Various Projections of United States Primary Minerals Demand in 2000**

| | 1973 | Mineral Facts & Problems | | U.S. Bureau of Mines | Ronald G. Ridker Resources for Future | |
|---|---|---|---|---|---|---|
| | Actual | High | Low | 1/11/74 | High | Low |
| Chromium (M tons) | 543 | 1283 | 861 | 1090 | 1100 | 800 |
| Iron (MM tons) | 93 | 175 | 130 | 153 | 219 | 162 |
| Manganese (M tons) | 1554 | 2330 | 1836 | 2360 | 2880 | 2080 |
| Molybdenum (MM lbs) | 73 | 207 | 151 | 188 | 238 | 172 |
| Nickel (MM lbs) | 386 | 1100 | 765 | 770 | 1020 | 730 |
| Silicon (M tons) | 656 | 1471 | 975 | 1000 | | |
| Tungsten (MM lbs) | 15 | 90 | 58 | 74 | 82.5 | 60 |
| Aluminum (MM tons) | 6.2 | 36.8 | 18.5 | 26.4 | 17.4 | 13.0 |
| Copper (M tons) | 1912 | 7860 | 4900 | 5400 | 4000 | 2880 |
| Lead (M tons) | 1059 | 2800 | 1300 | 1430 | 2400 | 1680 |
| Platinum Group (M oz) | 1485 | 3310 | 1770 | 1965 | | |
| Tin (M tons) | 54 | 98 | 71 | 90 | 96 | 78 |

| | | | | | | |
|---|---|---|---|---|---|---|
| Zinc (M tons) | 1556 | 4000 | 2090 | 3100 | 4420 | 3120 |
| Vanadium (M tons) | 8.5 | 37.5 | 25.5 | 31.0 | 46.0 | 34.0 |

Note: The first two estimates were made by the U.S. Bureau of Mines in the 1970 edition of *Mineral Facts and Problems* (Bureau of Mines Bulletin 650). These estimates were based on a contingency forecasting technique, which consists of "predicting and simulating alternative futures, based on contingencies assumed for technological, economic, social, environmental and other influences. The contingencies and the assumptions for these are identified, quantified and analyzed through 'scenarios'."

Separate scenarios are prepared for each end use, based on "threats or opportunities for each end use in terms of predicted technological, social, political, economic, environmental and other relevant influences."

The fourth column represents a more recent update by the U.S. Bureau of Mines of the median forecast, using the same techniques as in the 1970 study.

The last two columns are projections made in 1972 by Ronald G. Ridker of Resources for the Future, Inc., as a contribution to the Commission on Population Growth and the American Future (Vol. 3, *Population Resources and the Environment;* Chapter 2, "The Economy, Resource Requirements and Population Levels.") They were derived from an input-output model of some 185 economic sectors. The high forecast is based on the assumption of a high population growth (1.5 percent annually from 1970 to 2000) and high economic growth (4 percent); the low forecast assumes low population growth (7/8 percent) and low economic growth (1 2/3 percent). In addition, Ridker presents two intermediate cases (not shown here) of high population growth, low economic growth and low population growth, high economic growth.

This comparative table reveals wide areas of disagreement, due partly to differences in the historical base series. In the cases of chromium, molybdenum, manganese, tungsten, and tin, the projections are consistent with one another. The zinc projections would be consistent only if Ridker's low assumptions for both population and economic growth are realized. The current projections of the Bureau of Mines exceed Ridker's high estimates for aluminum and copper. They are below his low estimates for iron ore, vanadium, and lead.

**Table III-3**
**Forecast Growth Rate in U.S. Primary Minerals/Demand**
(% – annual average) units

| | 1950-1972 | 1972-2000 | 1970-2000 |
|---|---|---|---|
| | (U.S. Bureau of Mines | | (Res. for Future) |
| Chromium | 3.7 | 2.8 | 2.2 |
| Iron | 1.3 | 2.2 | 2.3 |
| Manganese | 1.3 | 2.0 | 1.5 |
| Molybdenum | 4.4 | 4.7 | 5.3 |
| Nickel | 2.5 | 2.9 | 3.1 |
| Silicon | 3.3 | 2.1 | – |
| Tungsten | 3.3 | 6.2 | 5.3 |
| Aluminum | 8.1 | 6.1 | 4.8 |
| Copper | 2.0 | 3.7 | 2.6 |
| Lead | 1.5 | 1.4 | 3.2 |
| Platinum Group | 5.0 | 1.7 | – |
| Tin | –1.8 | 2.2 | 1.3 |
| Zinc | 1.2 | 2.7 | 3.6 |
| Vanadium | 8.9 | 5.4 | 4.7 |

Source: Resources for the Future, Inc., U.S. Bureau of Mines, and "Commodity Statement Summary Tables," prepared for Commodity Statements, 1974 series, February 1974.

A combination of factors in addition to technical considerations, continues to hold down the percentage of secondary products which contribute to meeting the U.S. demand for materials. Among these are the following three constraints:

1. Freight rate regulations which are alleged to favor virgin materials over secondary materials;
2. Failure of federal buying practices to favor recycled fibers in government purchases of paper materials and other recycled products;
3. Tax benefits for various virgin materials industries, such as depletion allowances, foreign tax allowance and expensing of capital expenditures and capital gains treatments, which have tended to keep the prices of certain virgin materials lower than the prices of recovered materials.

These factors are discussed in more detail later in the report.

*Product Design and Substitution.* Innovations in materials application can encourage the use of those materials that are the most abundant and help conserve those materials where a potential scarcity is indicated. Products can be made more recoverable, thereby reducing the volume of waste.

**Table III-4**
**Forecast U.S. Per Capita Primary Minerals/Demand**

| | 1950 | 1972 | 2000 | 1950-72 | 1972-2000 |
|---|---|---|---|---|---|
| | | (pounds) | | (% avg. annual change) | |
| Chromium | 3.0 | 4.8 | 7.3 | 2.2 | 1.5 |
| Iron | 814.2 | 795.0 | 1020.0 | –0.1 | 0.9 |
| Manganese | 13.6 | 13.1 | 15.7 | –0.2 | 0.6 |
| Molybdenum | 0.1 | 0.2 | 0.6 | 3.2 | 4.0 |
| Nickel | 1.3 | 1.6 | 2.6 | 1.0 | 1.7 |
| Silicon | 3.6 | 5.4 | 6.7 | 1.9 | 0.8 |
| Tungsten | 3.6 | 0.1 | 0.2 | – | 2.5 |
| Aluminum | 12.0 | 48.7 | 176.0 | 6.6 | 4.7 |
| Copper | 16.7 | 18.7 | 36.0 | 0.5 | 2.4 |
| Lead | 9.2 | 9.3 | 9.5 | 0.1 | 0.1 |
| Tin | 1.1 | 0.5 | 0.7 | –3.6 | 1.2 |
| Zinc | 15.1 | 14.3 | 20.7 | –0.2 | 1.3 |
| Vanadium | – | 0.1 | 0.2 | – | 2.5 |

Source: U.S. Bureau of Mines.

The better we understand the properties of materials and how to control them, the more efficiently can materials be designed into products. Safety margins can sometimes be narrowed without hazard, thus reducing the amount of material needed in the product. Where physical properties, such as strength, can be upgraded, again less materials may be needed. Knowledge can also improve design by clarifying the functional requirements of specific parts of a product—for example, if only the surface must resist corrosion, coating or cladding may cost less or use less material than employing a corrosion-resistant material throughout. Improved durability of products can reduce pressures on material resources. Product design can help ease the dismantling and separating of components for recycling—metals like those in a shredded automobile tend to be degraded with each recycle and it will be important to develop secondary and tertiary level applications for these degraded alloys. The same is true of recycled plastics, ceramics, and glass.

Substitutions may take the form of material substitution, where a material that is more abundant or environmentally less offensive substitutes for one that is less abundant or less desirable. For example: silicates are the most abundant materials in the earth's crust; can their physical properties be improved so that they can be more readily used in structural applications, thereby easing the pressures on metals for such purposes? The Soviet Union is already extracting aluminum from anorthosite, instead of the scarcer bauxite. The U.S. Bureau of Mines has a major study underway in cooperation with a consortium of

**Table III-5**
**Projected Minerals Demand—Volume**

| | United States | | | | Rest of the World | | | |
|---|---|---|---|---|---|---|---|---|
| | 1972 | 2000 | Increase 1972-2000 | % Per Yr. | 1972 | 2000 | Increase 1972-2000 | % Per Yr. |
| Chromium (M tons) | 506 | 1,090 | 584 | 2.7 | 1,678 | 3,800 | 2,122 | 2.9 |
| Iron (MM tons) | 83 | 153 | 70 | 2.2 | 396 | 780 | 384 | 2.4 |
| Manganese (M tons) | 1,366 | 2,360 | 994 | 2.0 | 8,646 | 18,300 | 9,654 | 2.7 |
| Molybdenum (MM lb) | 51 | 188 | 137 | 4.7 | 107 | 345 | 238 | 4.2 |
| Nickel (M tons) | 172 | 385 | 213 | 2.9 | 353 | 915 | 562 | 3.4 |
| Silicon (M tons) | 561 | 1,000 | 439 | 2.1 | 1,284 | 3,800 | 2,516 | 3.9 |
| Tungsten (MM lb) | 14 | 74 | 60 | 6.1 | 65 | 125 | 60 | 2.4 |
| Aluminum (MM tons) | 5 | 26 | 21 | 6.1 | 8 | 49 | 41 | 6.7 |
| Copper (M tons) | 1,951 | 5,400 | 3,449 | 3.7 | 5,270 | 18,300 | 13,030 | 4.5 |
| Lead (M tons) | 970 | 1,430 | 460 | 1.4 | 3,083 | 5,000 | 1,917 | 1.7 |
| Platinum Group (M oz) | 1,180 | 1,965 | 700 | 1.8 | 3,075 | 9,120 | 6,045 | 3.9 |
| Tin (M tons) | 49 | 90 | 41 | 2.2 | 191 | 270 | 79 | 1.2 |
| Zinc (M tons) | 1,489 | 3,100 | 1,611 | 2.6 | 4,551 | 9,200 | 4,649 | 2.5 |
| Vanadium (M tons) | 7 | 31 | 24 | 5.3 | 18 | 33 | 15 | 2.2 |

Source: U.S. Bureau of Mines.

aluminum producers to explore extraction of aluminum from clay, alunite, anorthosite and coal mine washings.

Patterns of demand in certain materials can be changed through functional substitutions. Examples include adhesives in place of nails and rivets; transistors in place of vacuum tubes; satellites in place of underground cables. Such new technologies and techniques come about through bold research programs which are solution-oriented to the need to decrease dependence on certain materials.

It must be recognized, however, that substitution possibilities are finite. Industrial substitutions may often be at the expense of quality, convenience and cost. Complex systems, such as nuclear reactors and integrated circuits, are

**Table III-6**
**Cumulative Demand, 1972-2000**

| | U.S. | Rest of World | World | U.S. as % of World |
|---|---|---|---|---|
| Chromium (MM tons) | 22.0 | 74.0 | 96.0 | 22.9 |
| Iron (MMM tons) | 3.2 | 16.2 | 19.4 | 16.5 |
| Manganese (MM tons) | 51.0 | 365.0 | 416.0 | 12.3 |
| Molybdenum (MM lb) | 2,820.0 | 5,840.0 | 8,660.0 | 32.6 |
| Nickel (MM tons) | 7.5 | 17.0 | 24.5 | 30.6 |
| Silicon (MM tons) | 21.5 | 66.7 | 88.2 | 24.4 |
| Tungsten (MM lb) | 1,020.0 | 2,620.0 | 3,640.0 | 28.0 |
| Aluminum (MM tons) | 380.0 | 660.0 | 1,040.0 | 36.5 |
| Copper (MM tons) | 96.5 | 297.4 | 393.9 | 24.5 |
| Lead (MM tons) | 33.4 | 111.2 | 144.6 | 23.1 |
| Platinum Group (MM oz) | 13.0 | 159.0 | 202.0 | 21.3 |
| Tin (M tons) | 1,910.0 | 6,390.0 | 8,300.0 | 23.0 |
| Zinc (MM tons) | 62.8 | 186.0 | 248.8 | 25.2 |
| Vanadium (M tons) | 473.0 | 710.0 | 1,183.0 | 40.0 |

Source: U.S. Bureau of Mines.

composed of highly interdependent materials, each carefully adapted to its role in the process structure, and, therefore, substitutability for a particular component may not be possible.

It should also be recognized that the economic equations in materials substitution are sometimes reversible. Aluminum was in overabundant supply a decade ago, due in large part to the ready availability of large amounts of cheap power in many parts of the world. As the price of aluminum decreased, it was substituted for copper. Now, the changing energy situation is drastically modifying the future prospects for aluminum, as well as for plastics. Building construction, in particular, uses a large amount of aluminum and plastics, in addition to taking about 23 percent of the copper market. This is where all three materials—aluminum, plastic, and copper—may be interchanged to a high degree, both among themselves and with wood and cement.

**Table III-7**
**Cumulative Primary Mineral Demand (1972-2000) and Mineral Reserves Recoverable at U.S. 1972 Prices**

| | United States | | Rest of World | | World Total | |
|---|---|---|---|---|---|---|
| | Demand | Reserves | Demand | Reserves | Demand | Reserves |
| Chromium (MM tons) | 22 | 0 | 74 | 1,713 | 96 | 132 |
| Iron (MMM tons) | 3 | 2 | 16 | 97 | 19 | 97 |
| Manganese (MM tons) | 51 | 0 | 365 | 577 | 416 | 577 |
| Molybdenum (MMM lb) | 3 | 6 | 6 | 6 | 9 | 12 |
| Nickel (MM tons) | 7 | 0 | 17 | 46 | 24 | 46 |
| Silicon (MM tons) | 21 | A | 67 | A | 88 | A |
| Tungsten (MM lb) | 1,020 | 175 | 2,620 | 2,575 | 3,640 | 2,750 |
| Aluminum (MM tons) | 380 | 11 | 660 | 3,566 | 1,040 | 3,577 |
| Copper (MM tons) | 97 | 83 | 297 | 287 | 394 | 370 |
| Lead (MM tons) | 33 | 36 | 111 | 60 | 144 | 96 |
| Platinum Group (MM oz) | 43 | 2 | 159 | 584 | 202 | 586 |
| Tin (M tons) | 1,910 | 5 | 6,390 | 4,175 | 8,300 | 4,180 |
| Zinc (MM tons) | 63 | 30 | 186 | 101 | 249 | 131 |
| Vanadium (M tons) | 173 | 115 | 710 | 10,025 | 1,183 | 10,140 |

A = Adequate reserves.

Source: U.S. Bureau of Mines.

**Technological Advances.** In the past, much of the increased supply of raw materials has come from technological advances. The development of better methods of locating, mining and processing ores has been the main reason why predictions seventy years ago of imminent materials shortages have been proven wrong.

In terms of new ore deposits, we have only begun to scratch the surface. The world's mineral resources are still enormous, and for some minerals could prove virtually inexhaustable. New techniques can enable the mining industry to locate these deposits, to exploit those low-grade deposits that are now not economical to mine, and to use less minerals input per unit of final product output.

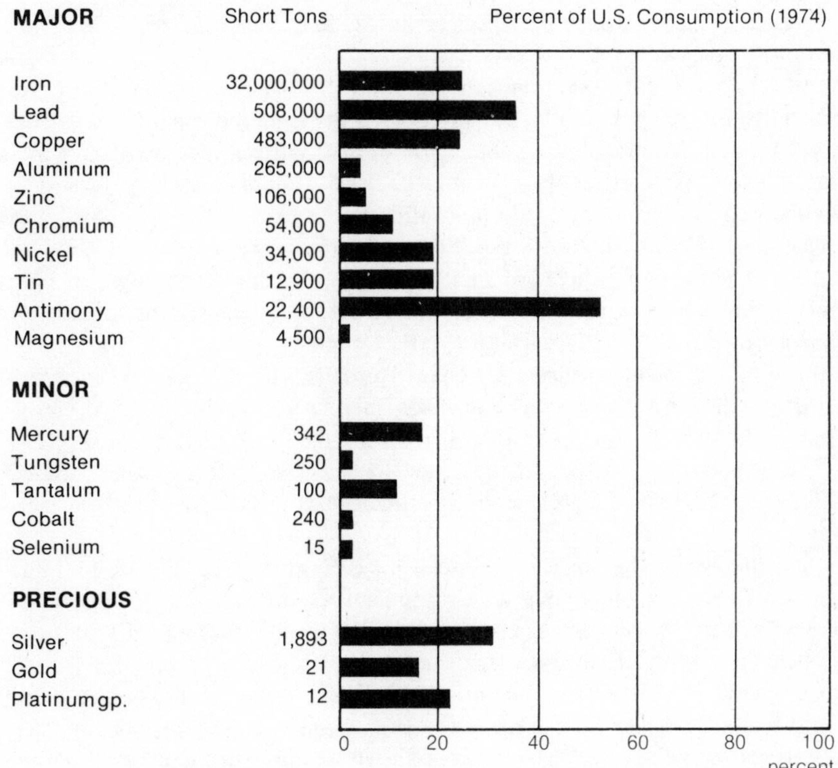


[a]Includes exports.

Source: U.S. Bureau of the Mines.

**Figure III-2.** Old Scrap Recycled in the U S.–1974

The sciences of geology, geochemistry, and geophysics provide models that help to predict the location of mineral deposits. Recent results from the solid state sciences and atomic physics are being applied in new exploration tools that allow the detection and sampling of ores without disruption of land surface.

New technology has entered this field only in recent years. Examples are the Geiger counter, the flying magnetometer, and the use of neutron activation techniques. There are great expectations for the Earth Resources Technology Satellite and the techniques of scanning computer searches to discover sources of minerals by analogy with existing deposits.

A major technological effort is required to work deposits that are currently marginal or noneconomical. These are often the low-grade deposits that remain after the high-grade ores have been extracted. Technological advances in extracting, handling, concentration, and refining of these ores has already enabled many older mining properties to continue to operate. Overall, however, progress has been slow, in part because of the long time it takes to reactivate previously marginal mines.

As long as supply and demand were roughly in balance, there was no imperative for major technological advances. The opening of major areas of the world to exploration and the stabilization of international markets after World War II made exploration on a worldwide scale a more financially rewarding alternative to uncertain or costly innovation in the exploitation of known, but submarginal deposits in the United States. Companies considered the development abroad of new sources of minerals, using available technology, to be a more desirable expenditure than a large R&D effort to increase the recovery of mineral ores from currently mined domestic deposits.

In addition, as Dr. William O. Baker, president of Bell Laboratories, has stressed,[4] the high technology industries–such as chemicals, electrical equipment, and communications–have been receiving the lion's share of R&D effort, to the neglect of the basic materials industries. These latter industries "shared little in the Federal and high technology stimulus of the '50s and '60s."

*Ocean Mining.* Technological advances may eventually enable us to mine significant amounts of the ocean's vast mineral resources. The potential of the oceans' mineral resources, particularly those lying on the seabed, has been receiving increasing attention. The interest stems in part from the United Nations Law of the Sea Conference, begun in the spring of 1974, but, more importantly, from the realization in the United States and other industrialized countries that seabed mineral resources are enormous. They consist primarily, but not exclusively, of magnanese, copper, cobalt, and nickel. Potentially, these reserves form a vast alternative source of supply for major metals.

At least thirty common minerals are known to exist in the sea, either in the seawater itself, as sediments on the ocean floor, or within bedrock. Today, the vast majority of all mining in oceans involves oil and gas. From the standpoint of the future, however, the greatest potential of the seas appears to lie in the mining of manganese nodules–small, potato-shaped concentrations on the ocean floor that form, almost literally a vast highway of raw materials. Although containing concentrations of many minerals, the nodules are economically important because of the large amounts of cobalt, copper, manganese, nickel, and zinc they contain. Many of these minerals are precisely the ones where potential shortages threaten.

Most countries, developed and developing, would like to resolve in the United Nations the question of who has the right to mine the seabed and under what conditions, with multilateral conventions regulating the uses and abuses of the ocean. A few companies, however, have been urging their governments to legitimatize their right to mine the seabed–under existing laws or new national legislation–either because they do not wish to be subject to international control or jurisdiction, or because they fear losing their technological edge over potential rivals by waiting for international arrangements to be agreed upon. There is concern that progress in ocean mining will continue to be bogged down in UN debate.

The United States thus faces three basic choices as regards the future development of ocean mining:

1. To continue to work toward a solution under the auspices of the United Nations;
2. To seek a multinational solution among interested parties outside of the United Nations;
3. To adopt a nationalist solution, such as by claiming a 200-mile limit beyond the shoreline as U.S. territory.

### *The Relationship of the U.S. to International Developments in Raw Materials*

**Increasing Dependence on Imports.** Domestic production of minerals has generally been satisfying less of the United States' growing minerals requirements, even though U.S. production has been increasing steadily and is now more than twice the level reached at the end of World War II.

This country has never been self-sufficient in all minerals, but its dependence on foreign sources is now steadily increasing. In the first quarter of this century, the United States provided some 90 percent of its own mineral requirements. It had to import quantities of manganese, chromium, tungsten, nickel, and asbestos. But, the United States was, in effect, able to pay for these imports with large exports of other minerals—copper, lead, zinc, and phosphate, as well as petroleum.

From 1930 on, the overall U.S. mineral position has shifted further away from self-sufficiency—especially so since the end of World War II. All in all, some one-third of the country's net supply of primary minerals and metallic ores is now obtained from foreign sources, and the gap between the U.S.'s mineral imports and exports continues to widen. Net minerals imports (including processed and unprocessed minerals) reached a record level of $9.5 billion in 1974, based on imports of $13.8 billion and exports of $4.3 billion. For the major unprocessed minerals, the U.S. experienced a large net import position (see Table III-8).

The share of total U.S. consumption that is covered by imports is indicated in Figure III-3, which also shows the major foreign sources of supply of minerals to the United States.

**Growing Economic Nationalism.** Growing economic nationalism could jeopardize the availability to the United States of foreign raw materials. Many

**Table III-8**
**Value of U.S. Mineral Imports and Exports**
($ million, 1974) units

| Net Imports | Imports | Exports | Balance |
|---|---|---|---|
| Copper | 1,119 | 303 | –816 |
| Iron | 722 | 86 | –636 |
| Nickel | 459 | 22 | –437 |
| Zinc | 475 | 42 | –433 |
| Tin | 326 | 54 | –272 |
| Aluminum[a] | 830 | 567 | –263 |
| Lead | 74 | 42 | – 32 |
| Net Exports | | | |
| Phosphates[b] | 91 | 478 | +387 |
| Nitrogen | 345 | 566 | +221 |
| Molybdenum | 1 | 151 | +150 |
| Magnesium | 5 | 49 | + 44 |
| Boron | 1 | 41 | + 40 |
| Platinum | 32 | 63 | + 31 |

Source: U.S. Bureau of Mines. Data refer mainly to unprocessed minerals.
[a]Includes alumina, bauxite, and aluminum.
[b]Includes super-phosphates.

extractive operations were started abroad in the postwar years. After having explored the main U.S. deposits, the U.S. companies found more geological opportunity and more economic reward in exploring for high-grade deposits abroad, especially since labor was cheap and the host governments quite hospitable.

Now, in a period of spreading economic nationalism, more and more governments are claiming that ownership of their countries' mineral wealth belongs to the host states. These states are no longer content to be passive landlords collecting rents or royalties on such minerals as may be developed; they want to be active participants in the key policy-making decisions of the operations, as well as mineral owners.

The stimulus for private sector exploration–the prize of undisputed title to a valuable ore body–is being rapidly eroded as ownership is increasingly being assumed by national agencies. In these circumstances, the discoverer is not *ipso facto*, the exclusive operator, and importantly, the operator does not have absolute title linked to the rights of discovery. For the mining corporation, this development changes its role from owner-operator to free-earning operator. Manifestations of this development are the policies of Mexicanization and Zambianization, as well as, in some cases, total expropriation of foreign ownership.

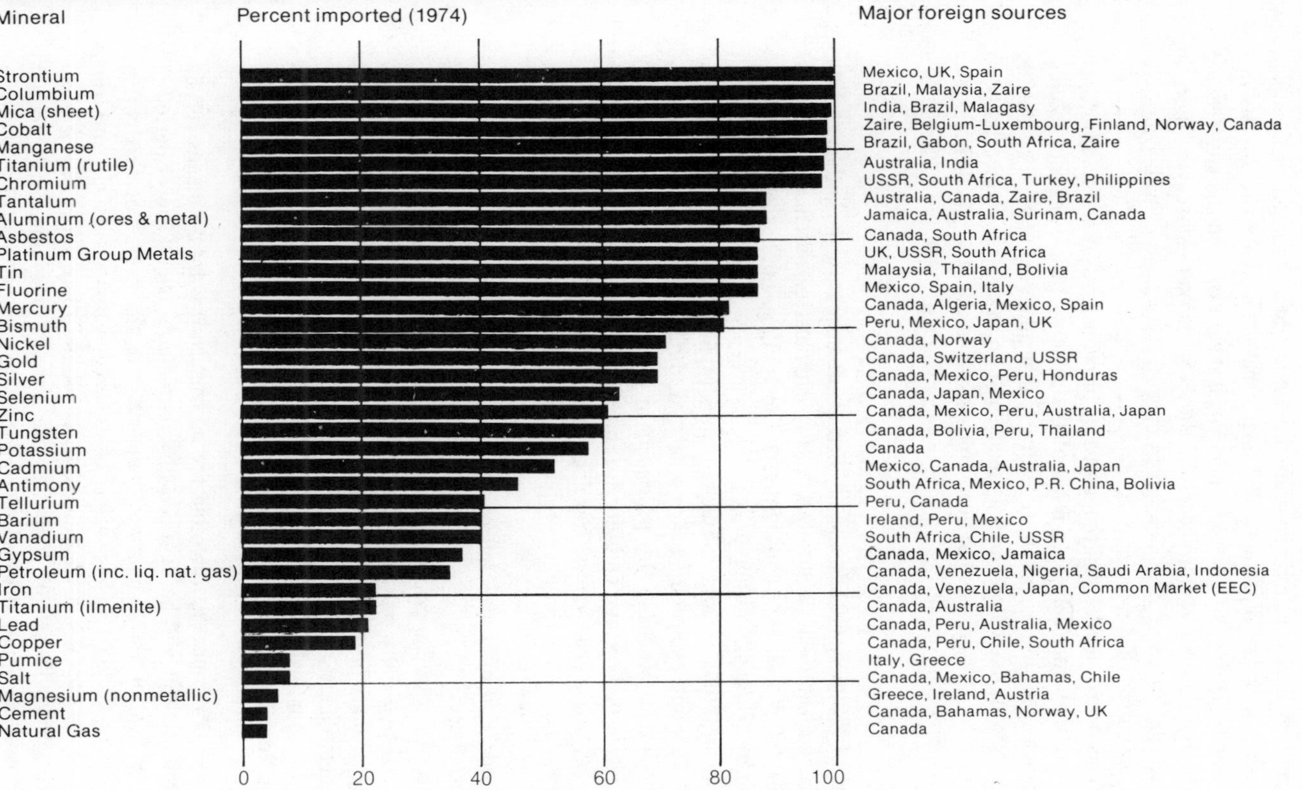


Source: U.S. Bureau of Mines (import-export data from U.S. Bureau of the Census).

**Figure III-3. Imports Supply Significant Percentage of Total U.S. Demand**

As a result of this continuing trend, the United States must now compete more actively and more diplomatically with other countries to secure its raw materials requirements. With state ownership, foreign raw material supplies are less directly tied to the requirements of the U.S. market. Moreover, there is concern that public control of foreign mining operations may well delay the pace of development of foreign mineral deposits.

Another concern relates to the growing insistence of the less developed countries that they themselves do most of the minerals processing and fabrication in order to gain more income from the higher added value of the resulting product. As already indicated, such a trend could increase U.S. vulnerability to foreign producers; it could also affect employment in the U.S. metals industries and the U.S. balance of trade.

**The Threat of Producer Cartels.** Closely tied to the increasing dependence of the United States on imports is the danger that producer cartels may be formed which disrupt the U.S. economy, either by restricting supplies of needed raw materials or by artificially raising prices.

The Arab oil embargo and subsequent quadrupling of world oil prices have heightened the apprehension that markets of other basic materials may be similarly exploited, especially by producers in the developing world. Warnings have been raised of U.S. vulnerability to Third World cartels in bauxite, copper, and other key materials. Several developments have served to reinforce these fears:

1. Establishment of effective control over the world coffee prices by the leading coffee producers;
2. A tripling of phosphate prices through coordinated action by producers;
3. Formation of the International Bauxite Association and the demand for six times higher taxes in royalties by Jamaica;
4. The raising of banana prices by joint imposition of export taxes;
5. A move by four major copper exporters—Chile, Peru, Zambia, and Zaire—to provide a floor on the price of that commodity.

While these developments resemble the oil cartels, it is by no means certain that any such attempt will be as successful, particularly over a longer period of time. Only a few of the major raw materials have the degree of production concentration necessary for a cartel to succeed—bauxite, nickel, and tin. Minerals are more easily substitutable than is oil and there appear to be good prospects for conservation of materials use through recycling and product design. Moreover, as opposed to oil, the minerals exporting countries are not as financially able to withhold supplies from world markets for any length of time.

The United States is thus not as vulnerable to foreign mineral cartels as it is to the oil cartel; nevertheless, some countries may still seek to emulate the OPEC success and their actions could bring short-run dislocations to U.S. industry and to the overall economy.

The following describes the world sources of supply for a number of the major minerals. The degree of concentration of production in Third World countries varies substantially for the different raw materials. Thus, the prospect for the markets of the various raw materials to be successfully cartelized also differs considerably.

*Iron Ore.* This is one of the few materials that exist in quantities sufficient to permit a really considerable growth in use over a long period. Total world production is on the order of 800 million tons a year, and is scattered over numerous countries. At least thirty-five countries each produce over 1 million tons of iron ore a year. The centrally-planned, Socialist countries combined produce about one-third of the world total. Among the Third World countries, the largest iron ore exporters are Brazil, Venezuela, Liberia, Chile, and Peru. However, these countries account for only about 13 percent of the total world production. Australia and Canada are the two developed countries that are substantial exporters. If these two countries join the five developing countries in concerted action, they could jointly control some 25 percent of the world output. The United States itself produces about 10 percent of the world total, although it imports (net) about 25 percent of its total needs, mainly from Canada and Venezuela.

*Bauxite.* World resources of bauxite are also abundant, but the concentration of production is far greater than for iron ore. Jamaica, Guinea, Surinam, Guyana, and the Dominican Republic supply about 40 percent of the total world output of 70 million tons. The share of Jamaica alone is about 20 percent. The world's largest producer is Australia which accounts for about 28 percent of the total and is the only developed country that is a major exporter. No other developed country supplies a major portion of its own requirement. However, the United States possesses huge resources of aluminum-bearing clays which are in the process of being developed and which could become an important substitute for bauxite in the long run. The United States imports over 85 percent of its needs, with roughly 60 percent of the total imports from Jamaica.

*Copper.* The concentration of copper production in the developing countries is also high. About 30 percent of world mine production, or 36 percent of free world mine production, is accounted for by Chile, Peru, Zambia, and Zaire. These countries supply about half of the copper entering world trade. The Philippines is also a major exporter, supplying about 5 percent of the world's exports. Canada, Australia, and the Republic of South Africa are the important exporting countries in the developed world. They account for about 18 percent of the world mine output and 25 percent of the world's export supply. The United States is the largest producer and supplies almost all of its own needs.

*Lead and Zinc.* The bulk of the production of these two metals is from joint operations and comes from the developed countries. The United States, Canada, and Australia together produce about half of the free world's primary lead and zinc. Significant mine production of lead and zinc is also found in Japan and many European countries. Some twenty developing countries together account for less than 35 percent of the free world mine production of lead and about 30 percent of that of zinc. Among them, Peru, Mexico, Yugoslavia, Morocco, and Southwest Africa together account for about 25 percent of the world mine production of lead. These five regions, plus Zambia and Zaire, also supply about 22 percent of the world's mine production of zinc. The United States is the world's largest producer of lead and the second leading producer of zinc. It imports about 20 percent of its consumption needs for lead and over half of its needs for zinc, mainly from Canada.

*Nickel.* Canada and the French territory of New Caledonia are the two dominant producers, together supplying about 55 percent of the world production or about 70 percent of the free world total. Australia has recently become a significant producer, accounting for about 5 percent of the world output. A number of developing countries—the Dominican Republic, the Philippines, Indonesia, Guatemala, and Colombia—are carrying out major expansion programs. These five countries, together with Cuba, now supply only about 12 percent of the world production, but their share is expected to increase sharply in the future. The United States relies on imports for over 70 percent of its consumption needs, with approximately 70 percent of the total imports coming from Canada.

*Tin.* Six developing countries—Malaysia, Bolivia, Thailand, Indonesia, Zaire, and Nigeria—produce over 80 percent of the free world tin output, or 70 percent of the world total. The only developed country with a significant tin production is Australia, which accounts for only about 6 percent of the free world total. Among Communist countries, only China is a substantial producer, supplying 10 percent of the world total. The United States produces virtually no tin, but has over 200,000 tons in its stockpile, the equivalent of about one year's production in the free world.

Concentration of production of most major minerals is sufficiently high for cooperation on output restrictions. Among major metals, production of copper, bauxite, nickel, and tin is more highly concentrated than iron ore, lead, and zinc and thus is relatively prone to cartel control. In the case of copper, however, the United States is substantially self-sufficient. And, except for tin, Canada and Australia are important exporters and their cooperation with the developing countries is essential to the latter's attempt to form cartels. It is too early to tell whether these two developed countries will join cartels of Third World producers. Even if they do, the success of the resultant cartels is by no means assured. Because of the cyclical nature of minerals demand, world economic downturns could still strain the ability of the cartels to keep prices high. The relatively high price elasticity for the cartelized minerals would also add to the pressure.[5]

**Potential Problems for the U.S.** Continued reliance by the United States on foreign imports to close the gap between domestic production and consumption can portend problems for this country.

*National Security.* As long as the United States increases its dependence on foreign imports, it runs the risk that short-run supply dislocations due to arbitrary decisions by foreign suppliers could seriously impair this country's national security objectives. Reliance on imports also depends on freedom of the seas, so that foreign supplies can find their way into U.S. markets. Any disruption of the sea lanes, as by Soviet threats or during local conflicts, could weaken U.S. national security.

*Balance of Payments.* Potentially serious is the implication for the U.S. foreign trade accounts of the intensifying production shortfall for certain minerals. A rough approximation of future import requirements is given in Table III-9, which compares forecasts of primary mineral production within the United States (based on the trend over the past twenty years) to forecasts of U.S. primary mineral demand in the year 2000.

The United States primary minerals gap for a total of sixty-two major minerals could reach some $40 billion annually by 2000. This represents a significant expansion over the 1950 and 1972 deficits.[a] The minerals with the three largest production shortfalls—aluminum, iron ore, and copper—together account for two-thirds of the total deficit. (To the extent that domestic resources or substitutes are developed, particularly for aluminum, this gap could narrow significantly.)

**Summary of the Problems.** The cumulative effect of these problems—the increasing dependence on foreign imports and the related problems of threats of producer cartels and growing economic nationalism among raw materials producing countries—is to leave the United States in an uncertain position as regards the raw materials it requires to uphold its high standard of living, to meet its national security requirements, and to prevent an unfavorable balance in its foreign accounts.

At present, the United States has:

1. No assurance against future shortages of key materials;

[a]By projecting domestic production on the basis that the 1972 ratio between production and demand will be maintained, the gap in the year 2000 comes to a still large $27 billion.

**Table III-9**
**Value of U.S. Primary Minerals Gap**
(millions of 1972 dollars) units

| | Primary Mineral Production | | | Primary Mineral Demand | | | Surplus or Deficit | | |
|---|---|---|---|---|---|---|---|---|---|
| | 1950 | 1972 | 2000[a] | 1950 | 1972 | 2000 | 1950 | 1972 | 2000 |
| Chromium | 0 | 0 | 0 | 52 | 75 | 149 | – 52 | – 75 | – 149 |
| Iron | 4,126 | 3,760 | 4,497 | 4,737 | 6,030 | 11,965 | – 611 | –2,270 | – 7,468 |
| Manganese | 33 | 2 | 0 | 143 | 73 | 150 | – 110 | – 71 | – 150 |
| Molybdenum | 52 | 193 | 338 | 37 | 89 | 323 | + 15 | + 104 | + 15 |
| Nickel | 2 | 47 | 116 | 184 | 481 | 1,178 | – 182 | – 434 | – 1,063 |
| Silicon | 110 | 161 | 318 | 120 | 168 | 335 | – 10 | – 7 | – 17 |
| Tungsten | 5 | 21 | 6 | 9 | 35 | 226 | – 4 | – 14 | – 220 |
| Aluminum | 239 | 215 | 320 | 585 | 2,338 | 15,312 | – 346 | –2,123 | –14,992 |
| Copper | 691 | 1,698 | 3,574 | 967 | 1,990 | 7,452 | – 276 | – 292 | – 3,878 |
| Lead | 207 | 186 | 312 | 335 | 291 | 543 | – 128 | – 105 | – 231 |
| Platinum Group | 3 | 1 | 3 | 44 | 86 | 219 | – 41 | – 85 | – 216 |
| Tin | 0 | 0 | 0 | 283 | 194 | 560 | – 283 | – 194 | – 560 |
| Zinc | 312 | 172 | 361 | 574 | 536 | 1,860 | – 262 | – 364 | – 1,499 |
| Vanadium | 12 | 28 | 58 | 8 | 39 | 167 | + 4 | – 11 | – 109 |
| Total of 62 Minerals | 7,877 | 10,080 | 17,418 | 10,423 | 17,150 | 57,629 | –2,546 | –7,070 | –40,211 |

[a]Assumes past twenty-year production trend continues.

2. No assurance against temporary disruptions in the supply of needed materials;
3. No assurance against unreasonable price increases by foreign suppliers.

## III. Long-run Critical Choices

### *Reliance on Market Forces*

In forecasting the demand and supply for various raw materials in the background section, we have assumed no change in the real prices of these materials (i.e., after allowance for inflation). While this assumption makes it easier to project future magnitudes, it is not realistic. In our market economy, shortages are reflected sooner or later in higher real prices, which, in turn, bring on demand and supply adjustments that work to eliminate the shortages.

On the demand side, higher prices for a scarce raw material tend to:

1. reduce final product demand;
2. increase the use of substitute materials;
3. encourage the development of substitute systems that do not use the higher-priced raw material;
4. encourage the development of processing and fabricating technologies that use less of the higher-priced material per unit of output;
5. stimulate recycling efforts.

On the supply side, higher prices tend to:

1. encourage the mining of existing deposits;
2. permit lower grade ores to be mined which, at lower prices, were economically sub-marginal;
3. encourage the exploration for new deposits;
4. stimulate R&D efforts to develop more efficient mining technologies.

In these ways, market forces work to eliminate potential long-run shortages of raw materials. However, the market system does not always work smoothly or quickly, especially when it comes to raw materials. Prices are subject to so many influences that it is often very difficult for business to distinguish the long-term trend. Speculation and the excessive accumulation or unloading of stocks cause highly volatile, short-term price movements. If materials consumers and producers are to make the necessary adjustments, they must be convinced that the price increases are of a sustained nature, reflecting a long-run shortage.

The expansion of production often involves major capital and operating costs for existing mines, let alone for new mines. The development of new technologies in either the mining, smelting, or fabricating stages is also very expensive, in time and money. Even the substitution of one material for another can be costly. These expenses can be justified only if there is reasonable certainty as to future demand/supply forces.

The long-run price increases must be high enough to stimulate the desired adjustments. For many minerals, high prices are more likely to expand supplies than to reduce demand. The demand for minerals is usually a "derived" demand, where the final consumer demand is for the finished product and not for the raw materials used in its manufacture. In most applications, primary mineral costs are a small fraction of the total product cost. Higher mineral prices can generally be absorbed by the fabricator without too much difficulty, or can be passed on to the final consumer as a marginal price increase. Either way, final product demand—and the derived demand for the raw materials—may not be significantly reduced.

On the supply side, prices have to be high enough not only to cover expected costs of incremental production (labor, energy, environmental regulations), but also to exceed the rise in the general price level. If this happens, the real profits of the industry on existing production will automatically rise and thus provide the necessary incentive and the resources for undertaking investments to open new mines or to work the marginal veins in existing mines or to utilize what might otherwise be "dump ore."

**What Is Needed.** The price mechanism could work more effectively if the private sector had more information and analyses on materials properties, substitution possibilities, underlying demand and supply forces, and projections. Much of this information is already available, but it is essential that it be brought into a central data storage and retrieval system, as well as be better organized and disseminated. A continual updating of demand/supply projections, both for the United States and abroad, would be especially useful, both for the government and the business sectors.

But data alone are not sufficient. There would have to be a policy framework for making the best use of these data. Price rises for raw materials should be encouraged where they represent a legitimate and desirable response to emerging long-run shortages; they bring corrective adjustments on both the demand and supply sides. Public policies also could be utilized to dampen volatile short-run price movements, without distorting the long-run trend. The problem is that in practice, it is difficult to discern long-term trends, let alone try to follow them.

**Impact on Economy.** The rise in prices required to prevent materials shortages will contribute to inflation, but probably less so than if materials bottlenecks were allowed to develop. Also, the increased supply generated by high prices will work to bring down these prices. Indeed, the experience of the materials sector is such that the supply response may be so great that companies may find that they have overexpanded and be forced to close down facilities, with a capital loss to themselves and to the nation.

A policy of reliance on market forces would encourage the shipment of minerals to the U.S. market from foreign sources, by reducing artificial barriers to the importation of foreign ores. Such imports are often competitive in the U.S. market, despite heavier transportation costs, because the higher grade of the foreign ores reduces overall production costs.

**Impact on Environment and Energy.** Use of foreign ores would reduce the environmental problems associated with domestic mining: scarring of the land, piles of tailings, pollution of streams. They also enable us to conserve our own supplies. Further environmental benefits would result from the internalization by the domestic mining industry of environmental and other social costs. This would give the mining companies a financial incentive to reduce such costs. Because mining is an energy-intensive activity, use of foreign ores could reduce domestic energy requirements.

**Impact on Public-Private Sector Relations.** A policy geared to reliance on market forces requires an efficient price mechanism that gives prompt and accurate signals to the private sector. Spot and futures metals markets may have to be strengthened. Such a policy orientation would tend to enhance the role of the private sector in economic decision-making.

**Impact on Quality of Life.** Members of the raw materials industry foresee two major shifts in the way Americans live under a market-oriented policy that involves rising materials prices, coupled with increased energy costs. One change would be in the cars Americans drive; the other would be in the composition and size of new housing.

Automobile manufacturers predict a weight loss in standard automobiles of between 400-1,000 pounds as the cost of gasoline increases. Thomas A. Murphy, chairman of General Motors Corporation, says that massive car redesigns are now underway "to offer motorists cars suited to an energy-short world ridden by inflation; cars large enough or small enough to meet their particular needs."[6] To accomplish this change, greater emphasis will be placed upon the use of aluminum and plastics in building cars and less on steel and iron.

Members of the housing industry predict a shift away from single family homes to multiple dwelling apartments to save materials and energy costs. Those single dwellings that are produced are likely to be small, with less emphasis on wood and greater emphasis on insulating materials.

**Impact on National Security and Foreign Relations.** This choice would encourage the flow of world trade. By increasing our purchases of raw materials from the less developed countries, we would be contributing to their export earnings and their economic growth. They, in turn, would become better markets for our own export manufactured products, as well as food.

This choice would also result in a continued import dependence. In some commodities, the level of dependence may increase if foreign sources of supply are much cheaper than domestic sources. This dependence, however, may pose less of a threat to the United States than is the case with oil. The countries that supply raw materials are much less financially able to withhold their products from the world market, especially for any length of time. They need the export revenue to finance their import requirements. As we have already seen, there are few key commodities where supplies are concentrated among a few countries. The possibility that other countries, including the United States, would develop their own deposits or substitutes further limits the freedom of action of potential cartels.

However, as already indicated, any heavy reliance on foreign mineral sources will require freedom of the seas to allow foreign materials to reach our shores. Without such freedom, our industrial structure and standard of living could be in serious jeopardy.

### *Limited Dependence*

There are many people who believe that market forces alone will not bring us the adequacy and stability of supply we need without the risk of serious dislocations—to the price level, to domestic economic activity, and to the balance of payments. Therefore, they seek to limit dependence on the price mechanism and on imports by policy measures, especially in the fields of technological development and resource management. However, the basic thrust of a raw materials development program would still be left to the private sector.

**What Is Needed.** The measures to be taken to limit dependence are:

*Technological Development.* In the past, much of our increased supply of raw materials has emanated from technological advances. Future technological progress, however, is by no means assured. It requires incentives, financial investment and hard work. Indeed, there is already some evidence of lagging efforts by the private sector in this important area, which could justify governmental stimulation. Over the past decade or so, the pace of innovation may not have been at a sufficient rate to counteract the decline in ore grades and the increase in mining problems. As a result, unit production costs may now be rising. Moreover, the capital investment needed to bring on stream a ton of annual metal output continues to increase. Mining projects typically cost above $100 million today. The exploration and development phases of natural resource investments generally involve very high risk, especially considering the long lead times before projects become operational.

Lagging private innovation, heavy capital requirements, and high risks are seen as reasons why government support is required for the research needed to accelerate progress in the mining industry. Private companies cannot afford to be too speculative with their funds when the prospective return is too diffuse to be captured in their own sales or is too longterm to be a meaningful part of their overall business strategy. To some extent, the actual research, directed primarily to applied technology, process improvement or product substitution, could probably be done most effectively by the private sector. But the federal government may have to be prepared to assume a good part of the risks of research and development.

Among the more promising areas for government support of technological developments are geology, marginal deposits, and ocean mining. (The need for technological advances in product design and materials substitution is discussed later in the report.)

**1. Geology.** There is need for an accelerated geological effort, using improved techniques, to discover and evaluate new ore bodies in the United States. Prospecting for materials in the ground has had a long history in the United States, where the Geological Survey, the Bureau of Mines and state authorities have been engaged for years in mapping, sampling, and correlating data on the subsoil and various ores.

There is still a need to develop the capability to discover deposits of minerals hidden more deeply in the ground and to ascertain their extent and value. However, the largest deposits of highly mineralized ore bodies have often been located abroad, in areas of low-cost labor. The prime geological and exploratory talent has been active on this more rewarding terrain.

While the geological mapping program in the continental United States has assembled a wealth of data on existing deposits, more remains to be done in centralizing the available data. There also needs to be a complete and continuing appraisal and inventorying of materials reserves, and a continuing evaluation of the national position concerning the demand for and supply of materials.

Continuing geological advances could help prevent any serious depletion in the current reserve level of our major minerals. In the past, the reserves of many minerals have increased in line with growing demand, which is only appropriate if reserves are considered as an inventory of minerals that bears some relationship to demand. While there is no reason to believe that current and prospective geological efforts will not be as successful as they have been up to now in finding new deposits, failure to do so could have especially serious effects on our highly industrialized economy and on our national security.

Accordingly, some argue that it would be prudent for the government to support geological efforts and the development of new technology in this field. While we will never know the total extent of minerals resources, the more we do know, the better we can formulate policies to guarantee our future materials availabilities.

**2. Marginal Deposits.** We need accelerated technological progress in extracting, handling, concentrating, and refining of ores from deposits that are currently marginal or noneconomic. Government support would be especially helpful on the development of larger and more sophisticated mining machinery, better and more efficient flotation systems, and improvements in the design of concentration and refining installations.

The government would need to maintain an up-to-date inventory of mines that have closed production—where they are located, what their mineral potential is, and what would be required to reopen them.

**3. Ocean Mining.** International agreement on the use of the oceans and the seabed would do much to expand worldwide mineral availabilities. Until then, further U.S. support for R&D on ocean mining technology and on the efficient processing of the manganese nodules would help lay the basis for future expansion.

*Materials Management.* We can stretch our raw material supplies through public policies to improve the management of our domestic resources, thereby averting or at least postponing prospective shortages. There are two basic resource management methods: recycling—the economic use of secondary and "waste" materials; and the setting of performance and design standards that encourage durability and stimulate the development and use of substitute materials or systems for those materials in short supply. A policy of technological improvements is principally oriented to expanding supplies; a resource management policy is mainly concerned with easing the demand for certain primary materials. To be effective, a materials management policy requires strong public participation and this, in turn, involves greater education of the public on conservation matters and strong leadership.

**1. Recycling.** To a large extent, recycling is responsive to market forces: the more profitable it becomes to "mine" wastes, the more secondary sources of supply will be made available. It is no wonder that there is no need for an official policy to recycle diamonds. The high price does that. Similarly, rising copper prices in 1973 encouraged the voluntary recycling of copper products by businessmen.

However, the price mechanism is already heavily influenced by various government policies, which some people believe work against recycling.

*a. Freight Rates.* Transportation costs are an important factor in the competition between virgin and secondary materials. It is a key link in an effective recycling program, because without a market for secondary goods, all the technology and research and development into better recycling methods are wasted.

Spokesmen for the secondary materials industry complain that discrimination in the rates approved by the Interstate Commerce Commission (ICC) and the Federal Maritime Commission can run as high as 50 percent of shipping costs by rail and 75 percent by sea, with virgin materials enjoying the lower costs. The

Environmental Protection Agency (EPA) did find that in every secondary material studied, the freight rate, as a percentage of the delivered price, was higher than for the virgin counterpart. While there was evidence of discrimination based on economic criteria, it did not find discrimination "from a legal point of view." The EPA has recommended that the ICC and Federal Maritime Commission further study the rate structures.

*b. Federal Buying Practices.* In 1971, the General Services Administration was ordered to institute a program requiring a certain percentage of recycled fibers in government purchases of paper materials. The order reflected an Executive Order in 1971 by President Nixon requiring all federal agencies to "initiate measures needed to direct their policies, plans and programs so as to meet national environmental goals."

The EPA has found that there has not been a widespread utilization of secondary materials by the federal government. It points out that uncertainty of supply of the recycled materials, budgetary constraints, and implementation and administrative problems have constituted the major barriers.

The direct market effect of a widespread government program aimed at buying secondary materials would probably be small. But indirectly, it could have a significant impact, because federal buying practices are widely copied on the state and local levels. In addition, considerable savings are possible through more careful controls over the use of government office supplies in general.

*c. Tax Measures.* The virgin materials industry enjoys a tax benefit of over $200 million annually, primarily through depletion allowances, foreign tax allowances, expensing of capital expenditures, and capital gains treatments. The first of these, the depletion allowance, provides the greatest benefit to primary producers. It was originally intended to reduce the risk in the discovery and development of resources and to assure an adequate long-range supply of resources. The depletion allowance has also kept certain virgin material prices low—lower in many cases than prices of recovered materials—which has the perverse effect of actually inhibiting the search for new materials.

The secondary materials industry holds that the percentage depletion places metal ores in a more advantageous position on the marketplace than recycled materials. The mining industry, it feels, has a much lower effective tax rate than manufacturing industries—and the secondary metals industry falls into the category of a manufacturing industry.

**2. Product Design, Materials Specifications, and Substitution.** Suggestions regarding product control cover a wide spectrum of the materials industry, and generally have two purposes: reducing the volume of waste and making products more recoverable. This raises the question of whether the private sector can adjust adequately to the pressures of scarcity and waste, and to what extent the public authorities can hasten that adjustment through policies and through their own buying practices. Policies could encompass direct regulatory measures, as well as fiscal approaches. The former policies could go as far as outright bans of certain products or materials, while the latter policies could involve a product tax based on weight or size of material components.

Use of substitute materials or systems could conserve those materials in short supply. One problem is that the designers, engineers, and processors of materials have to work within a framework of regulations, specifications, and standards that often result from competitive pressures, trade-offs, and consumer attitudes that cannot be easily set aside just to conserve materials.

We need a much more precise knowledge of the properties and relative availabilities of materials. Better integration is needed between such areas of knowledge as minerals exploration and assessment, minerals extraction, and materials science and engineering. All need greater emphasis and more clearly focused objectives. In these ways, a materials management system can combine with a technological strategy to reinforce the working of the market system in the effort to overcome potential long-run shortages of key materials.

**Impact on the Economy.** Reliance on limited government policies in the areas of technology and resource management need not have a major impact on the economy. While more investment in materials R&D will surely be required, the effort need not cause serious economic dislocations. Policies regarding better resource management, in particular, may involve relatively little additional expenditures.

However, this program will reduce imports below the level that would otherwise be if only market forces were operating. Such an import reduction would not be the result of direct import restraints which could impair our international economic relations. Rather, it would reflect the impact of the government programs designed to accelerate the development of the domestic minerals industry. Nevertheless, public intervention per se is bound to have some ripple effects on the overall economy–on resource allocation and prices.

**Impact on Environment and Energy.** The exploitation of new ore deposits and the accelerated development of known ore bodies may have a negative impact on the environment–especially the land and streams–probably more so than would the policy of relying mainly on market forces.

This negative impact would be offset, at least partially, by better resource management, in particular, recycling. Unlike primary mineral reserves, solid waste presents a problem when left in its undeveloped state. Its environmental effects, whether through burning, dumping, or littering, can be deleterious. The cost of collecting and disposing of waste has risen to the point where, in many communities, the expense of solid waste management programs now falls just below those of education and highway construction and maintenance. Recycling would reduce these environmental and financial costs.

In addition, increased recycling could lessen the energy burden on raw material production. The Citizens Advisory Committee on Environmental

Quality, for example, estimates that federal legislation requiring the use of refundable drink containers could serve the energy equivalent of 5 million gallons of gasoline a day.[7]

**Impact on Public/Private Sector Relations.** This choice would probably bring more government involvement in the economy; however, the thrust of public policies would basically be to support the private sector, especially in R&D activities. A resource management policy might involve the setting of mandatory standards on product design and materials specifications, which would limit the scope of private decision-making.

The impact under a limited dependence approach also could take the form envisioned by William S. Paley, chairman of the President's Materials Policy Commission (1952) and a member of the Commission on Critical Choices. Paley, in a statement before Congress in 1974, recommended that the United States establish an independent government agency to conduct an ongoing investigation into an evolving materials situation, with the cooperation of other government agencies and private and international organizations. The agency would have five specific functions:

1. Fact-finding, to maintain a running inventory of our natural resources and mineral reserves, the rate of their consumption and the status of alternative sources.
2. Projecting our future needs and potential shortages.
3. Defining and recommending areas where intensified research and development is called for.
4. Recommending to the Congress and to other appropriate government agencies a comprehensive national resources policy, and when and what nature of changes in that policy are required.
5. Determining the international aspects of our materials situation and recommending steps to deal with them.

The limited dependence approach would shift the main responsibility for helping the nation to meet its materials requirements to the U.S. government, while, at the same time, giving appropriate consideration to the needs of industry and to the desirability and need for international cooperation.

**Impact on Quality of Life.** The reduction in the volume of solid wastes on the streets and lands of the nation, especially abandoned automobiles and discarded cans, would contribute to an improvement in the quality of life of Americans.

**Impact on National Security and Foreign Policy.** Even though minerals imports would be somewhat reduced, this policy need not significantly affect U.S. international relations. The flow of imports and exports would still be large and determined basically by price and market considerations. However, our national security might be somewhat enhanced by the greater coverage of our domestic minerals requirements from domestic sources.

### *Complete Self-Reliance*

This choice reflected the concern that continuing dependence on foreign supplies, let alone a growing dependence, may jeopardize the industrial development and the national security of the United States. The objective of this strategy is to reduce U.S. dependence on foreign materials as much as possible. The price mechanism is not regarded as adequate for protecting the economic and the security interests of the United States. Instead, a host of government policies would be required to stimulate domestic minerals production, to cut back on domestic consumption, and to minimize competing imports.

**What Is Needed.** This policy would involve placing a high national priority on domestic materials development, possibly including the organization of a program similar to the one initially envisioned by Project Independence for energy. Major efforts would be required to locate new ore bodies and to develop the technology for extracting currently marginal and submarginal ores. Large government R&D expenditures will be required to underwrite this intensified program. At the same time, private development efforts would have to be encouraged through the maintenance of high minerals prices and/or financial subsidies. To encourage this domestic development and to protect high-cost producers from lower prices, imports of competing materials may have to be controlled through tariffs and/or quotas.

To cut back on raw materials demand, as part of the effort at self-sufficiency, a major public R&D program would be required in recycling, product design, and use of substitute materials and systems. The mandatory allocation of materials would be required where domestic production cannot be sufficiently expanded to reduce imports to negligible levels.

**Impact on the Economy.** Such an intense program is bound to put pressure on our resources—especially labor and capital. It would thus add to the inflationary pressures of an energy self-sufficiency program, of which it is a part.

To protect investments in the expansion of domestic output, barriers to competing imports may have to be created. Other countries may retaliate, thus hurting our exports; the overall volume of world trade could be seriously affected. Moreover, by accelerating the use of our lower grade and hence more costly mineral deposits, we would be making our entire industrial structure less competitive compared to those of other countries which utilize cheaper ores. Thus, a reduction in mineral imports could be at least partially offset by a reduction in our industrial exports.

**Impact on the Environment and Energy.** In a self-sufficiency approach, environmental standards may have to be substantially relaxed in order to accelerate the exploitation of domestic minerals resources. Our domestic energy requirements would increase, again with a negative impact on the environment, because the mining and processing of ores are such energy-intensive activities.

**Impact on Public-Private Sector Relations.** This policy of minerals self-sufficiency would involve, as a necessary cost, extensive government interference with the private sector. Mandatory regulations on the conservation of materials may have to be imposed. The federal government may not only support the R&D activities of the private sector, but may even decide to undertake production on its own. Import and export controls on minerals would further limit the private sector. In combination with a policy of energy self-sufficiency, this choice would considerably expand the influence of the public sector over our economy.

**Impact on the Quality of Life.** The choice of national self-sufficiency in raw materials would have a generally negative impact on the quality of life, especially if resources were diverted from social areas to support a large raw materials (and energy) program. At the same time, domestic employment opportunities might be increased.

**Impact on National Security and Foreign Policy.** Reduced imports of raw materials will make the United States less vulnerable to foreign political pressures. At the same time, the autarkic policy used to restrict imports may invite retaliation and thereby cause the international political climate to deteriorate. Other countries may be encouraged to promote their own national interests, narrowly defined, to the disregard of the impact on the international community.

## IV. Short-run Critical Choices

Even if we gear up successfully to prevent long-run shortages from materializing, we still must deal with the issue of sudden disruptions in supply and/or price caused by producer cartels, motivated either by economic or political considerations. One alternative would be to continue the strategy of no major changes in U.S. policy. This strategy gives heavy weight to the fact that, up to now, nonenergy producer cartels have not worked effectively and that, as already discussed, the economics are against their long-run viability.

We have already noted that, among the major metals, bauxite, copper, nickel, and tin are the most likely candidates for cartel control because of their high degree of producer concentration. However, in all these metals—except tin—Canada and/or Australia, two friendly nations, are major exporters. In the case of copper, the United States has already achieved a high degree of self-sufficiency. The United States, although not a member of the International Tin Agreement, holds a huge stockpile of tin which should protect the country against any threat of producer cartels. In addition, there are many substitute materials for tin.

A *status quo* policy, however, does risk short-run supply dislocations due to arbitrary decisions by foreign suppliers. This risk may be great enough to discredit this policy. Artificial shortages could disrupt normal economic activity and bring on temporary unemployment. Shortages could also involve higher import prices for our needed raw materials, which would adversely affect the U.S. balance of trade. Moreover, there is no guarantee that Canada and Australia will always regard it to be in their own self-interest to continue to supply minerals to the U.S. market—unless we adopt a conscious policy of mutual cooperation and development that will help bring this about.

If we choose an activist policy, we must then decide on the actual type of policy. There are four possibilities which are not mutually exclusive:

1. Economic Insurance Policies
2. Government Rationing
3. Deterrence
4. International Cooperation.

### *Economic Insurance Policies*

The United States can cushion the impact of unreasonable actions of producer cartels, and thereby possibly deter any such actions, by maintaining an adequate stockpile of scarce commodities and/or by developing domestic standby production facilities. The creation of a global stockpile among major consuming nations or a network of interdependent national stockpiles would be another way of insuring against precipitous acts of producers. A stockpile program, national or global, would enable the United States and other consumers to supply the domestic markets with commodities that are embargoed by cartels.

The current stockpile program was authorized by the Strategic and Critical Materials Stockpiling Act of 1946. It is managed by the General Services Administration, under the authority of Executive Order 11051. The stated objective of the stockpile act is to "decrease and prevent wherever possible a dangerous and costly dependence upon foreign materials for supplies of . . . materials in times of national emergency." Up to now, the "national emergency" has been interpreted to include only situations of potential military conflict. Thus, from 1947 to 1959, the stockpile objectives for the designated metals were based on the estimated requirements of fighting a five-year war. From 1959 to 1973, the stockpile objectives were reduced to the requirements for fighting a three-year war.

Since 1973, the stockpile objectives have been further drastically reduced to meet the requirements of a one-year war, with theaters both in Europe and Asia. It is also based on the assumption that imports of materials will continue to be available from all countries not in the war zone and not Communist-oriented. This change has meant that, for most stockpile commodities, the metals inventory exceeded requirements. The inventory was valued at $7.4 billion at the end of 1974, compared with the revised stockpile objective of $1.1 billion. As a result, the U.S. government has been actively engaged in disposing of such "excess" supplies. Such disposal has the added feature of helping improve the government's cash position.

Table III-10 indicates the extent to which the stockpile objectives for the various metals have declined.

In order to deal with real or potential shortages induced by the actions of foreign producers, the stockpile objective would have to be expanded to include economic requirements in addition to military considerations. Congressional action would probably be required to revise the Strategic and Critical Materials Stockpiling Act of 1945.

A second possibility would be the creation of a global stockpile arrangement among the major consuming countries. This would also require congressional action and administration approval. Such a stockpile would necessitate an agreement by participating countries on which materials to stockpile, how much of an inventory objective to set for each material, where to store the materials, and rules for acquisitions and disposals. Because of these complexities, it might

**Table III-10**
**Stockpile Profile**
(thousand tons) units

| | At Stockpile Peak 12/31/62 | 11/30/74 | New Objective |
|---|---|---|---|
| Tin | 347 | 207 | 40.5 |
| Chromium | 5,343 | 2,505 | 445 |
| Aluminum | 1,970 | 13 | 0 |
| Tungsten | 81 | 37 | 2 |
| Manganese | 10,028 | 4,201 | 750 |
| Lead | 1,386 | 599 | 65 |
| Zinc | 1,581 | 373 | 203 |
| Copper | 1,133 | 0 | 0 |

Source: General Services Administration.

prove useful to initiate a trial international stockpile for only one or two materials.

The development of standby production facilities, a third economic insurance policy, is a complex undertaking. First, it requires a determination of those commodities where there is or is likely to be a high import dependence and where a limited number of countries could control the market. Second, for these commodities, domestic mines that are no longer producing because of the costs of exploiting deep or low-grade deposits would have to be identified and kept in a ready condition. Third, ores on federal lands would have to be identified and plans prepared for their extraction in case of emergency. An inventory of "technology-on-the-shelf" might have to be maintained which could be drawn upon if cartels acted unreasonably. Such technology, especially new applied technology, would enable us to develop our domestic minerals resources as a substitute for dependence on foreign sources.

**Impact on the Economy.** The cost of any stockpile program depends principally on the number and the quantities of the materials to be stockpiled. The larger the stockpile program, the greater will be the financing and storage costs—which may or may not be offset by an increase in the value of the minerals held. Moreover, special care would have to be taken that the buildup of the stockpiles or the subsequent disposal of surplus stocks did not unduly disrupt private markets. If the U.S. stockpile program incorporates an economic objective, there may be a strong temptation to use the program for trying to smooth out short-run price movements, similar to the buffer stock arrangement under the International Tin Agreement.

Such an objective might involve daily purchases and sales in the market and could thus make the metals markets even more volatile than at present. Suppliers and purchasers would have to take into account possible decisions by the stockpile manager, in addition to assessing world demand and supply forces. There thus could be greater scope for speculative excesses. On the other hand, U.S. government initiatives during 1974, aimed at promoting international commodity arrangements with the producing countries, could provide a framework for limiting world price fluctuations in certain minerals.

A conscious effort to develop standby production facilities could prove to be costly. There are numerous expenses, which the government would have to cover in one way or another, in keeping currently uneconomic mines in a state of readiness—especially the need to maintain infrastructure (replace timbers, pump-out water, keep roads and rails in usable condition). There is a need to maintain a minimum inventory of trucks, equipment, and machinery and, to have a ready supply of trained manpower, who can be called upon when needed. Currently, such manpower is in short supply; a "reserve mining corps" would have to be created from heavy construction workers. It is generally very expensive and time-consuming to convert "technology-on-the-shelf" into actual production. By the time such technology is developed, the crisis may have long since passed. Moreover, if the technology is good, it would probably be worthwhile to take it off the shelf and apply it immediately.

**Impact on National Security and Foreign Policy.** A stockpile and/or standby facilities program is designed to protect the security interests of the United States by making our economy less vulnerable to the whims of foreign producers. Because we already have a stockpile program, its expansion to include economic criteria should not significantly affect U.S. relations with other countries. Indeed, a global stockpile program could encourage cooperation among the participating countries, including the lending of stocks to cover temporary shortages.

*Government Rationing.* If and when cartels exert unreasonable pressures against the United States—either by restricting raw materials supplies or by raising prices—the resulting disruptions to the U.S. economy could be minimized by a policy of rationing supplies among competing uses. Indeed, one reaction to the Arab oil embargo was the *ad hoc* rationing of gasoline sales by various state authorities. A more organized rationing system could be used to channel restricted materials to priority uses.

During the Second World War, the U.S. government adopted a Controlled Materials Plan (CMP) to allocate scarce materials to priority uses. In addition, the CMP helped set specific production and construction schedules in support of a wide range of programs. Some of the CMP experience would be applicable if there were a current materials shortage, caused either by foreign actions or by the need to support an expanded energy development program. The elements of such a control policy have been indicated by William C. Truppner of Robert R. Nathan Associates:[8]

1. Publish a specific definition of the program, similar to that currently in effect under the Defense Materials System.
2. Require manufacturers and construction firms participating in the program to identify their contracts and purchase orders with appropriate program symbols.
3. Undertake government action to break bottlenecks, shift shipping dates, reschedule production as necessary, to expedite delivery against identified orders.
4. Summarize new orders, unfilled orders, and shipments by program symbol.
5. Take appropriate policy or program action in light of program status information.
6. Issue production directories, as appropriate, to adopt production slates to meet needs.
7. Issue inventory regulations to control the level of inventories of products or materials in critical supply.

8. Employ the CMP "Claimant Agency" concept by assigning programs to specific government agencies.
9. Such agencies would be held responsible for developing programs, estimating materials requirements, justifying proposed levels, and "managing" the program after it is authorized.
10. The principle underlying the foregoing is to move gradually. This kind of development is likely to receive support from the business community, *a sine qua non* for the effective operation of any control system. If a more elaborate system is required in the future, let the events that cause it to be needed manifest themselves first. All control systems develop after they are initiated, not before. People are not smart enough to visualize the consequences of control measures in an economy as huge and complex as that of the United States. The damage has to be done before the repair can begin.

**Impact on the Economy.** A policy of rationing and allocating scarce raw materials involves a willingness to starve "nonessential" uses of needed materials. The Defense Department and the National Aeronautic and Space Administration (NASA) now receive priority allocations of materials. If the energy sector is added to the list, the rest of the economy will have to share whatever materials remain.

A control program requires widespread public support to be effective—support that in the past has been generated by wartime conditions. Without such support, the program deteriorates into black markets and economic distortions. Even the CMP was not that effective toward the end of the Second World War, according to David Novick of David Novick Associates:

> There were very few compliance or enforcement problems until 1944 when a general "we've won the war" feeling developed. Businessmen on the WPB (War Production Board) staff started to leave and even the military seemed more concerned about 'occupation' problems than production for war. The Battle of the Bulge changed this somewhat. But in 1945 it was difficult to keep businessmen in their WPB posts and impossible to recruit new ones. Black markets in materials developed to support unauthorized production and distribution of such things as table lamps and small parts for consumer durables. With VJ Day, WPB controls became a shambles despite the fact that we believed there would be major economic problems in converting from war production to that for peace . . . The reason the catastrophe was avoided was that business in 1944 and 1945 was not following Washington's direction on war production. Instead, most firms were devoting their major efforts to getting ready for the post-war fight for markets and profits. In fact there had been a small element of this in their activities throughout the period.[9]

**Impact on Public-Private Sector Relations.** A policy of rationing raw materials would involve extensive public influence over the production and distribution of goods. A large bureaucracy would have to be created to plan, coordinate, supervise, evaluate, revise, and police.

**Impact on National Security and Foreign Relations.** Another cost of a controls program would be the impairment of U.S. relations with other countries. To prevent controlled materials from being shipped abroad, either directly or in the form of finished products, some type of export control program would be required. This might adversely affect those countries that have become dependent on U.S. supplies, as well as hurt the U.S. foreign trade accounts at a time when there may be a need to generate as much foreign exchange earnings as possible.

*Deterrence*

The United States has tremendous mineral resources. Its greatest bargaining power vis-à-vis potential cartels would be to develop a viable domestic alternative to key minerals imports–i.e., accelerate development of these resources.

The United States is also the largest market in the world, especially for minerals. It can use its strong bargaining position coercively, to dissuade potential producer cartels from unreasonable actions. It could threaten such cartels not only with limited or no access to the U.S. market, but also with cutbacks in economic and military aid, in other capital flows, in technological transfers, in U.S. tourism. By so threatening to retaliate against harmful producer cartels, the United States would seek to prevent such cartels from being formed or being used in ways that adversely affect the national interest. To make this policy effective, the president would need standby authority from the Congress to be able to quickly adopt whatever of these measures the situation requires. Such authority by itself may deter cartels from taking hostile actions.

Alternatively, the United States might join with other major materials consuming countries for the purpose of developing a countervailing bargaining power against producer cartels. In so doing, this group, acting together, might effectively deter the cartels from taking unreasonable actions. In addition, if producer cartels restrict exports, the consumers could develop a mechanism for equitably rationing available supplies.

To be sure, cooperation among consuming countries is not easy to achieve, as the initial reaction to the OPEC oil embargo revealed. However, subsequent thinking has prompted the oil consuming countries to reach an agreement on allocations during any future crisis. Similar agreements might be made for those commodities which appear to be most subject to cartel manipulation.

**Impact on National Security and Foreign Policy.** The problem with coercive policies is that they could promote a more antagonistic world economy and lead to an exacerbation of world political tensions. If the United States acted alone, it could isolate itself from other countries that might resent such a policy. At the end of the Second World War, the United States was the world's technological leader and main economic power. Since then, other power centers have developed, which rival the United States, especially Europe and Japan. Thus, the bargaining power of the United States, while still substantial, is weaker than it once was and may not be sufficient to dissuade some cartels from adopting OPEC-type measures.

Agreements on consumer cartels would likely require the United States (and the other consumers) not to undertake special bilateral deals with raw materials suppliers. In any allocation arrangement, the United States might be required to share some of its own supplies with other materials consumers for the sake of an equitable distribution. This policy also has the drawback that it would pit consumers against producers, thus contributing to world tensions.

### *International Cooperation*

Another alternative is for the United States to decide that it can best meet its raw material requirements by establishing a long-term relationship of mutual trust and cooperation with key producing countries. By doing so, we would be encouraging them not to join cartels, but to continue to supply our market.

The implementation of this policy would require an identification of the significant producing countries for those major commodities that threaten to be in short supply around the world. Canada and Australia would likely be included in any such list. Acting alone, or in concert with other consuming countries, the United States would seek to integrate the economies of those favored producing countries into our own and possibly into the other consuming nations. We might provide special access to our markets, as through bilateral or regional trade arrangements. We might provide special facilities for the transfer of capital, aid and technology to these nations. In particular, the United States might seek to evaluate the long-range development needs of those countries and work out a program with them which could maximize the U.S. contribution to their development. By so doing, the United States would seek to increase the degree of mutual dependence so that both sides would have a strong incentive not to restrict trade. The basic startegy here is to use diplomacy and mutual self-interest to ensure that our raw materials requirements are met.

**Impact on National Security and Foreign Policy.** Bilateral deals between the United States and certain producing countries may be resented by other consuming countries, which may encourage them to out-bid the United States in currying the favor of the producers. The integrated world trading system could then break down into a discriminatory pattern. Multilateral arrangements, on the other hand, may minimize this trend, but they may not provide the United States with sufficient assurance that its overseas supplies will not be disrupted.

There is a possibility that such efforts by the United States, whether on a bilateral or multilateral basis, may be ineffective. The producing countries, especially the less developed ones but not exclusively so, may not want to establish special trade with the United States. They may fear too much U.S. influence over their own economic future. We have entered an era in which countries want full control over foreign investments, especially in the extractive industries. They are not interested in just selling raw ores abroad; they want the added value that comes from selling the more processed and fabricated products. Thus, while these countries may not be willing to tolerate too much U.S. influence over their economies, the U.S. may be unwilling to tolerate too much of the nationalized policies of the producers. The resulting conflict of interests could undo whatever mutual self-interest had been achieved.

Finally, this policy depends on freedom of the seas, so that foreign suppliers can find their way into U.S. markets. Any disruption of the sea lanes could nullify this policy and adversely affect the U.S. economy. Thus, it might be wise to combine this policy with a domestic stockpile program, which could counter this potential threat.

## V. Conclusions

We have seen how the effectiveness of the OPEC oil cartel and soaring commodities prices in 1973-74 prompted considerable concern in this country about the future availability and price of raw materials. This concern was heightened by the view expressed by some that our nation may be rapidly depleting its minerals reserves and thus sacrificing the economic well-being of its future generations for the sake of what some consider to be excessive consumption and growth at present. These causes for concern have since eased somewhat as world commodity prices have fallen sharply during 1975 and as the size of U.S. mineral resources and the possibilities of materials conservation have become better appreciated.

Nevertheless, estimates of U.S. mineral requirements through the year 2000 do indicate potential shortages in a number of key minerals. To be sure, the growth in demand for these minerals can be slowed by more recycling of scrap and waste materials, better product design and more substitution of abundant for scarce materials. Moreover, technological advances, such as in ocean mining, may expand future supplies considerably. Without such changes, and possibly even with them, U.S. dependence on imported raw materials can be expected to increase. Such a trend would heighten U.S. vulnerability to growing economic nationalism in the producing countries, including more foreign ownership and more foreign processing, and to hostile actions by producer cartels. Such vulnerability would create serious problems for the national security and the economic stability of the United States.

In evaluating the problem of long-run supply availabilities, we have focused on three critical choices. The first would rely basically on market forces to bring demand and supply into balance, regardless of the import consequences. The second would seek to limit dependence on imports, through more technological development at home and better materials management. The third would seek a maximum self-reliance on domestically produced minerals in order to minimize our vulnerability to foreign sources of supply.

In dealing with the shorter-run problems of supply disruptions caused by producer cartels, the American people face four alternative strategies, which are not mutually exclusive. They can expand the minerals stockpile for economic purposes and develop standby production facilities. Rationing of materials can be instituted in case of an embargo. The United States can try to deter producing countries from hostile actions, such as by threatening to retaliate. Or the United States can try to develop mutually beneficial relations with the producing countries in order to encourage them to act reasonably.

Indications are that the U.S. government has chosen this last course of action. In September 1975, the United States expressed its willingness to discuss special international commodity arrangements. This is an attempt to assure our nation the required flow of raw materials by improving relations with the producing countries. The success of this effort will depend, in part, on the following:

1. The return of the OECD countries to prosperity and regular growth at a high rate. It seems unlikely that these countries as a whole will increase their aid or significantly liberalize trade, as part of an effort to improve mutual relations with the developing countries, if their domestic economies continue to stagnate.
2. The willingness of the developing countries to set aside cartel arrangements and any use of their raw material exports for exerting strategic pressure.
3. Whether the agreements are designed to moderate world price fluctuations or seek to maintain prices at artificially high levels. This latter course could prove to be self-defeating, if only because it would tend to generate worldwide surpluses.

There is no assurance that another boom in world raw materials prices will not occur again. A return by the industrial countries to the high economic growth rates of the late 1960s might well bring this about. On the other hand, substitution of materials and increased efficiency of materials use work to ease the long-term demand for the scarce minerals.

What is clear is that the trend of increasing dependence on foreign sources of supply of raw materials represents a potential vulnerability to the national security and economic stability of the United States, especially since more of the imports are likely to be in a processed form. However, from the point of view of domestic and international economic development, such imports can have a positive influence.

The basic choice centers on whether or not we, the American people, should really be concerned about raw materials, about growing dependence on foreign sources of supply and about the possibility of short-run supply disruptions from actions by producer cartels. If we are concerned, we should carefully consider the key long- and short-run choices, ranging from the creation of an economic stockpile to the establishment of an independent agency to monitor our raw materials situation on a continual basis and to recommend policy changes. If we are not concerned, we should continue to rely basically on market forces to bring about adjustments in demand and supply, with no major policy initiatives other than possibly the establishment of a centralized and updated data base.

## Notes

1. Classification developed by Vincent E. McKelvy, director of the United States Geological Survey.

2. Donella H. Meadows, Dennis L. Meadows, Jørgen Randes, and William W. Behrens, III, *The Limits to Growth* (New York: Universal Books, 1972).

3. In Defense of Economic Growth, p. 219.

4. "Current Assessment of Industrial Research," prepared for the Commission on Critical Choices for Americans, April, 1974.

5. The data on specific commodities were derived from various U.S. government sources, especially the Bureau of Mines and the Department of Commerce.

6. *Journal of Commerce*, February 25, 1975.

7. *New York Times*, January 24, 1975.

8. William C. Truppner, "The Role of Government in the Distribution of Materials to Support the Energy Program," paper delivered at the Workshop on Resource Management, Washington, D.C., sponsored by the National Academy of Public Administration, August 21, 1974. U.S. Congress, Senate, Committee on Government Operations, *Materials Shortages: Workshop on Resource Management*, 94th Cong., 1st sess., February 1975, p. 26.

9. David Novick, "Resource Allocation Experience 1939-1948 and Its Application to 1975-1995 Energy Program Management," paper delivered at Workshop on Resource Management, sponsored by the National Academy of Public Administration, August 21, 1974. U.S. Congress, Senate, Committee on Government Operations, *Materials Shortages: Workshop on Resource Management*, 94th Cong., 1st sess., February 1975, p. 22.

# Members of the Panels

**PANEL I: Energy and Its Relationship to Ecology, Economics and World Stability**

Robert O. Anderson
Norman Ernest Borlaug
John S. Foster, Jr.
Walter Levy
Paul Winston McCracken
Russell W. Peterson
Wilson Riles
Laurance S. Rockefeller
William J. Ronan
Joseph C. Swidler
Edward Teller
Marina von Neumann Whitman
Carroll L. Wilson
John Winger
George D. Woods

**PANEL II: Food, Health, World Population and Quality of Life**

Bernard Berelson
Norman Ernest Borlaug
Lester Brown
Luther H. Foster
Nancy Hanks
J. George Harrar
Belton Kleberg Johnson
John H. Knowles, M.D.
Mary Wells Lawrence
Daniel Patrick Moynihan
Bess Myerson
Carroll L. Wilson

**PANEL III: Raw Materials, Industrial Development, Capital Formation, Employment and World Trade**

Robert O. Anderson
William O. Baker
C. Fred Bergsten
Guido Calabresi

**PANEL III** *(continued)*

John S. Foster, Jr.
Clarence B. Jones
Joseph Lane Kirkland
William S. Paley
Peter G. Peterson
Joseph C. Swidler
Edward Teller
Marina von Neumann Whitman
George D. Woods

**PANEL IV: International Trade and Monetary Systems, Inflation and the Relationships Among Differing Economic Systems**

Martin Anderson
William O. Baker
Guido Calabresi
Leo Cherne
Joseph Lane Kirkland
David S. Landes
Peter G. Peterson
Oscar M. Ruebhausen
Marina von Neumann Whitman
George D. Woods

**PANEL V: Change, National Security and Peace**

John S. Foster, Jr.
Clarence B. Jones
David S. Landes
Sol M. Linowitz
Clare Boothe Luce
Paul Winston McCracken
William J. Ronan
Oscar M. Ruebhausen
Edward Teller

**PANEL VI: Quality of Life of Individuals and Communities in the U.S.**

Ivan Allen, Jr.
Martin Anderson
Mrs. W. Vincent Astor
Daniel J. Boorstin
Ernest L. Boyer
Orville Brim
Lloyd A. Free
Nancy Hanks
John H. Knowles, M.D.
Sol M. Linowitz
Edward J. Logue
Daniel Patrick Moynihan
Bess Myerson
Russell W. Peterson
Wilson Riles
Laurance S. Rockefeller
Sylvester L. Weaver

# Index

# Index

ALLIED PRINTING
TRADES
UNION LABEL
COUNCIL
ESSEX COUNTY

# Vital Resources

presents the Reports of three panels of the Commission on Critical Choices for Americans with an Overview by Nelson A. Rockefeller.

The Reports cover the vitally important areas of energy, food and population, and raw materials. This work is the result of discussions and deliberations by distinguished authorities. The Reports set forth the urgent choices facing the United States and indicate the impact various courses of action would have on the United States and the world. They also point out that failure to make conscious choices at this time would also have significant worldwide consequences.

The Overview by Nelson A. Rockefeller sets forth his view on "Critical Choices and Emergent Opportunities." His distinctive and future-oriented essay shows the need for reassessment and reevaluation of our public policies in this rapidly changing world of today. For Nelson Rockefeller, "the Spirit of America has been one of energy and creativity to meet the needs of individuals." In his view, America's focus should continue to be directed toward increasing the opportunity for more and more individuals to attain that which their talents, capacities and aspirations can achieve.